What Did Jesus Know?

Matthew 24 -25

End Times and Judgment

By

Rev. Dr. Scott T. Arnold

Copyright

2-2018

Bedford, Massachusetts. USA

SHINE Publications

About the Author:

Scott Arnold is a compassionate creative Christian, a husband, father, pastor, chaplain and friend. Scott is also a cancer survivor with much experience ministering to people facing adversity, limitations, illness, grief and mortality. Jesus appeared directly to Scott one night while he had just begun cancer treatments, the Lord touched and healed him in a miraculous way that took the cancer away. At the time, Scott was in the fourth stage of advanced Non-Hodgkin's Lymphoma. Now, over 16 years later, Scott is Pastor at First Baptist Church of Bedford, Massachusetts and is currently a chaplain at Carleton Willard Village.

Scott's calling in ministry has led him to serve Baptist churches in Massachusetts, Rhode Island and Michigan. He has served as the Hospital Chaplain at Branch County Community Health Center, Branch County Cancer Center, and as a Kindred Hospice Chaplain.

Pastor Scott likes the outdoors, taking pictures, walking his dog, fixing cars, oil painting, playing guitar and singing, model trains, fishing and discovering New England history. He and his wife Marilyn enjoy ethnic dining, traveling and mission trips. Scott has written four previous books: "Soul Fruit: Bearing Blessings through Cancer", "Prelude: The Kingdom of God", "SHINE: A Celebration of Spiritual Gifts" and "Come Follow Jesus". His project after this book is: "What Did Jesus Teach? The Sermon on the Mount: Pure Discipleship".

Rev. Dr. Scott Arnold has been an ordained American Baptist minister since 1984 serving churches in Illinois, Massachusetts, Rhode Island and Michigan. Scott is now the Senior Pastor of First Baptist Church of Bedford, Massachusetts just outside of Boston. The Bedford Church is a vibrant and diverse church. Scott has been an advocate and coach to help the church grow in faith, witness and worship. Scott endeavors to help people discover, understand, and develop their Christian faith and spiritual gifts considering the Gospel of God's Kingdom in Jesus Christ.

Scott is blessed with his wife Marilyn (Penacerrada), they have been married 34 years. Their three adult sons are Mark, Thom, and John. Scott and Marilyn met in Chicago; Marilyn was born in the Philippines, she is a registered nurse.

Scott graduated from Midland High School, then at Delta College where he graduated with an emphasis in Art, at Michigan State University with a Bachelor's Degree in Urban Planning, at Northern Baptist Theological Seminary with a Masters in Divinity and Urban Ministry, and at Luther Rice University with a Doctorate in Ministry focused on

Discipleship and Small Groups. Scott serves as a church consultant for congregational renewal and has been a member of the American Baptist Churches think-tank for "Transformed by the Spirit" called "The Journey Team".

Preface

Excited with wonder and petrified with awe; my feelings about writing this book. God's grace, and the gentle voice of the Holy Spirit, spoke to my heart one morning in May of 2017, to delve into this study on Jesus' teaching in Matthew 24 and 25. Therefore, I began to prayerfully approach this "Olivet Discourse". Little did I know that many big things were about to happen in the summertime of writing this. The threat of a nuclear showdown with North Korea came, as Kim Jun Un fired missile tests over Japan and the Pacific and detonated a hydrogen bomb underground. Meanwhile, President Trump warned of "fire and fury like the world has never seen" as a threat. All this, while there was a nationwide total Solar Eclipse in America that was followed by three of the worst hurricanes in recorded history slamming Texas (Harvey) and Florida (Irma) and Puerto Rico (Maria). There were also several powerful earthquakes in Mexico and Japan, bombings and attacks by terrorists, continued suffering for refugees from Syria and many other incidents of violence and injustice everywhere around the world. All of this seems to be increasing with intensity, a warning and revealing of even more distressful times to come.

Therefore, while seeking God's leading and understanding in Matthew 24 and 25, I discovered again how wonderful and deep the knowledge of Jesus was and is. His warning was for people then, and is as relevant today. Reading, meditating upon and studying His words; I was given peace to hear my Lord speak to concerns about human survival, climate change and the end times leading to the Day of Judgment. While Jesus' words must have been overwhelming to His first circle of disciples, as He spoke to common people like us; even now, Jesus' words have an even greater pertinence to twenty-first century disciples and humanity. Jesus is speaking in ways that are intimate and global. The big picture of

God's work, and some fine details, are offered by the Lord as He paints a vision on an immense canvas. In close-up view, one discovers a personal call for faith, humility, reverence, respect and responsive service. From far away, the vision of Jesus reveals a picture of God at work to save and redeem humanity from its own sin and the corruption of evil. Jesus presented God's storyboard with both passion and balanced restraint. He tells us what we need to know about the future, and holds back on telling us too much. One could imagine the disciples listening intently, as Jesus gestured with His hands and arms. His face and eyes looking out upon the future, sometimes with eyelids closed, then open. Jesus went back and forth from immediate concern to a time yet to come, from the disciples and people of that time to people and disciples yet to come. Like many times before for me, reading the teachings of Jesus was not simply an academic exercise, but a profound encounter with the Living Lord whose word is current and life-changing.

Therefore, I ask you to join me in a patient journey of faith that may lead us upon a growing passionate hope on this subject of the coming of Jesus Christ and the Kingdom of God. Therefore, I pray that what I write is more than mere observation or pondering, but a response that helps to inspire deeper devotion to Christ and service that is Christ-like. Already there are too many commentators who have reduced Jesus' teaching to literary curiosity and speculators who have tried to rework Jesus teaching to fit their agendas. Instead, may we find that what Jesus said to His disciples then is just as helpful for us today. Jesus guides His disciples to have a bright faith vision of God's Kingdom to come. Faith can thrive amidst trials; practical principles of following Jesus are meant to be put into action. The Lord Jesus taught His disciples, and teaches people now, to operate with hope in God's sovereignty and providence.

Having faith in Jesus requires realistic discernment and faithful endurance. There is, after all, a spiritual war that is taking place in human history between good and evil. Jesus came to fulfill and initiate the Gospel of God's Kingdom on earth, and someday evil and wickedness shall be destroyed upon His return. During this era between Christ's first and second comings, people are called to be reconciled to God and actively participate in the message and service of God's Kingdom, in its current provisional state. Even so, service in God's Kingdom does not mean that people will establish the fullness of this Kingdom through their own doing. Indeed, while serving we must trust God's ultimate work of fulfillment and judgment. Jesus gave us enough information for us to anticipate the coming challenges that people shall face in the End Times. The Lord calls us to trust the work of God the Father in His Second Coming leading to the full manifestation and establishment of God's Kingdom in a New Heaven and Earth. Urgency and service are inspired in Jesus teaching for each generation until God's plan and purpose will be consummated in Christ's return.

I pray that this book may be encouraging and challenging to skeptics, doubters and believers. I pray that you and I together will discover the voice of God's Holy Spirit speaking through Jesus into the complexity of our existence and brokenness with prophetic hope and vision. Indeed, the words from Psalm 119:105 (*"Thy Word is a lamp unto our feet and light unto our pathway"*) serve as a perspective of how Jesus is God's word and light to us in the daily walk of faith, and for the whole journey that leads to the fulness of God's Kingdom coming on earth. Through His life and teaching, Jesus gave us the light of godly character as an example that inspires moral and practical steps of service for God's Kingdom. In addition, Jesus revealed a broad and dramatic vision of Heaven's bright horizon that is shining beyond our struggles, trials, frustrations and heartache. God's Spirit is at work to break into people's darkness and issue forth transformation. God has a plan to address the problem of evil; all this has relevance in the twenty-first century amid current and coming dynamic storm clouds of distress and judgment.

Jesus knew then, and Jesus knows now (as our risen Lord), what we need to know about the coming of the Kingdom of God as it will transform all things. The fact of Jesus Christ's inevitable return is what motivates this author to write, and not the obsession that some lunge for in determining exact signs or timing. The fact of God being Sovereign supports trust and belief that God's Divine plan shall unfold and become more and more immanent. Faith in God and Christ Jesus is what matters, not the denial of naysayers or the speculations of false prophets. Personally, this study has helped to inspire me and clarify God's purposes; I have greater inspiration for faith and service. Being overwhelmed is alright, in fact, it is quite healthy and reasonable. Nonetheless, I am even more motivated to work and serve with joy, desiring to see Jesus in the daily encounters, and not just when He returns to "take me home" (a day of personal judgment or the time of His coming on the clouds).

The words that Jesus spoke in Matthew 24 and 25 reveal the incredible foreknowledge of the One who was with God from the beginning of creation, this same One will be with God in the consummation of redeeming creation through judgment and the upcoming magnificent making of a New Heaven and New Earth. Jesus knew that His disciples had a desire to understand the big picture, to have a vision that all things would eventually work out according to God's ultimate plan of salvation. Jesus also knew that beyond the disciples' faith and the hope of the Jewish people, the diversity of humanity needed to receive the Gospel of God's Kingdom and be invited into the Covenant of God.

These two chapters, Matthew 24 and 25, are not just about end times and judgment, they are ultimately about living with the knowledge and vision of salvation and redemption. The urgent and patient work of the church to provide a witness of presence that shall prepare the world for the intervention of Jesus Christ, the inevitable, complete and necessary coming of God's Kingdom. The centrality of Jesus, in God's plan of establishing salvation and His Kingdom upon the earth, is pivotal. Christ is like a compass, He came from God as the center-spoke of existence, and in the span of God's grace and truth outstretched, the work of Christ and God's Kingdom reaches out to draw a wide circle, a circumference. How wide the circle is drawn upon the line and scope of history is God's divine mystery. What Jesus knew, and what He communicated in Matthew 24 and 25, is that God has a trajectory for history; there is a work of grace and truth unfolding. English Bible Scholar, William Barclay once said:

"The whole essence of the Christian view of history is that history is quite definitively going somewhere, that it has a goal, that it will have a consummation, and that the goal and consummation find their realization in the perfect reign of God and the return of Jesus Christ in the world." (p. 205 William Barclay; "The King and the Kingdom" Westminster Press, Philadelphia, 1968).

What any reasonable person must confess and consider is that this is an area to tread upon with humility, honesty and honor to God. The humility comes in awe and wonder of the grand and glorious nature of God. The honesty comes in realizing that we fragile human beings don't know very much, we are still learning. Nonetheless, we are made in the image of God and have great potential, enough so that Jesus believed we could handle the truth. For honoring God, Jesus taught us how to live and love all persons with integrity, respect and compassion. He also taught us to not live in denial about our physical mortality and of this world's inevitable undoing and coming encounter with God that would involve transformation, a sort of "global death and resurrection". In practical terms, Jesus taught us that life's purpose comes from joyfully, faithfully, lovingly serving others. By so doing, we serve Christ Himself while giving glory to God our Father in our deeds. In God's unfolding plan, we are called to prepare for, and participate in, Christ's Gospel of the Kingdom of Heaven. We serve through daily encounters, relationships and responsibilities. The best preparation is participation. If we wait for Jesus to show Himself upon the coming clouds of heaven, and not perceive or discover Him in the daily walk of faith in which we encounter people, then we shall miss His current presence, and the opportunity to participate in Heaven's Kingdom now.

This book has been a labor of faith and love for Jesus, and my duty to share Christ's leading with skeptics and believers alike. My paltry words of reflection pale in comparison to Jesus' words. I am like a barnacle talking about the solid rock that I cling to. The times we live in are tumultuous. Nature around us is reeling in hurricanes, storms, fires, earthquakes, flooding and many other disruptive factors that place biological ecosystems at risk of endangerment. Humanity is also struggling with conflict, war, racism, alienation, loss of compassion, deteriorating hope, toxic religious fundamentalism and increasing pessimism about the future.

I share this book in prayer that people will open their hearts to Jesus Christ in the days we are each given. The "Day of the Lord" is coming, one in which Jesus will return to earth in power and glory. The signs of the End Times and matters pertaining to Jesus' return for Judgment are explored in this book. However, the practical application of knowing about Jesus' teaching on this subject is that our Lord teaches us to be ready by faith and service. I am more convicted than ever that people need Jesus Christ. The time to believe in Him, and receive Him as Lord and Savior, is now. Jesus stands at the door, and He knocks. I pray that people will receive Him, know Him and be transformed within their hearts and minds, and therefore become salt and light in the world as part of the Kingdom of God. In a time that incongruity is rampant among believers, Christ's disciples must keep their focus on the Lord and not be fooled by false messiahs or politically charged crusades.

For the skeptical readers, don't wait until the sun and moon are darkened and the heavenly bodies are shaken; for then He (Christ Jesus) shall come upon the clouds of heaven when the angel trumpet sounds. The acceptable time of salvation is now. God's grace has been extended to each of us to receive by faith. God has given people a window of grace, the book of life is still being written within this time of preparation and service. The invitation is for people to come to faith in Jesus Christ, the one who mediates the covenant of God's grace. The work of God's Spirit is that we are to be born again. This gift comes by faith in the forgiveness and love of God.

Before we start this journey, in this book adventure, of hearing Jesus teach about the "End Times" and "Judgment", note that everything Jesus taught in this "Olivet Discourse" from Matthew 24 and 25 shall challenge assumptions people make about the Kingdom of God. One is left realizing that Jesus revealed both a profound knowledge of the future and a personal knowledge of the redemptive and righteous personality of God that is completely revolutionary, unique and trustworthy. Therefore, Jesus' message is both compelling and transformative.

-    Scott T. Arnold

Scripture Text: Matthew 24 -25

Matthew 24: *Jesus left the temple and was walking away when his disciples came up to him to call his attention to its buildings. "Do you see all these things?" he asked. "Truly I tell you, not one stone here will be left on another; every one will be thrown down." As Jesus was sitting on the Mount of Olives, the disciples came to him privately. "Tell us," they said, "when will this happen, and what will be the sign of your coming and of the end of the age?"*

Jesus answered: "Watch out that no one deceives you. For many will come in my name, claiming, 'I am the Messiah,' and will deceive many. You will hear of wars and rumors of wars, but see to it that you are not alarmed. Such things must happen, but the end is still to come. Nation will rise against nation, and kingdom against kingdom. There will be famines and earthquakes in various places. All these are the beginning of birth pains.

"Then you will be handed over to be persecuted and put to death, and you will be hated by all nations because of me. At that time many will turn away from the faith and will betray and hate each other, and many false prophets will appear and deceive many people. Because of the increase of wickedness, the love of most will grow cold, but the one who stands firm to the end will be saved. And this gospel of the kingdom will be preached in the whole world as a testimony to all nations, and then the end will come.

"So when you see standing in the holy place 'the abomination that causes desolation,' spoken of through the prophet Daniel—let the reader understand— then let those who are in Judea flee to the mountains. Let no one on the housetop go down to take anything out of the house. Let no one in the field go back to get their cloak. How dreadful it will be in those days for pregnant women and nursing mothers! Pray that your flight will not take place in winter or on the Sabbath.

For then there will be great distress, unequaled from the beginning of the world until now—and never to be equaled again. "If those days had not been cut short, no one would survive, but for the sake of the elect those days will be shortened. At that time if anyone says to you, 'Look, here is the Messiah!' or, 'There he is!' do not believe it. For false messiahs and false prophets will appear and perform great signs and wonders to deceive, if possible, even the elect. See, I have told you ahead of time.

"So if anyone tells you, 'There he is, out in the wilderness,' do not go out; or, 'Here he is, in the inner rooms,' do not believe it. For as lightning that comes from the east is visible even in the west, so will be the coming of the Son of Man. Wherever there is a carcass, there the vultures will gather.

"Immediately after the distress of those days "'the sun will be darkened, and the moon will not give its light; the stars will fall from the sky, and the heavenly bodies will be shaken.' "Then will appear the sign of the Son of Man in heaven. And then all the peoples of the earth will mourn when they see the Son of Man coming on the clouds of heaven, with power and great glory. And he will send his angels with a loud trumpet call, and they will gather his elect from the four winds, from one end of the heavens to the other.

"Now learn this lesson from the fig tree: As soon as its twigs get tender and its leaves come out, you know that summer is near. Even so, when you see all these things, you know that it is near, right at the door. Truly I tell you, this generation will certainly not pass away until all these things have happened. Heaven and earth will pass away, but my words will never pass away.

"But about that day or hour no one knows, not even the angels in heaven, nor the Son, but only the Father. As it was in the days of Noah, so it will be at the coming of the Son of Man. For in the days before the flood, people were eating and drinking, marrying and giving in marriage, up to the day Noah entered the ark; and they knew nothing about what would happen until the flood came and took them all away. That is how it will be at the coming of the Son of Man. Two men will be in the field; one will be taken and the other left. Two women will be grinding with a hand mill; one will be taken and the other left.

"Therefore, keep watch because you do not know on what day your Lord will come. But understand this: If the owner of the house had known at what time of night the thief was coming, he would have kept watch and would not have let his house be broken into. So you also must be ready, because the Son of Man will come at an hour when you do not expect him.

"Who then is the faithful and wise servant, whom the master has put in charge of the servants in his household to give them their food at the proper time? It will be good for that servant whose master finds him doing so when he returns. Truly I tell you, he will put him in charge of all his possessions. But suppose that servant is wicked and says to himself, 'My master is staying away a long time,' and he then begins to beat his fellow servants and to eat and drink with drunkards. The master of that servant will come on a day when he does not expect him and at an hour he is not aware of. He will cut him to pieces and assign him a place with the hypocrites, where there will be weeping and gnashing of teeth.

Matthew 25: "At that time the kingdom of heaven will be like ten virgins who took their lamps and went out to meet the bridegroom. Five of them were foolish and five were wise. The foolish ones took their lamps but did not take any oil with them. The wise ones, however, took oil in jars along with their lamps. The bridegroom was a long time in coming, and they all became drowsy and fell asleep. "At midnight the cry rang out: 'Here's the bridegroom! Come out to meet him!' "Then all the virgins woke up and trimmed their lamps. The foolish ones said to the wise, 'Give us some of your oil; our lamps are going out.' "'No,' they replied, 'there may not be enough for both us and you. Instead, go to those who sell oil and buy some for yourselves.' "But while they were on their way to buy the oil, the bridegroom arrived. The virgins who were ready went in with him to the wedding banquet. And the door was shut. "Later the others also came. 'Lord, Lord,' they said, 'open the door for us!' "But he replied, 'Truly I tell you, I don't know you.' Therefore, keep watch, because you do not know the day or the hour.

"Again, it will be like a man going on a journey, who called his servants and entrusted his wealth to them. To one he gave five bags of gold, to another two bags, and to another one bag, each according to his ability. Then he went on his journey. The man who had received five bags of gold went at once and put his money to work and gained five bags more. So also, the one with two bags of gold gained two more. But the man who had received one bag went off, dug a hole in the ground and hid his master's money.

"After a long time, the master of those servants returned and settled accounts with them. The man who had received five bags of gold brought the other five. 'Master,' he said, 'you entrusted me with five bags of gold. See, I have gained five more.' "His master replied, 'Well done, good and faithful servant! You have been faithful with a few things; I will put you in charge of many things. Come and share your master's happiness!' "The man with two bags of gold also came. 'Master,' he said, 'you entrusted me with two bags of gold; see, I have gained two more.' "His master replied, 'Well done, good and faithful servant! You have been faithful with a few things;

I will put you in charge of many things. Come and share your master's happiness!'

"Then the man who had received one bag of gold came. 'Master,' he said, 'I knew that you are a hard man, harvesting where you have not sown and gathering where you have not scattered seed. So I was afraid and went out and hid your gold in the ground. See, here is what belongs to you.' "His master replied, 'You wicked, lazy servant! So you knew that I harvest where I have not sown and gather where I have not scattered seed? Well then, you should have put my money on deposit with the bankers, so that when I returned I would have received it back with interest. "'So take the bag of gold from him and give it to the one who has ten bags. For whoever has will be given more, and they will have an abundance. Whoever does not have, even what they have will be taken from them. And throw that worthless servant outside, into the darkness, where there will be weeping and gnashing of teeth.'

"When the Son of Man comes in his glory, and all the angels with him, he will sit on his glorious throne. All the nations will be gathered before him, and he will separate the people one from another as a shepherd separates the sheep from the goats. He will put the sheep on his right and the goats on his left. "Then the King will say to those on his right, 'Come, you who are blessed by my Father; take your inheritance, the kingdom prepared for you since the creation of the world. For I was hungry and you gave me something to eat, I was thirsty and you *gave me something to drink, I was a stranger and you invited me in, I needed clothes and you clothed me, I was sick and you looked after me, I was in prison and you came to visit me.' "Then the righteous will answer him, 'Lord, when did we see you hungry and feed you, or thirsty and give you something to drink? When did we see you a stranger and invite you in, or needing clothes and clothe you? When did we see you sick or in prison and go to visit you?' "The King will reply, 'Truly I tell you, whatever you did for one of the least of these brothers and sisters of mine, you did for me.'*

"Then he will say to those on his left, 'Depart from me, you who are cursed, into the eternal fire prepared for the devil and his angels. For I was hungry and you gave me nothing to eat, I was thirsty and you gave me nothing to drink, I was a stranger and you did not invite me in, I needed clothes and you did not clothe me, I was sick and in prison and you did not look after me.' "They also will answer, 'Lord, when did we see you hungry or thirsty or a stranger or needing clothes or sick or in prison, and did not help you?' "He will reply, 'Truly I tell you, whatever you did not do for one of the least of these, you did not do for me.' "Then they will go away to eternal punishment, but the righteous to eternal life."

(New International Version, without verse numbers)

A Greenhouse and a Garden
(an Introduction)

To begin with, consider a metaphor that portrays existent parallel and interdependent realities in this world. Imagine that each of us have our own place, a sphere of influence, a "greenhouse" or "garden". Within your place or garden, God has given you relationships and responsibilities. There are also interrelationships you have with others, your garden is interrelated with others and the world and its environmental concerns. Since you are interrelated with others, you take on commitments and projects that involve the care and nurture of people utilizing the fruit of your labor you have grown, and exchange with others. The stewardship of life in your sphere involves both maintenance and improvement. In your greenhouse/garden one finds that there is an ongoing application of personal and shared knowledge, values and ideas that you and others orient to, creatively pursue and act upon. Ideally, one finds purpose, meaning and joy within the very life God has given. The Heavenly Creator has designed us for relationships that make up the process and outcome of qualitative life, spiritual health and growth. The fruit of your effort becomes beneficial (even beautiful) to you and the community you reside in.

On the path of ideals, one could go on to name the intrinsic outcomes or qualities of meaningful shared existence. The list may include what the Apostle Paul described as the "fruit of the Spirit"; this is evidence of the divine nature of God's Spirit at residence within healthy individuals and communities: *"love, joy, peace, patience, kindness, goodness, faithfulness, gentleness and self-control"* (Galatians 5:22-23). Such qualities supersede culture, race and nationality; they are germane to the core of faith covenants, healthy human nature and vibrant community life.

Now suppose that one sees their sphere or space as theirs alone, not even as a gift to be shared, not even as a purposeful place or world that is interrelated to other people in their spheres, gardens or worlds. Even worse, suppose that one sees other people and their spheres as threatening or even as persons, property and places to conquer, control or fear. When such a distorted perspective exists and grows in malignancy, people's vision and actions become fragmented, maligned and void of respect. There is a tragic loss of nurture, care and mindfulness of others and God. The result is deadly, caused by something diabolical and disruptive. Therefore, while the world God made is beautiful and full of wonders, the existence of corruption is real. Evil has smitten our fallen human race with sin and a rebellious spirit of false pride and consuming greed. How do we contend with this dilemma?

From the Garden of Eden onward, self-awareness has been at tension with awareness of "the other" and God. Patiently, even after Adam and Eve's fall, God initiated a working relationship of reconciliation and redemption. One may continue to see this in the very design of life. Creation is sustained by the goodness of interrelated diversity. Practically, this is stated in God's command to live in love and respect of one another. God, in creativity and through redemptive care, calls for us to come to a life of reconciled and redeemed faith. To have faith means that we shall respond to our Heavenly Creator's transformative existence, as evidenced in receiving God's very Spirit of grace, truth and love. We are given life, and a mindful conscience and soulful will, to respect one another in creation and give ultimate worth, "worship", to the One who created us. To this end, and for our reconciliation and redemption, Jesus gave His life, and continues to intercede on behalf of humanity before God our Heavenly Father. This is God's plan of salvation and redemption, initiated in the Abrahamic covenant and then fulfilled in the covenant of God in Jesus Christ.

Life, therefore, is best understood, truly purposeful and fulfilling, in healthy and loving relationships that are sustained in meaningful work within the context of community. This ideal is appealing because it was the design and plan that God intended. Yet we live in a world that is broken, alienated, polluted, corrupted, immoral and defaced. Our spheres, gardens, nations, cities and towns are not perfect; they have become infected and impersonal, they have both imploded into confusion and have collided into social, moral, spiritual shards. Yet still, God the creator has a plan for our salvation and redemption, and the need for all things to be made new. God is not a "throw away" creator. God is one who builds sustainability and renewal into creation. Jesus, the Prince of Peace, still speaks to our fears and chaos with a word of transformation, challenge, caution and hope.

The Gospel of *"God's Kingdom to come"* in the words of Jesus from Matthew, in chapters 24 and 25, have given us a glimpse into what Jesus knew about the future. Jesus Christ preached a message of caution, challenge, encouragement and compassion. His word speaks afresh today at a time that He foresaw. Christ's perspective, for His disciples, is to have faith within this imperfect life while anticipating God's coming Kingdom and judgment. Not only does Jesus reveal the big picture of God's plan of transformation, Jesus gave specific indicators of what to look for. These "signs" are comparable to "birth pains", and they shall precede the establishment of God's completed reign on earth (Matthew 24). Furthermore, Jesus spoke in parables and gave practical teaching (in Matthew 25) about how to live faithfully with engagement so that one is ready at any time to give account for their life.

Consider again the greenhouse/garden metaphor. God, the Creator and Redeemer, has designed us to willfully and freely do our part as good caretakers/residents. If we follow through in good faith, respect, wisdom and obedience, growth will most often lead to life sustaining leaves and fragrant beautiful blossoms. In time, with proper care, good fruit develops. Through responsive participation and creativity to the world and contexts we reside within, we may bear fruit and knowledge. The blessings that we are given are meant to be shared, they are to be brought out into the gardens of the world for mutual nourishment, encouragement and enjoyment.

Now, the plants and fruit in this metaphor may represent ways that we give, care for and feed one another, blessing souls and society. These plants that we are caretakers of are: Deeds of kindness, acts of mercy, sacrificial labors of love, words of truth and symphonies of grace.

Upon assessment, the greenhouse/garden metaphor is idyllic, blissful and sweet. A closer and more honest look at the greenhouses/gardens of this earth reveals that there are serious troubles and ills. Injustice, racism, abuse, neglect, addiction, hatred and violence have wrought ongoing chaos. Something evil is resident, and remains afoot, that is an affront to that which God first designed to be good. We no longer live in the Garden of Eden, but in a dynamic and dangerous place where there is life and death, joy and suffering, love and hate, peace and war, redemption and destruction. Close examination shows that many gardens suffer from invading weeds, conditions of blight, mold and various invasive pests. One could make the case that in social, political, economic, and spiritual realms there are rampant and pervasive forces at work amidst the "gardens" and "greenhouses" of humanity. People wonder: Why doesn't God intervene? Why does human suffering continue?

Without faith in God, these questions remain an enigma. However, people of faith in God ask: What is the plan of God to reverse or halt this decay? What is God's plan to redeem humanity and creation? The Apostle Paul wrote:

> 18 I consider that our present sufferings are not worth comparing with the glory that will be revealed in us. 19 For the creation waits in eager expectation for the children of God to be revealed. 20 For the creation was subjected to frustration, not by its own choice, but by the will of the one who subjected it, in hope 21 that the creation itself will be liberated from its bondage to decay and brought into the freedom and glory of the children of God. - (Romans 8:18-22)

Even though the Apostle Paul had discovered the purpose of God in the Gospel of God's Kingdom in Jesus Christ; there are many who doubt. They foolishly say: "There is no point"; "There is no God"; "Life has no meaning or ultimate purpose"; How could Jesus be the Son of God?" People deep down are denying the very reality and awareness that God gave us life and being, and our lives are meant to be experienced and shared in a meaningful way. Our questions only highlight the reality that we are more than material or social beings. Life has a spiritual core. God is to be honored and glorified, and our fruitfulness and freedom as humanity are meant to be blessed, and not cursed.

Our earth is both a greenhouse and a garden. There are small and larger spheres where people live out their personal and corporate lives, this is God's marvelous design. The microcosm of individual expression and personality is interdependent upon the macrocosm of shared community; this is God's intricate and interwoven design.

One wonders and ponders: "What is God's plan for dealing with the world in its broken state of dynamic conflict?" "Does God have a remedy for sickness, death, pain and sorrow?" Throughout the Gospels, and particularly in the Gospel of Matthew, we discover that Jesus knew more about God's Sovereignty and God's Kingdom than anyone else. How could He know so much? Jesus was the very Son of God; He stepped down from His position in Heaven at the right hand of God His Father to come to earth on a Mission of salvation for us. The life Jesus lived, and the words He spoke, have revealed enough truth and grace for us to have faith. This inspires people to believe and come to a working knowledge that God has a "Master Plan". In Christ, it has been revealed that each person has a purpose in life to serve for the coming of God's eternal Kingdom.

Jesus' teaching and prophetic words in Matthew 24 to 25 are the focus of this book. The goal will be to faithfully examine Jesus' Gospel of God's Kingdom with specific focus on End Times and Judgment. Jesus spoke with amazing awareness of what was soon to happen after his life in Jerusalem, and then word-painted an amazing set of pictures on a grand canvas of future time with a mix of brush strokes (large and precise). Still, Jesus clarified, that while He and the Father God are one, there are some things about the future that only God the Father knows about.

This was particularly true in the matter of exactly when Jesus (the Christ) would come back to earth in judgment and glory. If Jesus had needed to tell us exactly when He would return, God would have given Him this knowledge. However, there are some things in the sphere of existence that are better left unknown for the sake of discretion, innocence and motivation. If Jesus did know every detail of His Heavenly Father's plans within the human mind that He was temporarily given, then such knowledge could have been an awful burden for Him. One might likewise argue that the incarnation of Jesus into our human form was a gift that prevented Him from being set on a level that we could not understand or relate to. His human form and mind was given just the right amount of ability and knowledge to pour forth God's truth in ways that we could perceive and receive. The limitations God gave His

Son Jesus helped Him speak to our human condition and culture. More importantly, if we knew the exact timing and extent of God's plan, because of our current corrupted state, it would ruin and break us.

In Matthew 24 and 25, Jesus did not speak of His future millennial reign (a thousand-year period of Christ reigning), as may be found in Daniel and Revelation. Jesus kept it simple for this teaching moment. Sometimes, too many details can baffle people, and are not necessary to be spoken while getting to the point. Jesus went right to the point to present the nature and purpose of His second coming. The Lord did not mention, in this teaching moment, any details about a millennial reign and its time or placement in God's unfolding plan of redemption. For this study, therefore, I will leave the mystery of the millennial reign of Christ to that body of knowledge which is a matter of thoughtful consideration. I did write about the millennial reign of Jesus in a previous writing ("Prelude, The Kingdom of God" - 2012):

"God manifested His presence in many ways throughout biblical history and has continued to manifest His presence since then to today. Yet we realize that while this is true, there is a greater manifestation yet to come that is spoken of through the prophets and psalmists. The full manifestation of God's Kingdom shall be fulfilled in the second coming of Jesus Christ in a future millennial reign. These Psalms were written to give the people hope for the eventual full manifestation of God's Kingdom on earth. Because there have been, and will continue to be, counterfeits who will claim to be the Christ, it is important for us to take note of what the real Kingdom of God will be like when the Lord returns. Jerusalem will be the center of Jesus' reign upon the earth, and all nations will come and stand in awe of the Lord within the great New Jerusalem, the City of Zion. In Psalms 47 and 48, praise that began in Israel's history will continue until the future manifestation of

Christ Jesus and His rule upon the earth. These Psalms prepare us for that event, reign and future worship. There is an exciting, yet humbling, sense of awe. It won't be the current Jerusalem structure with political leaders taking the reins. The location will be the same, but the city itself will come down out of heaven from God. Jesus will reign in power and glory. There will be a radical change upon the earth and even in the heavens, such that all things shall be made new." (Arnold, Scott. "Prelude: The Kingdom of God. Signs, Salvation and Service". Shine Press, Quincy, MI, 2012. P. 54-55)

What God did, through Jesus' teaching of the Gospel, is give us a guiding awareness of God's master plan of salvation and judgment. Jesus Himself is the revealing gift from God. Through the Son of God, we are given motivation and vision to believe, we are also guided and empowered in Christ as He gave us God's Holy Spirit. Our ultimate purpose is to glorify God as we live, serve and care for people (that they too may come to faith, hope and eternal life). God worked through Jesus, and continues to work through His disciples. God's Son shall come again to complete salvation and issue a final judgment before the New Heaven and New Earth can be established.

A Preliminary Study from Matthew 13:24-30

Within this introduction, prior to considering Jesus' Olivet discourse in Matthew 24 and 25, a brief study of the "Parable of the Garden that has Weeds" in Matthew 13, will provide an essential summary of the eschatology of Jesus. (Eschatology is concerned with how God's Kingdom shall come to earth. Webster's Dictionary defines "eschatology" as "a branch of theology concerned with the final events in the history of the world or of humankind"). Here, in this succinct story, Jesus deals with the existence and problem of evil, and the response and plan of God and the Kingdom of Heaven.

Parable of the weeds. (Matthew 13)

24 Jesus told them another parable: "The kingdom of heaven is like a man who sowed good seed in his field. 25 But while everyone was sleeping, his enemy came and sowed weeds among the wheat, and went away. 26 When the wheat sprouted and formed heads, then the weeds also appeared. 27 "The owner's servants came to him and said, 'Sir, didn't you sow good seed in your field? Where then did the weeds come from?' 28 "'An enemy did this,' he replied. "The servants asked him, 'Do you want us to go and pull them up?' 29 "'No,' he answered, 'because while you are pulling the weeds, you may uproot the wheat with them. 30 Let both grow together until the harvest. At that time I will tell the harvesters: First collect the weeds and tie them in bundles to be burned; then gather the wheat and bring it into my barn.'" Matthew 13:24-30.

Throughout His ministry, Jesus described what the Kingdom of God is like in understandable terms. Nature revealed the character of God, and the problems within mankind's struggle in the natural realm reveals the result of the mankind's fall and sin. What would God do about the presence of evil, which is represented by the "weeds" that grew up around the "good seed/plants"? This parable addresses some of the false impressions people have about God being capricious or unconcerned. The "good seed" of the gospel of Jesus Christ has been sown into the world, and this "good seed" was a fulfillment and expansion of the teachings of the Old Testament that were sown through the Torah of the Jews. Sadly, alongside the teachings of God's word, there have been teachings of falsehood and treachery that are like weeds in the way they have taken root and spread. Jesus explains that both good and evil exist side by side until the harvest. God will wait to judge the earth until it is time to do so. Jesus' role is twofold: One, be the bearer of the good seed of God's grace and truth that gives life in God's Spirit to those who believe; and two, oversee and conduct the eventual harvest (Judgment Day).

When that Judgment Day comes, there will be a separation between the good wheat and the weeds (including the bundles of chaff) that will be burned separately. Jesus used imagery that people can relate to. The actual process and event will be far more involved and extensive than any image can portray. Nonetheless, the listeners are called to receive Jesus's parables like little children because of our limited our grasp of reality, compared to that of our Lord's awareness. Jesus revealed transformative truth because people are not innocent and without sin, we are called to repent, change our ways, seek the grace of God and serve the Lord with gratitude and hope in God's Kingdom plan. Simply put, we are to trust the strong, yet gracious and kind, hand of the Lord.

Considering Jesus' "parable of the weeds", we discover that it applies to how the choke-hold of sin and the seeds of strife have affected the gardens of human existence since the Fall in the Garden of Eden. These seeds are more than a nuisance, they often take over. Like the wild vine that climbs and chokes out other plants, evil has a way of competing to monopolize, dominate and destroy. Justice pleads for these to be checked and halted. What can be done to break the grip of evil and turn the devastating downward spiral around? How can we be saved from the consequences of our own sin, that were hatched by the Devil's sinister and evil plot? Jesus gave us some answers throughout His life and ministry, and particularly in Matthew 24 and 25.

In denial and doubt, there are people who will naysay the concern of "end times". (Perhaps the gravity of this topic may make our heads heavy, so Lord, help us to not nod off into "la la land"). Consider why we are to be awakened, the sobering reality that even the Scientific community is giving warning that coincides with biblical apocalyptic concerns. Evidence of global warming, concerns of nuclear radioactive fallout and the subtle threats of humanity inventing its own demise through artificial intelligence, are all on the table of debate and deep concern. Even though there is ample evidence for alarm, there are those who recommend that this topic be avoided or given light priority because it is too complex or controversial. The assumption that Jesus' teaching was only for a handful of disciples who would witness the destruction of the Jerusalem Temple in A.D. 70 is not faithful to the fullness of the scriptural text as Jesus taught upon the Mount of Olives. The antidote to such points of objection is that Jesus had a reason for transmitting this body of teaching. What Jesus revealed and taught continues to be informative, instructive and inspirational for each generation. What Jesus has given mankind is a warning and a word of hope. Jesus calls humanity to trust God's bigger purpose for life and God's ultimate plan of redemption.

Among skeptics, there are those who will rationalize avoidance of Jesus' teaching based on how previous generations, in various centuries, have over-anticipated the nearness of Christ's return. At any given time in history, there have been errant assumptions, or deceptive agendas, of people trying to manipulate various signs, trials or tribulations for their own attention or purposes. The problem of discernment for applying Jesus' teaching is to be a matter of prayer, wisdom and reason. For example, a distorted application of the Parable of the Weeds might be to say we should not address sin or evil until Jesus returns. The servants in the parable are asking, however, about full eradication through burning all the crops and weeds together. The land owner, God, decides upon patient realism. While the good crop and stifling weeds grow side by side until the harvest, the land owner cautions against a radical and complete weeding out until then. The workers in the field are still left with tilling, fertilizing and some remedial weeding in their care for the crops.

In a very real and humble way, the "parable of the weeds" (in Matthew 13) helps to point out that God's servants will always be uncomfortable about the presence of "weeds". Each generation will be aware that what is ultimately needed is a time of reckoning. The task of "pulling weeds" lightly, ad hoc, may help slow down the "weeds", but eventually the "weeds" coexist with "wheat/crops" until growth of the crop has reached its height of maturity and the time of harvest arrives. The crops shall be gathered, the weeds shall be burned. The importance of Jesus' teaching was not for people to figure out every detail of when God would do all these things, but to understand what to expect overall and why this is important for living with purpose, discernment, faithfulness and perseverance.

The depth of Jesus' teaching and knowledge is all the more evident in Matthew 24 and 25. However, even in Jesus' masterful teaching, He leaves us with a very honest and humbling truth: *"Only the Father knows the day and the time"* (Matthew 24:36). Jesus operated upon faith in His Heavenly Father, and this faith was founded upon a personal knowledge that was primarily relational. Christ's urgency and passion revealed the heart of the Heavenly Father, and how important it is for us to have a vision for ultimacy and direction while we await the coming of God's Heavenly Kingdom. People of faith in every generation are inspired by the vision Jesus portrayed of God's coming Kingdom. *"The Day is coming, here it comes. Ready or not?"* ("Chance the Rapper"). Christ's knowledge of these events was expansive and detailed, but the Father also called the Son to trust and obey in a way to inspire His disciples to follow in faith.

God' plan of redemption is to transform this current temporary world. The Kingdom of God is present in part, and still it has not yet come in completion. The Kingdom of God is within believers, yet believers are not yet within the expectant Kingdom. Life involves both tension and expectation. God's Kingdom transformation involves the resurrection of individuals, and a New

Creation redeemed from this world to the next. Key to God's work of full transformation is the coming Day of Judgment. The author, George Eldon Ladd writes:

> "There is to be a day of judgment, a day of separation among men. Christ one day will appear as the Son of man in glory to bring salvation to the sons of the Kingdom and a just condemnation to the sons of darkness. The Kingdom of God will then appear in power and glory. But in His grace, God has sent His Son among men in advance of that day. Christ has come among us to confront us with the blessings and demands of God's Kingdom. "Repent, for the kingdom of heaven has come near." Receive it! We may make a decision for that future Kingdom long before it comes in glory and judgment, because He who will be the future Judge has appeared among men to offer to them the life and blessing of that Kingdom here and now." "The Kingdom demands decision as it confronts men – eternal decision. Tomorrow has met today. The Age to Come has entered This Age. The life of tomorrow is offered to us in the here and now. Heaven, if you please, has kissed the earth. What are we to do? One thing... Repent! Turn around, and receive the Good News." G.E. Ladd. (The Gospel of the Kingdom. W.M. Eerdmans Publishing Co. Grand Rapids, MI.. P. 106.)

If faith, and living out the teachings of Jesus, were so easy, then the Gospel of the Kingdom would have already been shared in beautiful testimony throughout the world by now. However, the reality of just how hard it is for people to repent and receive God's gift of grace and new life in Christ has resulted in a patient work of God's mercy. While the "Age to Come has entered this Age", the embrace and love of heaven has not always been met with faith and love for God. Until the Day of Judgment, there will be a mix of responses. What is essential to note is that God will not let His

Kingdom plan be thwarted or delayed forever. A Day of reckoning, with dread and hope, is coming.

The point of this book is not only to declare the coming of the Lord Jesus to judge the earth and its peoples; the point is to help people consider three questions:

1: What did Jesus know about the End Times and Judgment that is essential for us to understand?

2: What does this mean for us today as we live and examine our relationships and shared existence as humanity?

3: How can we share the Gospel of God's Kingdom through faith and service? What would this look like for the Church, and for individual witness?

Hopefully, this exploration of Matthew 24-25 will help us to explore answers to these questions and discover the voice of Jesus speaking into our life and existence. The message of the Lord has great import and consequence for anyone who is willing to listen carefully to the truth contained and the mystery being revealed. No one should promise that all questions will be answered, nor should they be answered. Nonetheless, Jesus offers four essential blessings to all who believe and receive His word, and His presence:

1. The light to walk in faith and trust in God, and this as revealed in the Holy Bible.

2. The grace to know that we may receive forgiveness and new life through Jesus Christ, and be born-again in God's Holy Spirit.

3. The inspiration to see Jesus in all of life, every relationship and each moment of service.

4. The security of hope to believe in God's Kingdom plan and the believer's complete transformation.

In navigating life and the times ahead, I see a parallel to sailing. When I was growing up in Michigan, our family had a sailing canoe. Imagine the balancing act and attention to the wind and waves needed to sail a canoe without capsizing. My dad taught us how to steer the rudder and hold on to the rope that went to the boom of the sail, sometimes pulling it in tight to closely capture the wind and other times letting it out to adjust to the strength and direction of the wind, with thought to our intended destination. In the center of the canoe, we had boards that went up or down and would act as a keel to either side. Without this "centering" it was difficult to go forward at various angles of the wind. Constant vigilance, discernment and adjustment were required to navigate, otherwise one would lose control or drift far off course. Sailing required watching the waves, feeling the wind and keeping an eye on the weather.

Navigating the seasons of life, and the tumultuous times we live in, is as essential now as it was almost 2000 years ago when Jesus promised that He would return. We are called to steer wisely, hold fast to the sail rope and not give up or let go until we reach Heaven's shore (or He returns to bring us home). We have been taught here in Matthew 24-25 to watch for the signs of the end times with awareness, caution and adjustment to the wind and waves. The Lord teaches us to be discerning, not to listen to ill winds of false messiahs that could lead us astray. The Lord calls us to follow Him to steer in the direction that will balance speed and control, and catch the winds of the Holy Spirit that lead to helping those in need, caring for those lost on life's troubled seas. The analogy of sailing reminds us that we are on a journey.

If origins are to be considered in our journey, then God is to be trusted as the One who desires to help bring us safely into the harbor of His grace and truth from which all of us have our being. The choices we make in the journey relate to others in the sea of life, these choices affect the direction we take and our ultimate destination. Even if the seas get rough, and the rope of the sail slips from our hands and our boat capsizes; there is One who is our Savior and Deliverer. May we never forget Christ's promise:

27 Peace I leave with you; my peace I give you. I do not give to you as the world gives. Do not let your hearts be troubled and do not be afraid. – (John 14:27)

When this age ends, it will come to an end amidst a time of great trial and tribulation. Jesus will authorize God's angels to gather "the elect" from around the world. Eventually, the great tribulation will lead to a time when all people shall appear before Jesus the Christ for judgment. Jesus teaches in Matthew 24-25 that readiness involves:

(1) Faithfully believing and following Him

(2) Not being fooled by false messiahs

(3) Serving others as God would have us to with compassion, mercy and loving sacrifice.

While the world may grow cold and impersonal, the life of God's people will radiate love through humble service. Kindness will be shown to those who are hungry, thirsty, homeless, naked, sick and imprisoned. People will struggle with depression and dehumanization. Amidst natural catastrophes and limited resources, we shall struggle to meet all the intense needs of the world. Despite everything, the Body of Christ, the Church, is to be present in ways to show God's love, forgiveness and the eternal hope of Heaven. The faithful will overcome through the help of the Holy Spirit to worship God with their deeds of joy, and offer a sacrifice of praise with their helping hands and hospitality.

Questions for Discussion –
Introduction and Matthew 13:24-30

1. In your life, what were you taught about the Second Coming of Jesus? How is this a concern to you?

2. How does the Parable of "The Crops and Weeds" (Matthew 13:24-30) help to explain God's plan of salvation and judgment?

3. Why is it difficult in the parable for the servants of God to live with the weeds still in the garden?

4. How do we encourage one another to keep strong in the faith while we wait for God's plan to unfold?

Dedication and Thanks

Before going further into this adventure, I want to thank my wife Marilyn for her love and patience with me. She inspires me daily by her gift of mercy and ability to see through people to discern their motives. She is a great witness to the presence of God as a Christian. I also want to thank my mother and father, Gene and Esther Arnold, for their faithfulness to show the love of Christ.

I specifically dedicate this book to our three sons (Mark, Thom and John) for their questions, desire for truth and searching for answers at a time that their generation is facing incredible challenges. There is hope, the book of life is still being written.

I am thankful for my grandfather, Rev. Forrest Gilmore, and the example of pastoral care he gave me which informs and inspires my own pastoral ministry and chaplaincy. I am thankful also for each church I grew up in, and for every church I was honored to serve. The spiritual battle throughout life has been challenging, but Jesus is still shining His light unto my steps and path, and our Lord is faithful to the humble and meek who love Him, so that we will finish the race and see His Kingdom come.

I am particularly thankful to my current church family and place of service at First Baptist Church of Bedford, Massachusetts. They are gracious and kind, willing to work together as a genuine Body of Believers as we follow and serve Jesus together.

– Scott T. Arnold

Table of Contents:

"What Did Jesus Know?"
"Matthew 24 & 25 - End Times and Judgment"

Historical and Scriptural Context and Application:

While we shall delve into this passage of the Bible, especially one that carries such weight as Matthew 24 and 25, a summary of the historical, scriptural and theological significance of Jesus must be stated. The purpose here will be to relate Jesus' life and teaching to the context of what people were perceiving and experiencing at that time, and then to make correlations to today. What is important to note was that many God-fearing Jews and Gentiles were as interested in God's intervention to redeem humanity then as we find in our times.

Belief of a coming Messiah and a New Age that would fulfill the words and visions of the prophets Isaiah, Daniel, Micah and Ezekiel was strong, especially since the Romans had taken more control of Jerusalem and the Temple. Hopes of Jesus being the Christ, the Messiah, were growing as people witnessed Jesus' miracles and heard God's word with authority in His teaching. The expectation was that Jesus would take the next steps to establish the Kingdom of God on earth with might and power. Instead, "Jesus left the Temple", immediately following His confrontation of religious and political leaders. He refrained from the using His Divine authority to enforce the Kingdom of God or establish His rule through force. Jesus follows His Father's will by choosing the path of mercy and following the way of love that leads eventually to the cross. Victory would be won through atonement of sins and empowerment through the resurrection. The battle Jesus chose was not the sword of man, but the sword of God's Spirit that can conquer sin and death with forgiveness and the power of love.

Applied to today, we learn from Jesus that the way of God is the way of mercy and grace first. Judgment and justice will come, and yes, the Kingdom of God will be established, and a New Age will accompany a New Heaven and Earth. However, until then, we learn from Jesus the essence of God's redemptive care: *"Be merciful as your Father is merciful. (Luke 6:36)"*. Jesus revealed that God is at work as we reflect the nature of God, disciples are called to be transformed and led by God's Holy Spirit. Until the work of God's redemption and re-creation is completed (in Christ's return), God is extending His covenant to all who will repent and then receive the gift of God's forgiveness and grace. Jesus came for this purpose, and He has entrusted believers with the joyful (yet very challenging) service of bringing people into the Kingdom through faith, not force. Jesus ministered to the heart of humanity, and the nature of God has been revealed as forbearing and forgiving. God is holy and righteous, and the reign and rule of God will be established upon the earth in the fulness of time. Therefore, while we live and journey in faith, the work of God's salvation is unfolding, and the Kingdom of God is moving in ways that are initially transforming but ultimately fully redemptive.

God is not absent. Indeed, the Spirit of God that moved upon the face of the deep at creation's dawn is still moving upon the faces of humanity who come to behold God's light in Jesus Christ. Therefore, even though the days and world seem dark, may people of faith continue to spread the good news. God's redemptive plan in Christ is actively restorative and resplendent; as Habakkuk, the prophet wrote *"For the earth will be filled with the knowledge of the glory of the Lord as the waters cover the sea."* (Habakkuk 2:14 NIV). With the second coming of Jesus Christ in Glory, God's plan of salvation, judgment and redemption shall be made complete. The earth shall be filled with the Glory of the Lord in that conclusive, yet inaugural, moment. The current book of history shall end, and a new book shall begin.

Part 1: "Jesus has left the Temple."
(Prophecy of destruction)
Matthew 24:1-3

1 Jesus left the temple and was walking away when his disciples came up to him to call his attention to its buildings. 2 "Do you see all these things?" he asked. "Truly I tell you, not one stone here will be left on another; every one will be thrown down." 3 As Jesus was sitting on the Mount of Olives, the disciples came to him privately. "Tell us," they said, "when will this happen, and what will be the sign of your coming and of the end of the age?" Matthew 24:1-3

Introduction: "God's timing"

Consider the timing of Jesus walking away from the Temple in Jerusalem. He loved the city and its people, and He had many good memories of praying there, worshipping there since He was a young lad. At twelve years of age, He was the prodigy child teaching with wisdom and great knowledge in the Temple courts; young Jesus was so carried away with doing the work of His Heavenly

Father that He didn't pay notice to His family leaving for Nazareth. Jesus had been dedicated and brought up in the ways of Yahweh. Jesus would eventually be greeted with cheers and palm branches as the Messiah. Jesus, in His righteousness, could not stand for injustice and would turn over the tables of the corrupt money changers who had turned the Temple into a den of thieves. In His last days in Jerusalem before His passion, He would speak truth to power in Matthew 21-23, He would confront the Pharisees and Sadducees, speaking of seven woes to these religious leaders as they were gathered in Jerusalem's Temple:

"*Woe to you, teachers of the law and Pharisees, you hypocrites! You shut the door of the kingdom of heaven in people's faces.*" (Matthew 23:13)

"*Woe to you, teachers of the law and Pharisees, you hypocrites! You travel over land and sea to win a single convert, and when you have succeeded, you make them twice as much a child of hell as you are.*" (Matthew 23:15)

"*Woe to you, blind guides!*" (Matthew 23:16)

"*Woe to you, teachers of the law and Pharisees, you hypocrites! You give a tenth of your spices—mint, dill and cumin. But you have neglected the more important matters of the law—justice, mercy and faithfulness.*" (Matthew 23:23)

"*Woe to you, teachers of the law and Pharisees, you hypocrites! You clean the outside of the cup and dish, but inside they are full of greed and self-indulgence.*" (Matthew 23:25)

"*Woe to you, teachers of the law and Pharisees, you hypocrites! You are like whitewashed tombs, which look beautiful on the outside but on the inside are full of the bones of the dead and everything unclean.*" (Matthew 23:27)

"Woe to you, teachers of the law and Pharisees, you hypocrites! You build tombs for the prophets and decorate the graves of the righteous. 30 And you say, 'If we had lived in the days of our ancestors, we would not have taken part with them in shedding the blood of the prophets.' 31 So you testify against yourselves that you are the descendants of those who murdered the prophets. 32 Go ahead, then, and complete what your ancestors started" (Matthew 23:29-32).

Jesus did not mince words to make this moment of prophetic woe more palatable. People wondered if Jesus was the Messiah, the "presence" and "truth of God" incarnate? The question of Jesus' identity and authority then is still a pertinent question now. In this poignant and raw confrontation, which the Lord had with Israel's teachers and religious leaders, Jesus was contending with their deceit and denial. Still, He chose love over hate, forgiveness over condemnation.

"You snakes! You brood of vipers! How will you escape being condemned to hell? 34 Therefore I am sending you prophets and sages and teachers. Some of them you will kill and crucify; others you will flog in your synagogues and pursue from town to town. 35 And so upon you will come all the righteous blood that has been shed on earth..." (Matthew 23:33-35).

Jesus did not use His divine authority as the Son of God to enforce the Kingdom of God. Instead, He desired that they be saved from the ultimate condemnation of hell. Jesus tried warning them, but their willful rejection had culminated in this moment, and now Jesus sought to prepare them for His upcoming perfect sacrifice. The crucifixion would be used by God, through the freely offered gift of His Son, as the divinely appointed means of reconciliation and redemption.

To conclude this final Temple discourse with the religious leaders, Jesus cried out in compassion:

> *"37 Jerusalem, Jerusalem, you who kill the prophets and stone those sent to you, how often I have longed to gather your children together, as a hen gathers her chicks under her wings, and you were not willing. 38 Look, your house is left to you desolate. 39 For I tell you, you will not see me again until you say, 'Blessed is he who comes in the name of the Lord.'"* (Matthew 23:37-39)

With this statement, Jesus' words rang out, tolling the trouble that was ahead. Jesus had spoken with God's truth and grace, conviction and compassion. The Word of the prophet Jesus, the Son of God, the King of the Jews, the Son of Man, the Good Shepherd, the Way, Truth and Life was revealed. As the Lord and Savior left the Temple, what would the result be? Jesus gave a promise, He would return. Though He would die upon a cross for our sins, we would see Him again. There would be a resurrection after His death. Jesus, in God's plan, has ascended to Heaven to intercede for us at the right hand of the Thone of God; He shall return someday in triumph and glory to establish the Kingdom of God on earth as it is in Heaven. How are we to live and prepare for Christ's Kingdom? That is what Matthew 24 and 25 is all about.

Outline of Scripture Study: Matthew 24:1-3

I. What was Jesus walking away from? (v.1a)
    A. Jesus left a building
    B. Jesus left unaccepted
    C. Jesus left misunderstood
    D. Jesus left with a purpose and direction

II. What were the Disciples fixated upon? (v.1b)
    A. The disciples perceived a change in Jesus
    B. The disciples tried to redirect the attention of Jesus
    C. The disciples were fixated on the material and political

III. What did Jesus know that made Him see things differently? (2)
    A. Jesus points at the symbols of man's glory (2a)
    B. Jesus wants them to see beyond the immediate (2b)
    C. Jesus prophecies the destruction of the temple (2c)
    D. Jesus prophecies the devastation coming (2d)

IV. What would you like to ask Jesus? (3)
    A. Jesus waits for us to ask. (3a)
    B. Questions about when (3b)
    C. Questions about what to look for (3c)

V. How will Jesus answer their questions and ours?

Study on Matthew 24:1-3.

I. What was Jesus walking away from? (v.1a)

1 Jesus left the temple and was walking away...

A. Jesus left a building -

Jesus left the Jerusalem Temple that was rebuilt by Herod the Great. Herod was the very same Roman-approved monarch who entertained the Three Wise Men who followed celestial signs in search of a messianic newborn king. Herod then used deception to carry on his own search in Bethlehem for the one prophesized. In the cloak of darkness and evil, Herod ordered the slaughter of young children in the City of David. Jesus may have considered all this in looking at these buildings. Jesus didn't see the temple complex and surrounding buildings as sacred in themselves. He saw it as a sacred place for the people of God to worship. Others had built temples there before, Solomon and Zerubbabel, not near as large and massive, but still symbolic and guided by the instruction of God's anointed kings, priests and prophets. Times of favor and disfavor from God had surrounded this place of worship. During the Babylonian exile, in the time of the prophet Ezekiel, God even gave a vision of His Spirit's presence leaving the Temple. After Israel had learned many lessons pertinent to being faithful to God, and not to give in to the deception of false teachers and idols, God helped them to return to Jerusalem. The first project of renewal was to rebuild the walls of Jerusalem with the leadership of Nehemiah. Eventually, the second Temple was built with the leadership of Ezra and Zerubbabel.

Now, centuries later, this second Temple was built larger by Roman engineering under the prideful watch of Herod. This was an impressive structure, with work beginning in 20 B.C. and the final decorations and appointments concluding in 26 A.D. just a few years prior to Jesus' ministry. Josephus, the Jewish historian notes that "*In that temple were several stones which were 45 cubits in length, 5 cubits in height, and 6 cubits in breadth;*" (converted to feet, some of these stones were more than 70 feet long, 10 feet wide, and 8 feet high). This was Roman engineering at its height of human glory.

Jesus leaves all this structure with its strength and decorated beauty. He left not just one building, but a succession of buildings, courts and various people in worship. The procession from the center sanctuary courts to the peripheral walls and beautiful gates of the temple mount was viscerally moving and visually inspiring for Jesus' disciples. Jesus, however, experienced and saw things differently. He was not impressed by the material and temporal attempts of man that fell short of the glory of God. This was not the actual temple where the perfect sacrifice would be given. Indeed, He was the vessel and temple of the living God. His body was the living temple, the abiding place of God in human flesh. Jesus would give the perfect sacrifice in love by His body and blood, the very symbols He would hold in His hands at the Lord's Supper. Jesus identifies that the bread and the cup relate to His mission as the ultimate Passover Lamb of God for the sins of the world.

Jesus teaches us not to place our hope in buildings, or in the glories of man. Jesus teaches people to worship God in Spirit and in Truth. The walls, towers, bridges, structures, facades and porticos of man are often constructed in blood, even though they are pointed to in pride. God desires something better. Our Heavenly Father is looking for people who will seek His presence and not substitute their worship with idolatry, apostasy, or symbols of false security. Today, the symbols of success and security are not only great buildings or personal palaces, they may be automobiles, the ever-handy smart phone, tablet or computer, clothing of status or tools of technology and convenience. People create many types of vessels or temples, often their motivation and use are detrimental to their spiritual, social and psychological well-being. Walking away can sometimes be necessary, even healthy and wise.

B. Jesus left unaccepted -

When Jesus left the Temple, it was not with fanfare and applause. He left rejected with only a few disciples tagging behind. The religious leaders did not hear His teachings and did not heed His warnings of woe. Jesus clarified His authority as the Son of God in parables of the Kingdom, but they could not accept His authority. Why? Perhaps they were so far out of touch with the Spirit of God that they could not hear the truth. Repentance is difficult when self-righteousness blinds people. Jesus didn't fit their agendas and He certainly did not fit the shape of a conquering Messiah. Jesus was rejected by both the religious leaders and the revolutionary religious Zealots.

Acceptance by others feels good, we are after all, social beings. Jesus did feel the sting of being rejected. This did not deter His willingness to serve and His ability to love people in accord with His service to His Heavenly Father. One might even say that Christ's perspective and purpose was clarified in rejection. The work He was sent to complete was not to reform the existing religious and worship structures. Jesus came to bring about a radical new work that fulfilled the rituals of sacrifice in the Temple, through His perfect sacrifice. In so doing, God would create a new covenantal relationship in Christ's resurrection, and the impartation of New Life in the Holy Spirit. In Christ, God's truth and grace fulfilled both the law and the words of prophecy for the Kingdom of Heaven. The eventual fulfillment of God's Kingdom shall be completed in the Second Coming of Jesus Christ.

In our time, and in the end times, people will need to distinguish between when the church or the temple is being faithful or heretical, when the church needs to be confronted or when a person needs to find another church to fellowship and serve in.

There is a time to reform, and a time to give space and walk away. Being accepted is not the issue, being faithful to God, to Christ, and to service for the Lord in His Church is a matter of utmost importance. One should not try to justify themselves over minor matters, but trust the Lord when it comes to the important matters of God's Kingdom. The Church must cleanse itself from political entanglements and follow Jesus' example of unconditional love.

C. Jesus left misunderstood -

Jesus presented Himself as clearly as one could, but people just didn't understand. When people's ignorance and blindness keeps them from perceiving the truth about what is happening, then it is essential that we give them time. We need to trust that God's Spirit is at work to reveal truth and get through to people eventually. For Jesus, He knew that a big revealing event was ahead, His passion, death and resurrection. This event was not simply going to reflect His own character and that of God His Father in love and forgiveness; Jesus' death on Calvary would be an event where the very atoning and redemptive work of God would be accomplished. Three days later, the resurrection of Jesus at the Garden tomb would validate how Jesus death was purposeful, and eternal life itself was revealed. Some things are not understood until they happen and the evidence is in provided. Jesus' ministry was not understood until well after it all took place. Even now, people are still catching on to the Gospel of God's Kingdom in Jesus Christ.

Believers should not be surprised if people without faith may not understand. Trusting God and His Son Jesus will help believers to endure people's ignorance and blindness. If you are a person who struggles with believing, Jesus understands and can shine truth and grace into your life. If you are a person who has come to faith and yet struggles with friends or family that do not believe or understand, then trust in the ability of our Lord to shine truth and grace into their lives. None of us are the Savior, only Jesus is. There is a work of God's Spirit and Word (in Jesus Christ) that alone can lead a person into a right and bright relationship with the Living God. Pray for others as you pray for yourself to understand the wisdom, Word and ways of God our Creator/Redeemer.

D. Jesus left with a purpose and direction -

When Jesus left the Temple, He left a physical set of buildings. There was something more to this moment, however. In fact, He walked away from the trappings of political maneuvering, abuse of authority and temptation to use power for selfish gain. Instead, He embodied the very work of God by "being the Temple", the abiding place, our very High Priest as the Son of God. His purpose was to lay down His life for the lost sheep, for those He called friend, and even for those who despised and rejected Him. Jesus' purpose was our salvation, His direction was the Cross of Calvary as the bridge to God's gift of grace and eternal life. This was a purpose and direction that He did not need for Himself, but one that He chose to walk upon and go through on our account, for our being blessed and not cursed. The words of the prophet Isaiah speak of how Jesus, the suffering servant messiah, would conduct Himself:

> *4 Surely, he took up our pain and bore our suffering, yet we considered him punished by God, stricken by him, and afflicted. 5 But he was pierced for our transgressions, he was crushed for our iniquities; the punishment that brought us peace was on him, and by his wounds we are healed. 6 We all, like sheep, have gone astray, each of us has turned to our own way; and the Lord has laid on him the iniquity of us all.* Isaiah 53:4-6

When big changes are needed, the level of sacrifice becomes difficult to comprehend, seemingly impossible to bear. Not only did Jesus take up our pain and bear our sorrows on the cross (in a way that only He could do to accomplish God's work of personal salvation); Jesus also calls us to follow His way of life and service by picking up our crosses and following Him. The purpose and direction of God's people, the Church of Jesus, is to serve unselfishly and follow the teaching and example of our Lord. What the Church in the End Times will be challenged with is the fallout (consequence) of the Church's historical hypocrisy (imperfections) and the Church's theological move away from Scriptural orthodoxy. It is vital that Christians renew the priority of living like Jesus to be faithful disciples, and to embody the good news with the redemptive quality of the Gospel. Jesus is calling the Church, His true disciples, to shine the light of His grace and truth, especially as the times call for faithfulness and service.

II. <u>What were the Disciples fixated upon?</u> (v.1b)

… when his disciples came up to him to call his attention to its buildings. (Matthew 24:1b)

A.   The disciples perceived a change in Jesus -

The disciples, and many other people, were watching Jesus as He proceeded to leave the Temple. His facial expression and body language communicated a disturbing message. He was not looking back as He walked, He was not looking side to side. Jesus was focused on leaving, and the disciples came up to Him because the Lord's determination to leave was surprising and concerning to them.

B.   The disciples tried to redirect the attention of Jesus -

Anxiously, the disciples came up to Jesus to deter His departure and draw His attention back toward Jerusalem. Here was a city and temple that meant everything to the people of Israel. It was a city that Jesus had wept for, a focal point of history and hope. The priests and prophets spoke of God abiding in the Holy Place within the Temple, and of a time when God's Kingdom would come to earth and replace all earthly kingdoms (Daniel 7:26-27). The disciples and many devoted Israelites hoped that Jesus was in their midst for a radical, messianic, socio-political shake up.

In the twenty first century, people still try to redirect Jesus to bless their temporal hopes, and to assuage their insecurities. There is a danger and deception that occurs when people expect Jesus to fit their preconceptions and prejudices. Jesus is not smitten by the illusion or need to grasp for power. Indeed, He would use His divine authority and power to humble Himself in the form of a servant. He was leaving Jerusalem to fulfill a different role than that of political revolutionary and reformer. The resolute face of Jesus was now focused upon the passion, the cross. Jesus would bring a spiritual victory and reality in His death and resurrection. Jesus walked away, trusting in His Heavenly Father's intervention of atoning grace to be poured out as a result.

C.   The disciples were fixated on the material and political -

Buildings have a fascination and interest for most people. Structures like the Great Pyramids of Egypt, the Eifel Tower of Paris, the Taj Mahal of India, the Greek Parthenon, the Cathedral of Notre Dame, the Empire State building in New York, the Great Wall of China, and a great host of modern day skyscraper marvels, imprint a sense of wonder and imagination. Identification and fixation is placed on buildings as symbols of culture, religion, safety, beauty, progress and power. Some structures even give the impression or illusion of something transcendent, grand or glorious. When Jesus was being tempted by Satan in the wilderness (just after His baptism), the glory, power and greatness of the buildings and civilizations shown by the devil to Jesus were called to the Lord's attention (Luke 4:5). Now, a few years later, the disciples were calling attention to the glory of the buildings that composed the Temple Complex of Jerusalem. Jesus knew better than to fixate upon these temporal structures or give heed to these political symbols of power. Jesus was focused upon seeking the Kingdom of God, His Heavenly Father, first. Jesus was fully oriented and directed to trust that His Father's work was to establish a different Temple, with His very own body as the vessel that alone could provide the perfect living sacrifice for Divine grace and truth to abide in and prevail.

Many times, in human history, the material and political is given far more weight than the spiritual. While temporal things and socio-political matters are important, they are passing and transient. What we do as stewards and caretakers of this material world is vital, and our responsibilities relate to the importance of being the spiritual community God calls us to be. What is problematic, however, is when people start to over-manipulate our physical existence and socio-economical structures in ways that harm and malign. Jesus saw through the motives of the different factions in Jerusalem. The Pharisees wanted to preserve their artificial peace through keeping power. The Zealots wanted to create peace through violent revolution and deposing Roman rule and established Jewish leaders. Throughout history, the coalition of religious leaders with political entities of power has consistently proved damaging to the actual tenants and practice of peaceful religious adherence. The separation of Church and State among Christians was advocated by Jesus when He asked for a Roman coin, a denarius that had the image of Augustus Caesar on it. Jesus lifted the coin up and said: *"Render unto Caesar what is Caesar's and render unto God what is God's"* (Mark 12:16-17). Temporal concerns and responsibilities under governmental and social organization are given unto mankind by God, but ultimate worth, worship and purpose are to be given to God.

Because we live in a corrupt world, it is dangerous for any religious group to wed religious matters with state matters. Moral and ethical concerns are the domain of all who live. Still, no religious group can usher in the Kingdom of God by force, law or legislation. The way of God cannot be established by man's effort alone, or be enforced outside of the free will of people to respond in faith and obedience to the moving, and greater power, of God's Spirit. For those who believe the Gospel of the Kingdom of God in

Jesus Christ is a matter of crusade or conquest, the Lord Jesus Himself has given His teaching and example as a preventative to such error and deception.

III. What did Jesus know that made Him see things differently? (2)

> 2 "Do you see all these things?" he asked. "Truly I tell you, not one stone here will be left on another; every one will be thrown down."

A. Jesus points at the symbols of man's glory (2a) -
"Do you see all these things? He asked."

Jesus saw the Temple buildings and décor that the disciples pointed to. Gesturing with open hands to the Temple structures, the walls, the towers, the artwork and fine details adorning the structures; Jesus pointed at everything standing above ground. He may have even pointed out a few more things that the disciples had missed. Yes, Jesus could see all these structures and architecture, but these seemingly mighty stones and ornate walls were doomed for destruction. Their majesty and beauty were fleeting, soon to be toppled and laid waste.

This moment of Jesus remaining calm, during the whirlwind of controversy that surrounded Him, reminds me of a piece of art I once viewed at the Isabella Stuart Gardner museum in Boston. It was a large and dramatic painting by Rembrandt that showed Jesus and His disciples in their fishing vessel on the Sea of Galilee during a storm. A few years after I saw this painting, some thieves came in and stole this priceless masterpiece, along with others. Now, many years later, the painting is still missing. What a shame! While I would like to see it again, the message of the painting however, has stayed with me: "Through the storms of life, trust in Jesus. He can still the waters." The painting by Rembrandt was taken, but they could not steal the message of the Gospel. I believe the artist had rendered a message that symbolized something beyond the wealth and temporal valuations of human economy and culture. Jesus came to accomplish something greater than we could imagine, something priceless.

There are many ways that people can be diverted and distracted from a vital and personal relationship with God. The idols and symbols of mankind can be powerful visual focal points. Faith, and the life of the Spirit, must see through and beyond the constructions of human endeavor. Ultimately, we are called to seek, find, acknowledge and worship God in His Glory.

B. Jesus wants them to see beyond the immediate (2b) -
"Truly I tell you,"

Have you ever noticed that Jesus would often challenge His disciples to think more deeply, to question and consider life beyond their initial thoughts and assumptions? *"Truly.."* were the words Jesus spoke so that the disciples would pay attention, listen carefully, and become discerning. Truth may also reveal something that we may have no inkling about. Ignorance may give us a false sense of bliss and security, but more often Truth will set us free to be alert, ready, prepared. Truth, some may say, is a relative matter to each person as experience varies. This reduction of Truth to personal subjectivity and opinion is a poor substitute and rationalization (born of evil) that avoids the inevitable reality of God. Here was a moment when subjectivity and false assumptions about the future of Jerusalem, and the Kingdom of God, needed to be set aside. For Jesus, the Truth of what was about to happen was not guesswork, or some prescriptive approximation. Here, in this moment, an important Truth needed to be revealed about what was about to happen to the Temple of Jerusalem.

Jesus began His departure from Jerusalem with a startling prophecy about what would befall the people, the mighty Temple and its impressive walls. Truth is often difficult to receive, and even more difficult to digest. Looking at the Temple, perhaps even pointing to it from the outer courts just outside the structure, Jesus will tell them something disturbing and alarming. Their beloved city and Temple were in jeopardy, both would be destroyed. Jesus will eventually answer the resulting questions of the disciples after they leave the city and go to the Mount of Olives. They were in shock, however, as they walked with Him and began to wrestle with the significance of their Lord's words of foreknowledge.

C. Jesus prophecies the destruction of the temple (2c) -
"not one stone here will be left on another;" -

About 40 years after Jesus' death, resurrection and ascension; the Temple of Jerusalem, built by Herod the Great, would be destroyed (70 CE). This event would come because of the Judean resistance to Roman rule in part, but also due to the moral decay of Judaic society and the religious apostasy brought on by politically charged zealots whose conduct became appalling and abhorrent. Various reports (from both reliable and questionable sources) in Rome gave rise to contrasting views of the Jewish people. In addition, suspicion was also directed to Christians as an offshoot of Judaism. Both Jews and Christians were scattered throughout the Roman empire, and many were living peacefully outside of Judea as Roman citizens. However, in Judea and Jerusalem, resistance to Roman rule was met with ferocity and unscrupulous behavior, and so Emperor Titus justified the destruction of the Temple in Jerusalem:

> *"At any rate, with the temple in ruins, Titus set about depicting the religion of the Jews as not worthy to exist, and the Temple's destruction as an act of piety to the gods of the Roman world."* (Martin Goodman, "Jerusalem and Rome: The Clash of Ancient Civilizations").

The Jewish historian, Josephus, was a direct witness to the destruction of Jerusalem and was aware of each side, himself being a Jew and yet advocating a truce with the Romans. As much as Josephus tried to be an advocate of peace, He was viewed by Zealots as a traitor. In human conflict, there is a tendency for one group to demonize another group to commit horrendous acts of violence in the guise of subduing evil or immorality. The Romans were not above slander, and neither were the Jewish Zealots and Nationalists who also demonized their opponents.

Jesus tried to intervene and be a reconciler in His ministry. During the childhood of Jesus, as He grew up in Nazareth and traveled frequently to Jerusalem. He would have noted the ongoing struggle between Jews and Romans that existed all throughout Judea. Jesus welcomed Romans during His ministry and gave the gift of healing to their servants. Pilate found no fault in Jesus, and Jesus did not curse Pilate or the Roman soldiers who mocked and beat Him. Jesus was a peacemaker, and such was the path He exemplified for His true followers.

D. Jesus prophecies the devastation coming (2d)
"every one will be thrown down."

Did Jesus know that the level of conflict between Romans and Jews would grow so intense that it would involve a complete destruction of the Temple? It's fascinating that Jesus foretold the Temple's destruction with detail as He stopped to view Jerusalem at the beginning of His Peaceful Palm Sunday procession. Weeping for the city, Jesus had specific foreknowledge of what would happen:

> *41 As he approached Jerusalem and saw the city, he wept over it 42 and said, "If you, even you, had only known on this day what would bring you peace—but now it is hidden from your eyes. 43 The days will come upon you when your enemies will build an embankment against you and encircle you and hem you in on every side. 44 They will dash you to the ground, you and the children within your walls. They will not leave one stone on another, because you did not recognize the time of God's coming to you." Luke 19:41-44*

Jewish historian Josephus recorded that Jerusalem was conquered by the Romans building a wall around it to starve its residents. Eventually, a terrible battle ensued between the Romans and those Hebrew Zealots who did not leave, this refusal to yield to the Romans eventually involved the violent deaths of women, children and the elderly among the holdouts in Jerusalem. Finally, a decision needed to be made by the Roman leader Titus (Caesar) as he held counsel with his advisors concerning the destruction of Jerusalem's Temple:

> *Titus summoned his council, and before taking action consulted it whether he should overthrow a sanctuary of such workmanship, since it seemed to many that a sacred building, one more remarkable than any other human work, should not be destroyed. For if preserved it would testify to the moderation of the Romans, while if demolished it would be a perpetual sign of cruelty. On the other hand, others, and Titus himself, expressed their opinion that the Temple should be destroyed without delay, in order that the religion of the Jews and Christians should be more completely exterminated.* ("Jerusalem and Rome" p.421.)

Further details of the actual event of the Temple's destruction are given by Josephus:

> *At this moment, one of the soldiers, awaiting no orders and with no horror of so dread a deed, but moved by some supernatural impulse, snatched a brand from the burning timber and, hoisted up by one of his comrades, flung the fiery missile through a low golden door, which gave access on the north side to the chambers surrounding the sanctuary. As the flame shot up, a cry, as poignant as the tragedy, arose from the Jews, who flocked to the rescue, lost to all thought of self-preservation, all husbanding of strength, now that the object of all their past vigilance was vanishing. Titus was resting in his tent after the engagement, when a messenger rushed in with the tidings. Starting up just as he was, he ran to the Temple to arrest the conflagration; behind him followed his whole staff of generals, while in their train came excited legionaries, and there was all the hubbub and confusion attending the*

disorderly movement of so large a force. Caesar (Titus) both by voice and hand, signaled to the combatants to extinguish the fire; but they neither heard his shouts, drowned in the louder din which filled their ears, nor heeded his beckoning hand, distracted as they were by the fight or their fury... As they drew nearer to the sanctuary they pretended not even to hear Caesar's orders and shouted to those in front of them to throw in their firebrands. The insurgents, for their part, were now powerless to help; and on all sides was carnage and flight. Most of the slain were civilians, weak and unarmed people, each butchered where he was caught. Around the altar a pile of corpses was accumulating; down the steps of the sanctuary flowed a stream of blood, and the bodies of the victims killed above went sliding to the bottom. ("Jerusalem and Rome" p.421-422)

The capture and destruction of the Temple came amidst chaos and confusion, a reminder that "Evil", "Satan", has a way of using such moments. How was it Jesus had foreknowledge of this event? Indeed, Jesus wept. Jesus would also warn people prior to His first messianic entrance (which was as a servant to lay down His life). In the Olivet Discourse of Matthew 24 and 25, Jesus had given details of this upcoming destruction, along with forewarnings of future events within the bigger picture of God's plan. Jesus was not only the bearer of the Gospel, the Good News of God's grace and salvation; Jesus was also the bearer of prophetic doom, the destruction of Jerusalem and everything above the foundation of this temporal house of worship, Herod's Temple.

IV. <u>What would you like to ask Jesus?</u> (3)

3 As Jesus was sitting on the Mount of Olives, the disciples came to him privately. "Tell us," they said, "when will this happen, and what will be the sign of your coming and of the end of the age?"

A. Jesus waits for us to ask. (3a) -

As Jesus was sitting on the Mount of Olives, the disciples came to him privately.

Jesus positioned Himself to be available, to answer the questions of the disciples on the Mount of Olives. Jesus did not entertain questions or go into detail while on the Temple grounds, or while they were in the city proper. Here, in a safe place, a set aside time, a holy moment, Jesus will speak freely and openly. Our Lord calls us to ask, to inquire, to seek.

B. Questions about when (3b) -

"Tell us," they said, "when will this happen,"

The disciples were filled with questions, they were compelled by a desire for truth and knowledge, even if it would be difficult. They also had been expecting Jesus to fulfill the hopes of prophetic engagement regarding the Messiah, to bring radical change.

> *As far as the apostles were concerned, the ominous words of Jesus concerning the destruction of the temple could point only one direction: to the experiencing of the eschatological judgment. This was a subject to which Jesus had often alluded in his teaching ministry and therefore something they may well have expected him to indicate. They were accordingly eager to know how soon this might occur and what sign they might anticipate to indicate its approach... From their perspective, the destruction of the temple must have meant the coming again of Jesus, not as he now was with them when his glory was veiled but as the clearly revealed Son of God for all to see. Jesus had now to instruct them more closely about these matters, about the future he had intimated in his dramatic oracle of judgment."*
>
> (Donald A. Hagner, Word Biblical Commentary. Word Press, p. 688-689)

Jesus appreciated the interest of His disciples. He anticipated their questions. The matter of when it would happen had to be clarified by Jesus as a long-term work of God. Many Jews were hopeful, Jesus' disciples were hopeful. They wondered if Jesus could be the powerful messiah they had hoped for. They continued to ask Jesus, as they sat with Jesus while He was overlooking the "Valley of Jehoshaphat". They waited and watched from this vantage point, the Mt. of Olives. What would Jesus say as they looked down upon was thought to be the "Valley of Decision"? This was considered, by many Jews, to be the place of the final battle involving the defeat of evil and a time when the nations would receive judgment from their future Messiah.

C. Questions about what to look for (3c) -

.. and what will be the sign of your coming and of the end of the age?"

Jesus is about to answer these essential questions with a mix of specific and broad answers. At the heart of His answers is the reality that Jesus understood much more than we could ever begin to fathom or receive. Nonetheless, Jesus reveals enough to help the disciples gain a perspective of humility, awe and respect for God's Kingdom plan. They were already aware that Jesus, the Son of God, had come to reveal the nature of God in a way that personally communicated God's grace and Truth. Now, they longed to know how Jesus would apply Himself to address the power structures of Jewish hypocrisy and Roman rule that were colliding in Jerusalem and Judea. They believed that Jesus was about to act, and perhaps to even manifest the power of God to inaugurate something radically transformative of God's Kingdom; but when and how? How would they know when He would do this? What would be the sure signs? Their optimism that Jesus could bring an end to this world's madness was well-placed, but little did they know that the process and work of God required a bigger plan than their immediacy and limited knowledge could perceive.

V. How will Jesus answer their questions and ours?

We learn from Scripture that God works in ways that are not our ways. The purpose and plan of God will accomplish God's will. The seed of God's Son, which is the seed of the Gospel of God's Kingdom, built upon the seed of the Law and Commandments given through Moses to the Jews, and fulfilled in Jesus Christ, will yield a harvest in the fullness of time:

> "For my thoughts are not your thoughts, neither are your ways my ways," declares the Lord. 9 "As the heavens are higher than the earth, so are my ways higher than your ways and my thoughts than your thoughts. 10 As the rain and the snow come down from heaven, and do not return to it without watering the earth and making it bud and flourish, so that it yields seed for the sower and bread for the eater, 11 so is my word that goes out from my mouth: It will not return to me empty, but will accomplish what I desire and achieve the purpose for which I sent it. - Isaiah 55:8-11

The disciples discovered that Jesus, the Son of God, revealed the patient salvation-mission of His Heavenly Father. Through Christ's own obedience He fulfilled the righteousness of the law for the Gospel of God's Kingdom plan to be offered to all who repent and believe. There are still questions that remain. God will eventually answer our questions, but not always in the way we want our questions to be answered. Indeed, God will answer us according to what is truthful, timely, right and good in His will and proceedings. God's work to address human sin through Jesus was manifested in sacrificial love first, and this is still offered in this time of grace that we live in prior to the time of judgment. This extension of God's grace was therefore revealed in Jesus teachings there on the Mount of Olives. This was for His disciples then, and it was for generations of people to come.

Not every question we ask shall be answered in this present time. There are some things that can only be understood when the work of God's full transformation, His Kingdom, shall be completed. Therefore, we live with paradox, tension, and eager expectation for the Kingdom of God to be revealed. We bring our questions, our concerns and fears, in prayer to Jesus and listen to message of assurance and hope, warning and wisdom, that He has given.

Questions for Discussion:

1. What were some of the false assumptions people had about Jesus?

2. What false assumptions do people have today?

3. Why did Jesus leave Jerusalem and not use His divine power and authority to bring in the Kingdom of God in the way that the people wanted?

4. What do we learn about the disciples (and ourselves) as we consider how they wanted to know more about "signs of Jesus' coming and the end of the age"?

5. What are some of the big questions you would like to bring to Jesus concerning the coming of His Kingdom, end times and judgment?

Part 2: "Watch Out"
(Birth Pains, Proclamation and Persecution)
Matthew 24:4-14

4 Jesus answered: "Watch out that no one deceives you. 5 For many will come in my name, claiming, 'I am the Messiah,' and will deceive many. 6 You will hear of wars and rumors of wars, but see to it that you are not alarmed. Such things must happen, but the end is still to come. 7 Nation will rise against nation, and kingdom against kingdom. There will be famines and earthquakes in various places. 8 All these are the beginning of birth pains. 9 "Then you will be handed over to be persecuted and put to death, and you will be hated by all nations because of me. 10 At that time many will turn away from the faith and will betray and hate each other,
11 and many false prophets will appear and deceive many people. 12 Because of the increase of wickedness, the love of most will grow cold, 13 but the one who stands firm to the end will be saved. 14 And this gospel of the kingdom will be preached in the whole world as a testimony to all nations, and then the end will come. -
Matthew 24:4-14 (NIV)

Introduction: Who will you trust?

"The Death of Truth" was the title page of a Time Magazine periodical in the Fall of 2016. The election season in the United States of America was so contentious and divisive that it led to unscrupulous and unethical dissemination of information. On the internet, on television, and on printed media, so much was being thrown at people; much of it based on error, mere suggestion and even outright lies. Political rhetoric was coming from various parties and questionable sources; the melee created divisive ill-will and scarring scorn. Election meddling was evidenced, even foreign nations were involved. Candidates and the voting citizens were dizzied from imbibing in an elixir of misleading rhetoric. Who could you trust? The concern of deception reared its ugly head, with a voice that mocked truth, decency and civility. Who could keep their head together with discernment? Who would name the culprits behind their social media masks? The "author of lies" was at it again, besetting humanity with vex and venom, now in the 21st Century A.D. as it was also a thorny problem for Jesus in the first century A.D.

When Jesus first encountered disbelief, people opposed Him for addressing corruption and injustice by prophetically speaking divine truth to power. He noted that if God was respected as their Father, then people would receive the message of truth that He brought. Indeed, the question of whether to listen to Jesus, to believe He was the Christ, the Messiah, was critical to receive the Gospel of God's Kingdom. Faith would result in repentance. People would then experience freedom and salvation; but because many did not receive Him, because they could not hear the truth Jesus Christ bore, it revealed something dire about their spiritual condition as Jesus addressed them:

> *"You belong to your father, the devil, and you want to carry out your father's desires. He was a murderer from the*

beginning, not holding to the truth, for there is no truth in him. When he lies, he speaks his native language, for he is a liar and the father of lies. 45 Yet because I tell the truth, you do not believe me! 46 Can any of you prove me guilty of sin? If I am telling the truth, why don't you believe me? 47 Whoever belongs to God hears what God says. The reason you do not hear is that you do not belong to God."
John 8:44-47 (NIV)

Jesus confronted His fellow Jews because they had forsaken God in their affections, in their essential worship and devotion, even as their superficial actions approximated following the law of Moses. They were fooling themselves by not receiving Jesus and the message He came to bring. Jesus spoke the Truth, and they did not believe Him because they did not belong to God via a genuine faith like that of Abraham and Moses. Jesus saw through their false assumptions and pretense, and behind it all was the deceiver, the devil, the "father of lies".

What exactly are the issues at hand, then and now? Who you trust is not simply a matter of being dismissive and saying, "trust no one"; that is a rejection that God is Truth and one may know God. The issue is also not that Truth and facts are unavailable or undiscernible. Jesus did teach that *"You shall know the Truth and the Truth shall set you free"* (John 8:31-32). Non-sense has been reasoned, and chaotic conclusions have been reached by those who operate from the presumption that "truth is fully relative and never absolute". On the contrary, people have an innate desire to know what is right, good and true. To discern what is true or false, and to operate from a base of trust, is essential for us to live, move and have our being. We are creatures who were born in the truth of being made with inherent value, that is, being made in the "image of God".

Because of humanity's fall; however, people trust deception, false competing voices, market manipulators, pundits, hackers, nutty professors, gossipers, liars, and myth makers. We have exchanged the Truth for lies that divert our attention and pollute our perceptions. The Apostle Paul put it this way as it mattered in the realm of faith: *"They exchanged the truth of God for a lie"* (Romans 1:25). The antidote for humanity is not simply that we try harder to tell the truth, for deep within our minds and hearts something needs to change. Jesus came for this very reason, He is the antidote from God, and the very presence of God as the Only Begotten Son, to lead us in the path of Truth and righteousness. He said: *"...If you hold to my teaching, you are really my disciples. Then you will know the truth, and the truth will set you free."* John 8:31-32. Then again Jesus said: *"I am the way and the truth and the life, no one comes to the Father except through me"* (John 14:6-7).

Focusing on Christ's teaching of warning about false messiahs in Matthew 24:4-14, a key question may be asked. What are the motives of people? What agenda do they have? Watch out! People will lie and deceive to achieve their own ends, not necessarily in respect of what is good for all, or in tune with our Creator's will and purposes. Jesus answers the questions of the disciples by beginning His "Olivet discourse" with the words *"Watch out that no one deceives you"*. His words ring out as a warning, a declaration, a clarion of prophecy for generations to come. Jesus sets the tone of warning and God's wisdom in approaching this difficult and controversial prophecy. His goal was not only to warn and prepare people for the centuries and millenniums to come, His goal was to give hope by revealing a glimpse of God's Kingdom plan that will address the problem of human sin and suffering. People are not exempt from involvement; indeed, people are in the mix of problem and potential. People are called to seek and represent the Truth and endure with faith, hope and love. There is a work in progress and we are called to grow in faith, repent from sin, trust God, name and overcome evil and deception, be faithful to God in service and become faithful bearers, protectors, communicators, of what is good, right and true.

Outline of Matthew 24:4-14

I. Jesus knows that they must become wise about deception (v.4)

II. Jesus warns about false messiahs (v.5)
- A. There will be many imposters (5a)
- B. They will make false claims and give false hope (5b)
- C. There will be many people who will be deceived (5c)

III. Jesus warns that times of trouble will come (6-8)
- A. Wars and rumors of war (6a)
- B. Faith must be greater than fear (6b)
- C. Patience and perspective are needed to endure (6c)
- D. God's Kingdom plan comes after much time and trial (7)
  1. Political turmoil and conflict (7a)
  2. Natural disasters (7b)
- E. Analogy of "birth pains" - The coming of God's Kingdom (8)
  1. The process is underway
  2. The process will take time
  3. The process will consummate in a good result

IV. Jesus warns that persecution will occur (9-11)
- A. False accusations, arrests and executions (9a)
- B. Hatred and rejection in every nation (9b)
- C. Denial, betrayal and strife (10)
- D. Apostacy and deception (11)

V. Jesus warns about the danger of losing faith, hope and love (12-13)
- A. Evil will infect many and bring about coldness (12)
- B. Believers will stay compassionate and committed to God (13)

VI. Jesus reveals God's mission and what needs to be fulfilled (14)
- A. The Gospel of the Kingdom will be preached worldwide (14a)
- B. The testimony of believers as a witness of Jesus Christ (14b)
- C. God's plan involves a fulfillment of invitation (14c)

Study on Matthew 24:4-14

I. <u>Jesus knows that they must become wise about deception</u> (v.4)

4 Jesus answered: "Watch out that no one deceives you.

Danger is present. "Watch out!" Jesus warned the inner circle of disciples then to make sure that they would not be deceived by false teachers. The concern was urgent, yet it was also set into the future. Jesus was about to teach them something that applied to their upcoming trials, and the trials of future generations. The dawning of the Age of the Gospel of the Kingdom, brought by Jesus' perfect example, life and sacrifice (the gift of God's grace and Truth in Christ), was accompanied by the power and baptism of the Holy Spirit of God that gives New Life. The light of salvation was shining anew in Jesus' life, death and resurrection. The spiritual hope, and the real battle for the souls of mankind, escalated with the "Church Age." This was not a replacement for God's covenant with Abraham, but an extension and fulfillment of God's plan and promise.

In studying history since Christ, one should not be shocked or surprised to see that there have been political and religious leaders who have violated people's trust and twisted the Gospel of Jesus to suit their agendas for power and personal gain. Jesus' first words of response to their questions about the coming of God's Kingdom, and the "signs of the end of the age", began with an alarm for discernment, a warning of danger which was both immediate and long term.

II. Jesus warns about false messiahs (v.5)

. 5 For many will come in my name, claiming, 'I am the Messiah,' and will deceive many.

A. There will be many imposters (5a) -
"5 For many will come in my name, "

Jesus was fully aware that people would come after Him with the potential of misrepresentation. Using the name of Jesus (which meant "savior"), imposters have justified their false authority and deceitful actions to achieve ends that are not in keeping with the will and timing of God. Because Jesus had given a good name to God, it is not surprising the devil would want to discredit Jesus' name and authority. False Christs would come. People claiming to be disciples of Jesus, but not living in harmony and spirit with the teachings and values of Jesus and God's peaceful Kingdom, would lead or join the wide path of deception.

The problem of speaking the name of Jesus upon one's lips, but not confessing Jesus as Lord in one's heart and living in faithful obedience to God, becomes the issue. Jesus didn't say that this was a minor problem of a few heretics and maniacs, He emphasized that there would be "many" who would falsely come in His name. This is consistent with Jesus' teaching from the Sermon on the Mount:
"Enter through the narrow gate. For wide is the gate and broad is the road that leads to destruction, and many enter through it. But small is the gate and narrow the road that leads to life, and only a few find it. Matthew 7:13-14

B. They will make false claims and give false hope
(5b) *"claiming, 'I am the Messiah,'"*

The claim of being the "Messiah" carries with it a magnitude of divine promise and hopeful expectation. There is only One who is to be "the Messiah" in the scope of Divine/Human redemptive history according to the Hebrew prophets and writings of the Apostles. There was debate among the teachers and Pharisees of Jesus' time as to the origin of the Messiah. On one hand, the prophecy stated that He would be of the lineage of King David, and on the other hand there was prophecy stating that the Messiah would be God, or God's Son, intervening in a direct way as *"the Most High"* (Daniel 7 and Isaiah 9:6-7). In the Temple, before leaving, Jesus questioned the Pharisees to challenge their assumption that He was not the Messiah:

> *While the Pharisees were gathered together, Jesus asked them, 42 "What do you think about the Messiah? Whose son is he?" "The son of David," they replied. 43 He said to them, "How is it then that David, speaking by the Spirit, calls him 'Lord'? For he says, 44 "'The Lord said to my Lord: "Sit at my right hand until I put your enemies under your feet."' 45 If then David calls him 'Lord,' how can he be his son?" - Matthew 22:41-45*

The results were telling of their presumption for a human political leader, and not a direct revelation, manifestation, of God's Son incarnate in human flesh in their midst. David knew the Lord Jesus as the pre-incarnate Son of God through the revelation of God in prayer and praise. David beheld the Son of God seated at the right hand of God the Father/Creator even before Jesus' incarnation.

> *7 For the king trusts in the Lord; through the unfailing love of the Most High he will not be shaken. 8 Your hand will lay hold on all your enemies; your right hand will seize your foes. 9 When you appear for battle, you will burn them up as in a blazing furnace. The Lord will swallow them up in his wrath, and his fire will consume them.* (Psalm 21:7-9)

The Pharisees were not just closed minded, they were jaded with skepticism as many Zealots and revolutionaries had led Israel astray before. What made Jesus different? How could they be sure Jesus was the Messiah, the fulfillment of God's plan of salvation?

The answer had been provided time and again by Jesus, whose teaching, miracles and character proved flawless and spirit-filled.

Many false messiahs would come soon after Jesus, prior to the destruction of the Temple in 70 A.D. One was known as the "Egyptian", a Jew who led his followers to the Mount of Olives as he claimed doom upon the Romans at Jerusalem and victory for himself. Jewish historian of the time, Josephus, writes:

> But there was an Egyptian false prophet that did the Jews more mischief than the former; for he was a cheat, and pretended to be a prophet also, and got together thirty thousand men that were deluded by him; these he led round about from the wilderness to the mount which was called the Mount of Olives, and was ready to break into Jerusalem by force from that place; and if he could but once conquer the Roman garrison and the people, he intended to domineer over them by the assistance of those guards of his that were to break into the city with him. But Felix prevented his attempt, and met him with his Roman soldiers, ("A History of the Jewish People in the Time of Jesus" Peter Connolly. 1983 p. 66)

The "Egyptian" (one of the false messiahs Jesus warned them about) somehow escaped, it was soon afterward that the Apostle Paul was arrested while teaching in Jerusalem. The Roman garrison assumed that Paul must be the "Egyptian" because people were stirred up. When Paul appealed to be given a fair trial as a Roman Citizen, and spoke clearly in fine Greek, they realized he couldn't be the "Egyptian". God used the moment of false identification to allow Paul the opportunity to be transported to Rome. Paul and the early believers participated in sharing the Gospel at a time when people were being bombarded by false messiahs who advocated the use of violence and used coercion to gain power.

Fellow Jews who were not following the way of peace, and wanted to keep fighting Rome, initiated a revolt in 65-70 A.D. that resulted in the Temple's destruction. Then, over sixty years later, the "Bar Kokhba" revolt, led by a Simon bar Kokhba, against the Romans took place from 132-136 A.D.. From that violent conflict the result was the forced dispersion of Jews and Christians from the region of Judea. Increased persecution was unfairly applied to innocent Jews and Christians throughout the Roman Empire, and an attempt of genocide of the Hebrew people was promoted by some Romans.

Historically, the danger of following messiahs who justify "holy war" affects all religions. Sadly, even as Christians gained influence, status and power during the later Roman Empire, the abuse of leaders and people following false leaders continued to be played out through the history of "church". Throughout Europe, the union of church and state brought about corruption within the Catholic church and the Church of England. Instead of unity being promoted among people of the Christian faith, there was conflict and war. Eventually, the anti-sematic antagonism of the Romans was kept alive for centuries through parts of Europe.

Leading up to World War II, Germans, and even some Americans with close European ties (particularly within the Ku Klux Klan), believed Hitler and his evil teachings that promoted "the Arian race" as superior, a "chosen people". Of course, the great African American boxer, Joe Lewis, beat that theory by defeating German boxer Max Schmeling in 1938. This was a rematch; Joe Lewis had lost to Schmeling in 1936. In America, the history of the Black people has been a difficult and inspiring saga, many times having to overcome the prejudice of people who put on the façade of church and the Christian faith. Throughout the world, the significant moral failings of people who pretend to be Christians has often been a negative witness, and the sins of a few have been applied to the whole. For that reason, people will often not listen to a faithful reading and application of the Gospel. The fault has never been with Jesus and His teachings, but with false prophets, "wolves in sheep's clothing", hacks, and those who have advocated violence and deceptive teaching to mask ill-intent, manipulation and evil.

C. There will be many people who will be deceived (5c) *"and will deceive many."*

Thus far, the focus of Jesus was on warning people of coming "false messiahs", leaders who would deceive. Now, Jesus indicates that deception has another side, those who receive lies and believe them. The mass deception of people leads one to consider three things:

1: How do people receive and process information?
2: How do people discern the reliability of given information?
3: Why do people end up believing deceptive information and then follow blindly in ways that prove to be damaging and destructive?

Psychologists and sociologists can point to reasons for such behavior, some of the answers relate to how people react or respond in their minds. Neurologists will tell us that If people use the "right frontal lobe of the cerebral cortex" of their brains more (the thinking, feeling and compassionate unselfish thought center), people would be slow to react and be more empathetic, considerate and caring. Instead, people stop short of clear thinking because the limbic system of the brain, the "amygdala and ventral tegmental areas" of the brain take over in aggressive, addictive and repetitive ways. (For further information see "The Emotional Nervous System", Dr. C. George Boeree, online).

While psychology and brain physiology are interesting, and are interrelated subjects for human behavior, they still can't fully address the existential problems of mental, social and physical disease. Jesus knew that we would need help. He came from God our Heavenly Father to be a Wonderful Counselor, the Great Physician. Jesus alone is the Messiah, who came to lead us to salvation, and Jesus will come again in unmistakable and majestic glory.

Jesus has opened the way to a new life, born of God's Spirit, for all people who repent and believe. Be warned that there will be others who will lead you astray on a path of spiritual deception. God's plan of redemption becomes a reality through a prayer of confession and through steps of faith. Be warned that there are people who will promise you great peace through meditation techniques, be wary and forewarned that many are fakes. Jesus has given us the sound teaching that we need, the best example for us to follow, and a promise of God's Kingdom and personal transformation that gives us hope. Jesus calls His disciples to grow in their faith, to discern truth from errant teachings. Jesus showed us how to be mindful of the prompting and counsel of the Holy Spirit through prayer and quiet reflection. Having a humble faith relationship with Jesus, the Prince of Peace, is the path of Truth and Life. Jesus came as God's Son, the True Good Shepherd who is God's antidote to deception. Accept no substitute for Jesus, the one True Savior and Lord who can reign in your heart, and who will come again.

III. Jesus warns that times of trouble will come (6-8)

6 You will hear of wars and rumors of wars, but see to it that you are not alarmed. Such things must happen, but the end is still to come. 7 Nation will rise against nation, and kingdom against kingdom. There will be famines and earthquakes in various places. 8 All these are the beginning of birth pains.

A. Wars and rumors of war (6a)
"6 You will hear of wars and rumors of wars,"

The disciples of Jesus fully expected to experience a significant conflict upon their return with Jesus to Jerusalem. This was part of their Jewish prophetic and apocalyptic expectation. Jesus did not meet their expectations, and for that reason it is presumed that Judas Iscariot may have betrayed Jesus to force the Lord's hand toward conquest. Jesus warns the disciples that they will *"hear"* of wars. The emphasis on anticipation may also be a warning for His disciples to beware of those who would promote war as the answer. This fits with the problem of the Zealots who advocated armed aggression with the Romans. In Jesus' time, and soon afterward, there were those who tried to justify violence in the name of God.

Jesus takes His warning further to those who feed into the rumors that give rise to misunderstanding, ignorance, manipulation and prejudice among people. He taught that people are called to love their enemies, to overcome hatred with forgiveness. Jesus' true disciples will hear of wars and give thoughtful and prayerful responses. Christians are ultimately citizens of the Kingdom of God, and are globally called to be concerned for God's grace to extend to all people of every nation. War is ultimately based upon deception and abuse of power. In His Sermon on the Mount, Jesus said: *"Blessed are the peacemakers, for they shall be called children of God"* (Matthew 5:9). The security of God's children is ultimately not based upon the strength of man, but upon the strength of God and His Spirit and Sovereignty.

B. Faith must be greater than fear (6b)

"but see to it that you are not alarmed."

In His humble example, through teaching God's character and Truth, and by communicating the vision of the Kingdom of God for people, Jesus taught that fear and anxiety must not be the motivation for His disciples. Jesus instructed people to pray with faith that God can bring down the mighty mountains of fear, or cleanse the lifeless structures that are unfruitful, like the fig tree.

20 When the disciples saw this, they were amazed. "How did the fig tree wither so quickly?" they asked. 21 Jesus replied, "Truly I tell you, if you have faith and do not doubt, not only can you do what was done to the fig tree, but also you can say to this mountain, 'Go, throw yourself into the sea,' and it will be done. 22 If you believe, you will receive whatever you ask for in prayer." Matthew 21:20-22

The key to faith is not taking the reins, but trusting in God's reign. Prayer is the beginning of wisdom, and wisdom is the beginning of being responsive and not reactive, attentive and not alarmed.

C. Patience and perspective are needed to endure (6c)

"Such things must happen, but the end is still to come."

Why God allows certain things to happen is a mystery that Jesus addresses. He doesn't give a comprehensive detailed answer. That would not be helpful anyway. However, Jesus does answer calmly with a firm tone of confidence that God is working things out. Things will happen, there is a process that must be played out. God is patiently working out a plan of salvation and redemption, and there shall be a time of judgment. People and entities with free-will and agency are given time, space and opportunity. How freedom and opportunity shall be used, and that within certain limits, shall involve ongoing and ultimate accountability. Jesus spoke in here about how "such things must happen", that God has a foreknowledge of how people will behave and how things shall occur in nature. The omniscience of God that exists parallel to the free will of intelligent beings and creatures is mind blowing. Yet here Jesus is talking about history and nature as being within God's full knowledge and sovereign reign. Jesus portrays the patience of God, allowing things to happen, while still giving humanity freedom. Within the plan that God has in place, God has the wisdom and power to let it all play out in time and to bring it all under control with a goal of salvation, an end plan that involves judgment and a new beginning.

In this oracle, Jesus declares that God has an *"end"* planned, a time to conclude this current epoch of life as we know it here on earth. How this "end time" shall incorporate a Millennial Reign of Christ before the final judgment is a topic that would require additional study beyond Matthew 24 & 25. However, what Jesus points to is an *"end"* that will be supplanted by a new beginning. God's promised covenant plan will be fulfilled in the New Heaven and New Earth. There will be a conclusion to the *"old order of things"*. We read in Revelation 21: 3-5:

> *3 And I heard a loud voice from the throne saying, "Look! God's dwelling place is now among the people, and he will dwell with them. They will be his people, and God himself will be with them and be their God. 4 'He will wipe every tear from their eyes. There will be no more death' or mourning or crying or pain, for the old order of things has passed away."* Revelation 21:3-4

D. God's Kingdom plan comes after much time and trial (7)

7   Nation will rise against nation, and kingdom against kingdom. There will be famines and earthquakes in various places.

1. Political turmoil and conflict (7a)

"7 Nation will rise against nation, and kingdom against kingdom."

Jesus continued to describe what His disciples, and believers of generations to come, must expect to endure as God's Kingdom plan unfolds amidst much time and trial. Nations will wage war, kings and leaders will oppose one another. Jesus is not advocating that Christians be aligned with allegiance to nationalistic movements, or be quiet and absent to oppose injustice by despots, dictators and regimes. He has already taught His disciples that believers are to practice non-violent resistance as a rule, to be peacemakers, show mercy and seek the welfare and salvation of all people. Political intrigue and games of power manipulation are a reality in human history; however, extremes of engagement and detachment have not helped represent the cause of the Gospel of God's Kingdom. Jesus' warning to Peter, at the time of His arrest in Gethsemane, was:

> *"Put your sword back in its place," Jesus said to him, "for all who draw the sword will die by the sword. 53 Do you think I cannot call on my Father, and he will at once put at my disposal more than twelve legions of angels? 54 But how then would the Scriptures be fulfilled that say it must happen in this way?"* Matthew 26:52-54

2. Natural disasters (7b)
"There will be famines and earthquakes in various places."

Natural disasters and calamities comprise the system of dynamic forces that are at work in our world and universe. Some of these events occur due to forces beyond our human control. Preparations are important, but there are events such as earthquakes, typhoons, tornadoes, hurricanes, draughts, floods and tsunamis that make us aware of our mortality and fragility. Still, we also discover the importance of community amidst the drama of survival and rescue.

What is troubling, however, are those man-caused disasters and tragedies; even our abuse of the world's resources indicates we have brought the whirlwind of global warming and climate change upon ourselves. Famines are often a result of war and violence. Refugees seek to find safety and food, and are often left destitute, hungry, homeless and in limbo. Who will be the Good Samaritan? Who will be moved by compassion and respond in mercy and care? Who will be responsible as good stewards of our limited resources, and share bread and water with the needy? Who will care for our environment, and take steps to recycle and reuse? Who will modify their lifestyle to decrease their "carbon footprint"? In so doing, widespread famines would be lessened if we slowed-down consumption to help prevent global warming. Climate change has already affected the production of food and the harvest of fish. Population growth on our planet, combined with limited resources and increased demand of goods, has precipitated a crisis that is just now approaching dangerous levels.

"Chasing Coral Reefs" is a video documentary (2016) that examines changes to the Great Barrier Reef which is over a thousand miles long, located off the eastern coast of Australia. Over 29 percent of this massive coral reef has died from 2011 to 2016. Around the world, other coral reefs are seeing the same phenomena. The warming of oceans by human activity is the cause. The death of more coral reefs will continue as ocean temperatures increase. Since coral reefs support small and large fish life, this will affect the fisheries of the world as the schools of fish will diminish. The result will be less food supply for the world's people. Shortages of food could spell overdependence upon some food supplies that are weather and soil dependent. Increased conditions for famine are on the horizon. The ocean researchers and divers who have chronicled this tragic devastation, give warning. Who will heed their voices? Environmentalists' love for this world that God has made. Their heartbreak for humanity's dire situation, and their advocacy for the bio-diversity of this planet, is not shared by all. People of faith, disciples of Jesus, should be strident among those who believe in good stewardship of this earth, and are to lead by example and sacrifice.

E. Analogy of "birth pains" - The coming of God's Kingdom (8) *8 All these are the beginning of birth pains.*

One of the most amazing analogies that Jesus makes about the coming of God's Kingdom is to compare it to the "birthing" of a child. God is at work in history as the Sovereign Heavenly Father. God has not given up on fallen humanity, but has instead devised a plan of salvation and new life. The analogy Jesus uses of birth indicates that God is up to something new.

Although the disciples would see big challenges in their lifetime, other believers for millennia following have also experienced the "birth pains" of the Kingdom as well. One may ponder if the time of the Adamic and Abrahamic Covenant, leading to the ministry of Jesus, was a sort of conception process leading to "pregnancy"; Judaism being the "fertile soil" in which the Gospel of God's Kingdom in Christ becomes the seed that takes root and grows within people of faith. That first epoch took many thousands of years until Jesus was incarnate. Since Jesus is talking about another *"birth"* beyond His own incarnation, the birthing He was referring to has been compared to the time of "pregnancy" and/or the "maturation" of the Church (in the womb of God's grace). The growth of the Church upon the earth will eventually reach its full term, and the time of His glorious return is something Jesus likens to the moment of delivery, the day and hour when the redeemed shall be welcomed into God's manifest Kingdom. This too, Jesus hints, may take many, many, years. One thing is stated clearly, there will be pain and travail near the end, leading up to the fulfillment of God's Kingdom, especially near to Christ's return. Beyond the refining and redemptive process of God's developing Kingdom plan, there are three things to note from Jesus' words and ministry:

1. <u>The process is underway</u> - God's Kingdom plan has been in place, and has been actively and redemptively at work, even though we may not perceive it from the surface of life (much like a pregnancy). God worked through the patriarchs, priests, prophets and kings of the Old Testament, eventually culminating a plan of redemption in Jesus the Messiah. Jesus' first coming was a humble incarnation with a ministry of exemplary service and perfect sacrifice. The call of Jesus to humanity: "Repent, for the Kingdom of God is at hand".

2. <u>The process will take time</u> - The several millennia since Jesus' ministry have involved the spread of the Gospel message, the conversion and spiritual transformation of many people throughout the world. The workers of the harvest of God's Kingdom, which involves all who believe, still have much work to do.

3. <u>The process will consummate in a good result</u> - Eventually, when the work of God's Kingdom declaration and preparations on earth are complete, the "birth pains" of God's Kingdom shall give way to the "birth moment". Jesus' powerful and magnificent return will occur. Christ Jesus will come again as the glorious and powerful Son of God. That will be an awesome, breathtaking and beautiful day. Who will be ready?

IV. <u>Jesus warns that persecution will occur</u> (9-11)

9 "Then you will be handed over to be persecuted and put to death, and you will be hated by all nations because of me. 10 At that time many will turn away from the faith and will betray and hate each other, 11 and many false prophets will appear and deceive many people.

A. False accusations, arrests and executions (9a)

"9 "Then you will be handed over to be persecuted and put to death,"

Knowledge of the *"birth"* to come is what will help the people of God overcome their travail of persecution and temporal death. Some individuals will be martyrs for the cause of the Gospel, but that does not prevent the spread of the Gospel of God's Kingdom of peace and new life in Jesus Christ. Over the centuries there have been false accusations, arrests and executions made against both Christians and Jews. The Holy Scriptures of the Bible are not accepted in some lands, and it is punishable by death to be teaching or reading the Bible. In the Early Church, the Romans justified killing Jews and Christians because they did not submit to worship the Roman Emperors or bring sacrifices to the Roman gods. Jesus knew that some of His disciples would be persecuted, and others would be put to death for their faith. The reality is that the "birth pains" involve having courage and Christ-like forgiveness to live as ambassadors of the Gospel.

B. Hatred and rejection in every nation (9b)
"and you will be hated by all nations because of me."

Persecution may vary in locale, but Jesus portrays global hatred. There are times within history that nations and cultures have claimed to be "Christian", but their "un-Christlike actions and attitudes had become a stumbling block, problematic. Claims can be misleading, especially when one considers the hypocrisy of nations bent on conquest in the name of Christ, or justifying slavery and oppressive colonization in the name of spreading Christianity. True followers of Jesus are often counter-cultural and radical in their lives, not consumed with power, but peaceful. The way of Jesus is not the way of war, and certainly not the way of ethnic exclusion or hatred. Believers of Jesus Christ will often be "hated" for their independent thinking and resistance to bow down to systems of injustice, racism, prejudice and oppression. The way of Jesus is love and forgiveness, and that is most often counter-cultural. If a person claims to be a Christian, and yet hates others, where is the Spirit of God of the love of Christ in them? The beloved disciple John confronted the church in his first letter to follow Jesus' example:

> *Do not be surprised, my brothers and sisters, if the world hates you. 14 We know that we have passed from death to life, because we love each other. Anyone who does not love remains in death. 15 Anyone who hates a brother or sister is a murderer, and you know that no murderer has eternal life residing in him. 16 This is how we know what love*

is: Jesus Christ laid down his life for us. And we ought to lay down our lives for our brothers and sisters. 17 If anyone has material possessions and sees a brother or sister in need but has no pity on them, how can the love of God be in that person? 18 Dear children, let us not love with words or speech but with actions and in truth. 1 John 3:13-19

The loss of Christ-like love is often evident within political discourse. When people use "religious nationalism" or "political triumphalism" in the "name of Christ", it has often led to un-Christlike behavior, even dehumanizing rhetoric and unethical behavior. False religious leaders do this too. People of faith sometimes follow "pseudo-messiahs" because they believe the end results will justify the means of achieving their misplaced hopes. Theological and missional dilemmas and ethical inconsistencies are often overlooked, even ignored if exposed. Use of force, and the disrespect of people through oppression, violence, racism and economic exploitation have occurred. Such activity is incongruent with the Gospel of Jesus. In contrast to the world, disciples of Jesus are to be filled with respect and love, and are to be moved by pure, righteous and redemptive motives whose fruit is evident in gracious actions.

C. Denial, betrayal and strife (10)

"10 At that time many will turn away from the faith and will betray and hate each other,"

In this statement toward a future time, Jesus is now specifying that there will be a distinct time when all the madness that has been building among mankind and our environment will reach a peak level of intensity, a breaking point. People will break away from the Judeo/Christian faith, and others will break away from loving and respecting one another, even within the Church. The decrease of the Church and its positive social/spiritual influence has already occurred in much of Europe and North America. Even so, the Church is still growing and impacting parts of Asia, Africa,

Australia and South America. While the seeds of discord and division have been sown, and are growing; this prediction of Jesus will involve an intense time of breaking apart, amid ardent apostasy. Within current generations of young adults in North America, the idea of spirituality has appeal; but the message of the Gospel has been polluted by hatred and division within churches and among people of the Christian faith. The result has been a growing dismissal of the Church's relevance and a deepening divide between what is seen to be secular and sacred.

This concern for the inconsistency of believers and the hypocritical witness of the Church was evident even in the origins of the Early Church. Throughout history, this has been a source of tension for Christ's Body in dealing with the lingering reality of human sin and alienation, the parallel existence of "the wheat and the tares". What Jesus is saying, in this poignant statement of Matthew 24:10, is that the proximity of His return will be marked by an escalation of these issues unlike anything experienced before. Apostasy will turn into hatred, and hatred will turn into a diabolical type of division. The hallmark of the Church is to be love. May Christ's disciples be vigilant in matters of grace and truth, kindness and patience, suffering and hope.

D. Apostacy and deception (11)

11 and many false prophets will appear and deceive many people."

The number of false teachers and their adherents will increase. People will fill their minds with the things they want to hear to "feel good" or to promote themselves and an agenda that hits their standard of righteousness. A few wise words in a Proverb from Solomon are in order:

> *Desire without knowledge is not good— how much more will hasty feet miss the way! 3 A person's own folly leads to their ruin, yet their heart rages against the Lord.* - Proverbs 19:2-3

The Apostle Paul lamented how quickly people forsook sound teaching in favor of deceptive teaching that suited their temporal desires, philosophical assumptions and ungodly lifestyles:

> *3 For the time will come when people will not put up with sound doctrine. Instead, to suit their own desires, they will gather around them a great number of teachers to say what their itching ears want to hear. 4 They will turn their ears away from the truth and turn aside to myths. 5 But you, keep your head in all situations, endure hardship, do the work of an evangelist, discharge all the duties of your ministry.* - 2 Timothy 4:3-5

Deception has been a problem since the Garden of Eden, but the level and language of deception will increase closer to the Second Coming of Jesus Christ. We will continue to see "Name it and claim it" evangelists, media savvy crowd dazzlers, illusive political manipulators, unbiblical philosophies, religious apostasy, racist religions, divisive nationalism, justification of violence, and a general focus on worship of all things human and the creation (instead of God the creator). These are the "marks" of those who "turn their ears away from the truth". The plea of Paul to Timothy, which also is evident in Jesus' teaching in Matthew 24-25, is to "keep your head", "endure" and "work". Being a Christian involves taking care of mental, spiritual and physical health. Care for self and others' well-being, and the earth we share, is a Godly matter of human responsibility, and even more essential at the "end times".

Jesus wants His Church to stand firm by faith in Him, and not to be fooled by false Messiahs. This will mean that the Church must be even tighter as a community to survive the spiritual onset that is to be expected in the last days. At the same time, the Church will need to be in "rescue mode" to keep people from being fooled by false messiahs and hollow philosophies. The urgency of the gospel and the need for maintaining sound biblical faith is always essential; testing and apostasy will increase as the time of Christ's return draws near.

V. <u>Jesus warns about the danger of losing faith, hope and love</u> (12-13)

12 Because of the increase of wickedness, the love of most will grow cold, 13 but the one who stands firm to the end will be saved.

A. Evil will infect many and bring about coldness (12)

12 Because of the increase of wickedness, the love of most will grow cold,

When Jesus said that the love of people will grow cold, He was not only speaking of people's love for God and one another, He was also referring to people's love for all life and this creation that God has made. A sign of the increase of wickedness is seen in man's inhumanity to one another; wars, genocide, human trafficking, exploitation, oppression, racism, intolerance, incivility, loss of mercy and a growing alienation among people. Another sign of the increase of wickedness is seen in mankind's abuse and neglect of this planet and the beautiful diversity of life contained upon it. The otherness of life's variety should lead us to awe, reverence, respect and preservation. Instead, as the time of human travail escalates, it seems that certain governments, corporations and their leaders are willing to endanger the life of the planet's global health so that they may pursue temporary gain, security and wealth. This kind of self/group exclusive thinking is not only short-sighted, it is cold and wicked.

Recalling a few scenes from the "Lord of the Rings" trilogy movies, the forces of evil were in opposition to the forces of good and nature. These evil forces blotted and destroyed the landscape, cities and various peoples of middle earth, all to dominate and feed their appetite for power and submission. When Tolkien wrote these books following World War II, it came from an awareness that spiritual forces underlie the life we lead on earth. Tolkien was giving a parallel world, in our world "Good versus evil" is a reality that also involves reckoning, and God has not been silent or unengaged. Indeed, the world is God's general revelation and the Scriptures leading to Jesus are God's personal revelation. God has a plan to judge all, and to destroy evil and heal the earth from its wicked ways. Now, as always, repentance and faith opens our souls to what we need. Faith is what brings people to the warmth of life born of God's Spirit and the very gift of redeeming love.

B. Believers will stay compassionate and committed to God (13) *13 but the one who stands firm to the end will be saved.*

The winds of adversity will blow. The waters of turmoil will rise and fall, toss back and forth. The image Jesus gave His disciples, then and now, is that we can stand firm in His strength, and that we will be saved. There will be a conclusion to this current human story of struggle and survival that has taken many twists and turns. This story culminates with God's decision and redemption. Judgment will involve justice measured with either mercy or condemnation. The assurance of salvation strengthens those who have come to believe and experience God's grace and have also found strength in obeying God's revealed truth.

People must always acknowledge that it is by grace, not works, that we are saved. However, the way we live does matter and does involve our will and resolve to endure, stand firm, serve faithfully and trust that Jesus is Lord and Savior. In the words of a hymn: "Faith is the victory that overcomes the world". John, now a mature believer, writes with years of faith, having a deepened awareness and tested experience of knowing Jesus and of walking by faith after the resurrection:

> "And his commands are not burdensome, 4 for everyone born of God overcomes the world. This is the victory that has overcome the world, even our faith. 5 Who is it that overcomes the world? Only the one who believes that Jesus is the Son of God. - 1 John 5:3-5

The word for *"world"* in the Apostles' letter is the Greek word *"kosmos"*; the application of this word on a generic level is to the *"overall system of life on earth and in the universe"*, it could also be used more specifically to refer to the *"system of humanity that encompassed corruption"*, a system that is "in tension" with faith in God. The application here is that of "tension" and a system that is errant and hostile to God. For the Church, for believers, life involves the challenge of living within, but not being consumed by, the corrupt system of man that been infected by evil and broken by chaos. Salvation comes by faith and endurance.

VI. Jesus reveals God's mission and what needs to be fulfilled (14)

14 And this gospel of the kingdom will be preached in the whole world as a testimony to all nations, and then the end will come.

The good news of the Gospel, the good seed of heaven's gift of grace and new life, will be spread throughout the entire world. Nations and cultures, tribes and islanders, urban dwellers, jungle dwellers, desert dwellers, mountain dwellers and Eskimos; people in cities of southern and northern hemispheres of the earth; all will come to hear the good news of God's Son, the Savior, Jesus the Christ. It will take time, and there are gaps to be filled along with an extension of God's grace and mercy.

A. The Gospel of the Kingdom will be preached worldwide (14a) *"14 And this gospel of the kingdom will be preached in the whole world"*

The phrase *"gospel of the kingdom"* is a potent seed of truth that contains the heart and essence of the ministry and message of Jesus. Jesus Himself is the "gospel" or "good news", the Word of God Incarnate. He is the One who is Savior; the One who not only represents God the Heavenly Father/Creator, Jesus was sent to be

Lord and King, Prince of Peace. The Kingdom Jesus ushers in is not another kingdom made from human effort; but is a Kingdom established upon the pre-existent, transcendent sovereignty and reign of God. The Kingdom that Jesus inaugurates, comes first within the hearts and souls of people of faith. This Kingdom is first preached through deed and word, this message of the Gospel of God's Kingdom is then received through repentance and faith. God's grace is dispensed within the seed of Truth in Christ and the New Life given by the deposit of God's Holy Spirit.

The extensiveness of how the *"Gospel of the Kingdom"* will be preached to the whole world implies a great expanse of time. The urgency of sharing the gospel is balanced by the transcendency of God's patient love, allowing for grace in the garden of human distribution and development. In God's plan, there is a fairness, a wholeness, a work that unfolds within and beyond human culture, rising above and beyond man's definitions of difference and distinction. God loves all, and the Gospel of the Kingdom in Jesus Christ is offered for all. Even if all do not believe, or receive Jesus as Savior and thereby forfeit Heaven, this does not deter the eminence of God's saving seed of grace in Christ, and it will not keep the appointed time of His return from occurring.

B. The testimony of believers as a witness of Jesus Christ (14b)

"as a testimony to all nations,"

The testimony of Jesus' disciples, and of the Church that Jesus founded, is for all the earth's peoples and nations to hear and respond to. Will people believe the Gospel? Will people turn in their hearts and experience new life born of God's Holy Spirit in Jesus Christ? *"The answer, my friends, is blowing in the wind"*; that is, it depends upon faith, catching the wind of God's grace and truth and letting that reality change one's life. For those who do believe, who share life and testimony as the Body of Christ, the Church; there must be authenticity. The testimony of the Church, those who proclaim to follow Jesus, must not be contentious, but instead be compassionate.

In the time given to the Church to share the Gospel and extend God's invitation of grace and New Life in Christ, endurance is essential. "Staying with" the task involves being with people the way Jesus was with people. In chaplaincy, (part of this author's vocation) one is willing to be present with others in a way that is open, vulnerable and unassuming. The objective, first, is to listen and discover the way in which God's Spirit may precipitate a spiritual connection with another person. People are not always open or interested to receive or share with the chaplain. Many times, a person will ask early on: "Why are you here?" "What's your interest?" The same question might be asked of a Christian who cares for a stranger, a new neighbor, a new coworker, a classmate, an estranged relative, the person waiting beside you at a coffee shop or a doctor's office. The fact is, the witness of a believer is not something one turns on and off. Witness, as well as worship and prayer, is non-stop; the flow of grace began and continues to flow with the leading of God's Spirit for the world to hear and know of Jesus.

This becomes real as the Church is led to be in redemptive, reconciling, renewing relationships with strangers, neighbors, friends and family. In the twenty-first century, mission to the nations is near and present. Indeed, the world has been brought together as seen in the diversity of nationalities in cities and towns throughout most of the world. The question is: What will the Church do to adjust? Can the Church desegregate? Will the Church overcome ethnocentrism, racism, and nationalism so that it can shine the true vision of Christ for the Kingdom of God? There are a few shining examples, some dividing walls that the love of God in Jesus Christ has brought down. I see signs of Christ's Kingdom in the Church I serve, where people of many nations, cultures, races and ages come together to praise God, serve Jesus and love one another.

C. God's plan involves a fulfillment of invitation (14c)

"and then the end will come."

The invitation of God through Jesus has been delivered personally by the Lord and then by His disciples. This message of what it means to be a child of God was witnessed in Jesus' ministry through miracles of grace and mercy, parables, dialogue with enquirers and direct preaching. This message Jesus entrusted to common people to share with others till the "end of the age":

> *19 Therefore go and make disciples of all nations, baptizing them in the name of the Father and of the Son and of the Holy Spirit, 20 and teaching them to obey everything I have commanded you. And surely, I am with you always, to the very end of the age."* - Matthew 28:19-20

The calling of all people in the "Gospel of the Kingdom" is that we be reconciled with God and one another. The Gospel of Jesus Christ is the good news that this reconciliation is possible, that forgiveness, grace and transformation can be a reality. The tone of the end times will involve a greater dichotomy between the redeemed community of faith and the corrosive community of the fallen world. There will also be many people whose hypocrisy and apostasy will be evidenced in a loss of love, compassion and mercy; manifested in the coldness of people betraying one another and being misled by false messiahs and deceptive teachings.

The theologian George E. Ladd makes this observation about the witness and testimony of the Church and Christians to be "salt" and "light":

> *The Church is the community of the Kingdom of God and is to press this struggle against satanic evil in the world. The sons of the Kingdom cannot help but exercise an influence in human history for they are the light of the world*

and the salt of the earth (Matt. 5:13-16). So long as light is light, it must shine; and so long as salt is salt, it must preserve. Thus, the mission of the Church is not only that of employing the keys of the Kingdom to open to both Jew and Gentile the door unto eternal life which is the gift of God's Kingdom; it is also the instrument of God's dynamic rule in the world to oppose evil and the powers of Satan in every form of their manifestation." (Ladd, "The Gospel of the Kingdom", p. 121)

In the twenty-first century, over 58 years have lapsed since professor Ladd wrote "The Gospel of the Kingdom". The potency of being faithful believers and of battling *"satanic evil in the world"* has intensified. Though the Church has diminished in much of North America and Europe, it has grown in Asia, Africa and South America. Wherever the Church is present, enduring darkness, struggle and persecution; believers are called to shine as *"light"* and preserve as *"salt"*.

Questions for Discussion:

1. Why is it important to be forewarned?   (24:4-6)

2. The image of "birthing" is a positive metaphor of what God is up to. How does this help you deal with the process of waiting and serving in Jesus' name and for God's Kingdom? (8)

3. What did Jesus want His disciples and people today to know about the end times?

4. How is it overwhelming to live in these times? (7-14) How then is Jesus calling people to live with faith, hope and love?

Part 3: "Understand"
(Fleeing and the Fall of Jerusalem, 70 A.D.)
Matthew 24:15-22

15 "So when you see standing in the holy place 'the abomination that causes desolation,' spoken of through the prophet Daniel—let the reader understand— 16 then let those who are in Judea flee to the mountains. 17 Let no one on the housetop go down to take anything out of the house. 18 Let no one in the field go back to get their cloak. 19 How dreadful it will be in those days for pregnant women and nursing mothers! 20 Pray that your flight will not take place in winter or on the Sabbath. 21 For then there will be great distress, unequaled from the beginning of the world until now—and never to be equaled again. 22 "If those days had not been cut short, no one would survive, but for the sake of the elect those days will be shortened. Matthew 24:15-22

Introduction: Doom for Dystopia

Why is it that people are intrigued with fictional stories that depict dystopia or cataclysmic destruction? The Merriam-Webster dictionary defines "dystopia" as "*an imaginary place where people lead dehumanized and often fearful lives* ". From "zombies" to robots, biological mutations to artificial intelligence, there is a dark fascination people have with our demise, and there is a realization that mankind has been infected with the germ of corruption. Our creations reflect our maligned imagination, and can become monstrosities, "Frankensteinish". On one hand, science and technology can be helpful and bring hope; yet on the other hand, science and technology can wreak havoc or be used adversely for exploitation. Can people be trusted with the wise use of science or knowledge?

One would hope that peoples' consciences and ethical considerations would overcome greed. The problem, however, is that science or knowledge is not as pure or objective as one would hope, it can be used for good or evil. With every step forward in unleashing the power of knowledge, who shall decide how it will be used? Who will discern, ask, discuss and consider the difficult moral questions? While science presupposes progress, the perilous truth we have witnessed is that knowledge and science has often been exploited, misguided or manipulated in application; this potential danger increases exponentially as knowledge grows. One wonders, are we capable of creating the ethical structures and social processes to safeguard and sustain life? Can we learn to survive and thrive through the respectful use of knowledge and science? Can we discover the vital connection of science and knowledge to the integration of faith and respect of God? In view of human limitations and history, are we doomed for dystopia, desolation and self-destruction? If left to our own devices and inner demons, what transcendent hope do we have?

In this passage, Jesus foretold the troubling reality that a severe time of doom was about to befall the city and Temple of Jerusalem. God could not allow His Temple and Jerusalem to continue in the shroud of darkness, corruption and evil. The Jewish Zealots had created a dystopia by their own uncooperative spirit, immoral behavior and political wrangling. They had stirred the ire of Roman rule, being willing to live and die by the sword. While there was a remnant of faithful and peaceful Jews and followers of Jesus, there was great havoc wrought by the Zealots and others who thought that they could "make Israel great again" via force. The lesson given by Jesus was that the Kingdom of God was not to be ushered in through violence or human effort and strength. The Kingdom of God first comes through repentance, faith and humility by trusting God and living at peace with one another. The work of God's grace and truth in Jesus is what must take precedence for God's Spirit to lead and transform this earth and its people.

Neither Jerusalem or Rome would stand forever upon military strength, as Jesus foresaw the fall of the Temple, the seeds for the eventual fall of the Roman empire were also evident. Historically, human imagination, desire, effort and technology, on its own, has not reliably sought or found the remedy to our brokenness. External governance, without internal conscience and constraint, will only produce more strain and another form of oppression or bondage. What can be done to save us from ourselves? While there is a residual element of our human nature that is "made in the image of God"; there is also a shadow of bankruptcy, a 'black hole within each soul'. Only the reality of God in truth and grace can bring healing to this void, and true freedom can then begin to restore us to our God-designed humanity. One might say that the overall operating system of mankind was infected with a virus in the "Garden of Eden", and now, no amount of eating of the "fruit of the tree of the knowledge of good and evil" will save us. The food we will be left with may be self-destructive; the "Soylent Green" of abomination.

(Spoiler alert: Note that "Soylent Green" was an old Science Fiction movie set into a dismal future of environmental catastrophe where overpopulation and poor food production collided with an abuse of politics and science. Without consent and knowledge, people in this dystopian world were then euthanized and processed into a food product named "Soylent Green" that was consumed by an unknowing public).

Is such a skeptical and pessimistic view of humanity fair? Witness, deforestation and the destruction of healthy habitats on land, lakes, rivers and seas for the sake of satisfying outrageous and wasteful consumption. Witness, the pollution of the earth, the spread of injustice, the rise of famine and disease. Witness, the reckless behavior of individuals and corporations that prey on the weak and poor for cheap goods and services. Witness, increasing alienation of people with one another, war, racism, violence, substance abuse and depression. While there is much that is good on earth and within people, sin and evil are pervasive and the need is dire for redemption and remaking at our core. Witness, Jesus knew what was about to happen to Jerusalem, its people and the Temple; to this concern and much more, He gave specific warning and instructions.

In this passage, Jesus is circling back in His warning to the disciples, telling them of the more immediate signs they should be alert to regarding the destruction of the Temple of Jerusalem. Upon the canvas of revealing/portraying what the disciples should know about the perilous times ahead, Jesus paints a dramatic, dangerous, vivid and spiraling spiritual atmosphere for the End Times. In Matthew 24:15-22 we watch Jesus give a vision of what is to come upon History's canvas. For one specific upcoming event, the destruction of Jerusalem, Jesus illustrates with detail and clarity. This prophecy was historically fulfilled with Jerusalem's fall and the destruction of the Temple in 70 A.D. While this small corner of Jesus' prophetic canvas is part of a greater whole, it is important to not automatically apply this one direct warning of Jesus to every future event of abomination and desolation to come. This specific prophecy was primarily fulfilled in the destruction of the Second Temple. Such times of apostasy and religious deception will be repeated until Jesus returns in power and glory. On a precautionary level, it is essential that believers do not become obsessed with spiritual "profiling", playing an assumed role of judgment that ultimately belongs to Christ. What is vitally important on a level of preparation, is for Christians to continue in the work of spreading the Gospel of the Kingdom to the nations through humble, simple, personal acts of kindness. Consistency of character like that of Jesus will carry greater weight than words.

Bible scholars will relate this passage (Matthew 24:15-22) to the prophecies of Daniel (Daniel 7-12), and this cannot be ignored, nor should it be dismissed. One may also consider the Revelation to John and prophecies to Isaiah, Jeremiah, Micah, Haggai, and Malachi and others. For this chapter's study, we will consider what part of Daniel's prophecy Jesus had in mind while we consider the specific word of doom for Jerusalem that is contained in this Olivet Discourse. While Jesus refers to the prophet Daniel, there are two clear purposes our Lord had in mind:

(1) Warn the people, Jews and Gentiles, and the ministry of the early Church so that they would leave Jerusalem before its destruction. This way they could survive and continue to fulfill the work of God's Kingdom.

(2) Prepare and protect people from not only that event, but for times in the future that would be similar, involving the destruction of a Third Temple which would be built and made an abomination by a final manifestation of deception and evil.

Jesus communicated to reach people in the near term of history and the far reaches of the future. Jesus spoke about a near and specific destruction of the existent Temple of Jerusalem, and yet Jesus was speaking in terms that signified an even greater tribulation for all the earth, prior to His return of judgment. Within the Hebrew prophetic tradition, God's word could have direct import several times, both once and then later for future events. The abomination and destruction of Solomon's Temple had occurred in 425 B.C., and now just after Jesus' ministry, the abomination and destruction of Herod's temple would soon occur.

The size of each of these temples increased, one upon the other. The level of abomination and desolation also increased with each succession. Jesus spoke specifically to the second destruction, within the lifetime of some of His listening disciples. Jesus spoke of the prophetic fulfillment of Daniel's prophecy, this involved the destruction of Herod's Temple. The third time that this will occur, shall involve a yet larger Temple that will become even more abominable in its pretense of religious pride and false peace. Meanwhile, true worship of God will be absent amidst strong deception and apostacy in that historic place at a future time. The Third Temple's desolation and destruction will be a global and final event that leads to the Day of Christ's return, the Day of Reckoning and God's Judgment.

What will Jesus teach us in this passage? Let's listen carefully and ask for God's wisdom to understand what Jesus warned His disciples about. May we be careful not to either miss or misapply Christ's warning for the future. The fulfillment of what Jesus spoke about has come true in part. Still to come in God's plan, there are some workings that unfold gently and other events that involve sudden revelation and immediate response.

OUTLINE OF Matthew 24:15-22

I. Jesus knew about the Destruction of the Jerusalem Temple (v.15)
    A. The abomination, desolation that led to the destruction in 70 A.D.
    B. The abomination and desolation of the end times (Daniel)

II. Jesus warns the people of Judea to flee (v.16-18)
    A. "Head for the hills" (16)
    B. "Up on the roof" (17)
    C. "Out Standing in your field" (18)

III. Jesus speaks of "Days of Dread" with a call for prayer (19-20)
    A. Jesus' concern for life and compassion for the vulnerable (19)
    B. Jesus' call for people to pray and be prepared (20)

IV. Jesus foretells the coming of the "Great Tribulation" (21)
    A. Great distress (21a)
    B. Worse than any other time in history (21b)
    C. Never to be equaled again (21c)

V. Jesus gives a glimmer of hope (22)
    A. Some will survive the "Great Tribulation" (22a)
    B. God will extend mercy and grace to the remnant elect (22b)

Study on Matthew 24:15-22

I. Jesus knew about the Destruction of the Jerusalem Temple (v.15)

15 "So when you see standing in the holy place 'the abomination that causes desolation,' spoken of through the prophet Daniel—let the reader understand—

A. The abomination, desolation that led to the destruction in 70 A.D.

What was this abomination standing in the holy place of the Temple in Jerusalem? In the fulfillment of Daniel's prophecy, scholars will often point to the conquest of Greek ruler, "Antiochus IV Epiphanes" (Greek, meaning: *"god manifest"*), who had centuries before entered Jerusalem: *"And at the temple he will set up an abomination that causes desolation, until the end that is decreed is poured out on him."* Daniel 9:27 Antiochus IV Epiphanes ordered that an image of Zeus be placed on the altar of the Lord's temple (the same temple begun by Haggai and completed in Jesus time by Herod). The entrance of Antiochus led to a revolt in which the Maccabees repelled the Greeks. Antiochus soon died suddenly of a disease in 164 B.C., the account is given in the book of Maccabees (2:9): *"But the all-seeing Lord, the God of Israel, struck him an incurable and unseen blow."*

All this occurred many years before Jesus ministry, it was an example from history of how God fulfills prophecy. However, why did Jesus refer to Daniel's prophetic visions for future events? Within a decade of Jesus' death and resurrection (32 A.D.), there was a new Roman Emperor, Caligula, who in 40 A.D. directed that his image be set up in Jerusalem's Temple (Word Biblical Commentary, p. 700-701). This aggravated the growing tension between Roman Emperors and Jewish and Christian believers who denied each Emperor's declaration of self-divinity. The imposed worship of the Roman Emperors was met by non-violent resistance that led some to martyrdom. Others reacted violently as Jewish Nationalists and Zealots, and they were obliterated by the Romans.

A period of about 30 years followed this sign of abhorrence placed by Caligula. One considers how God gave time for the people to be forewarned. This symbolic, and idolatrous, sculpture of Caligula signaled impending doom for Jerusalem and the Temple.

The unfolding chaos and violent reaction of the Zealots culminated in greater insistence by Rome for ultimate rule; the leveling of the Temple and destruction of Jerusalem in 70 A.D. was the result. There were some Jews who counted on this being the time of their triumph, the time of victory for God's Holy people. Yet such was not the case, the fulfillment of God's Kingdom to replace the beastly kingdoms of the earth (as foretold in the book of Daniel) would need to happen later.

B. The abomination and desolation of the end times (Daniel)

The events of Jerusalem's struggle with foreign occupation eventually led to the time of destruction by the Romans in 70 A.D. This is but a small part of Daniel's prophetic visions regarding the eventual replacement of world kingdoms and the coming of God's Kingdom. Daniel was given a vision of four beasts, each of which symbolized a different empire that would rise and fall. The fourth and last beast mentioned was of grave interest and concern for Daniel. We read of the terrifying vision God gave Daniel:

> 7 "After that, in my vision at night I looked, and there before me was a fourth beast—terrifying and frightening and very powerful. It had large iron teeth; it crushed and devoured its victims and trampled underfoot whatever was left. It was different from all the former beasts, and it had ten horns. - Daniel 7:7-8

Daniel watched the vision in horror, witnessing the beast's evil killing, exploitation, bloodshed, and disregard for life and habitats of all forms. He watched then, as the beast sprouted a talking horn that spoke boastfully. This horn of pride (an abomination manifested from the beast) was disrupted in the vision as God showed up in Sovereign glory and judgment:

"thrones were set in place, and the Ancient of Days took his seat. His clothing was as white as snow; the hair of his head was white like wool. His throne was flaming with fire, and its wheels were all ablaze. 10 A river of fire was flowing, coming out from before him. Thousands upon thousands attended him; ten thousand times ten thousand stood before him. The court was seated, and the books were opened." - Daniel 7:9-10

God is referred to in verse 9 of Daniel's vision as *"The Ancient of Days"*, harkening to the name *"Yahweh"* given to Moses, meaning *"I am that I am"*. God the Sovereign Creator will judge the nations and all people.

Following this vision of God being enthroned and opening the books of account/judgment; the *"Son of Man"*, Jesus the Christ is revealed in Daniel 7:13-14 as joining God's reign and rule on the earth. Church historian, Eusebius, believed that this vision from Daniel referred to Jesus. (see Paul Maier, "Eusebius" p. 26-27. Kregel publishing, 2007). Daniel beheld the pre-incarnate Christ:

13 "In my vision at night I looked, and there before me was one like a son of man, coming with the clouds of heaven. He approached the Ancient of Days and was led into his presence. 14 He was given authority, glory and sovereign power; all nations and peoples of every language worshiped him. His dominion is an everlasting dominion that will not pass away, and his kingdom is one that will never be destroyed. Daniel 7:13-14

While Daniel sees the coming of Jesus in human form first, Daniel watches as God bestows glory and authority to Him. Dominion and sovereign power is given to the Son, to jointly reign with the Ancient of Days, God the Father. Jesus own profession of authority was given following His death and resurrection, prior to commissioning His disciples: *"All authority in heaven and on earth has been given to me.*" Matthew 28:18. The theology of the incarnation, therefore, involves Christ coming as the "Word of God made flesh" (John 1:14) and as the "Son of God" who was sent into the world for salvation (John 3:16); this very Son of Man/Son of God would humble Himself to accomplish God's work of transforming grace and truth, with victory over sin and death.

The vision of Daniel then moved from the revelation of the "Son of Man" back to the reality of ongoing spiritual warfare. Daniel, being intrigued, wanted more clarity about the overall meaning of the fourth beast that he saw in the vision. He asked someone standing in the courts of Heaven for an explanation. In a few sentences, there is a summation of how God's ultimate judgment will be in favor of the holy people (those who are holy through faith, the covenants of Abraham and of Christ, the Son of Man):

> *21 As I watched, this horn was waging war against the holy people and defeating them, 22 until the Ancient of Days came and pronounced judgment in favor of the holy people of the Most High, and the time came when they possessed the kingdom.* (Daniel 7:21-22)

The "*Ancient of Days*" will share possession/inheritance of the Kingdom to His people. Daniel was given the big picture, but he still wanted to understand even more details about the fourth beast and kingdom:

> *23 "He gave me this explanation: 'The fourth beast is a fourth kingdom that will appear on earth. It will be different from all the other kingdoms and will devour the whole earth, trampling it down and crushing it. 24 The ten horns are ten kings who will come from this kingdom. After them another king will arise, different from the earlier ones; he will subdue three kings. 25 He will speak against the Most High and oppress his holy people and try to change the set times and*

the laws. The holy people will be delivered into his hands for a time, times and half a time. - (Daniel 7:21-26)

The word given to Daniel, from a servant of God, was that this fourth kingdom would advance and spread in such a way that it would devour the whole earth. One might draw a parallel to how the influence of Rome inspired much of western civilization and the whole world. It's use of law for peace (the "Pax Romana"), governance, technology and military conquest subdued the known world. The nations that arose from the Roman empire then went on to have their own empires/kingdoms; the methods and ideals of the original Roman empire have now been repeated for close to two millenniums. The ten horns are manifestations of crushing and subduing power that would be repeated over time; witness the global eras of conquests, colonialism and capitalism. Eventually, the vision given to Daniel was that there will come one last manifestation of this oppressive earthly kingdom, like the previous, and yet even more intense.

Coming back to the Olivet discourse in Matthew 24-25, Jesus referred to the written visions of the prophet Daniel for a reason. Jesus was not only the Son of Man revealed in these prophecies, He was unified with God the Father for this prophecy's understanding and fulfillment. Jesus also wanted His disciples to learn from Daniel that the realization of God's Kingdom plan is a very complex and multi-layered process. Their future would involve facing the oppression and opposition of worldly kings and kingdoms. In Matthew 24:15, Jesus was specifically warning people about the destruction that would come soon, within 40 years of his death and resurrection. The journey ahead for believers would involve much time, perseverance and vigilance. They were to have hope and faith, even though a horrendous king and kingdom would come and be overwhelming in size, scope and manifestation of evil. Ultimately, God's Kingdom plan of salvation and transformation will prevail.

Today we can see the signs of evil's sway in man's kingdoms; we look at the problems and troubles in the world with wars, economic disparity, racial inequality and greed. These have wrought havoc upon the earth's peoples, ecosystems and have perpetuated suffering to many people. The additional note of Jesus, *"let the reader understand"*, was likely added by Matthew to help the Early Church be careful to include the study of Daniel the prophet. What Daniel contributes is God's message that earthly kingdoms will come and go, but the Kingdom of God is Sovereign over all earthly kingdoms and shall in time replace these temporal and broken systems. For the disciples, like Daniel, their focus was to be faithful in serving God by being ambassadors of God's grace and truth. They had to be ready to respond to God's leading, and they could not put their hope in Jerusalem and those who promised hope in political reform or revolution by human means.

II. Jesus warns the people of Judea to flee (v.16-18)

16 then let those who are in Judea flee to the mountains. 17 Let no one on the housetop go down to take anything out of the house. 18 Let no one in the field go back to get their cloak.

A. "Head for the hills" (16)
16 then let those who are in Judea flee to the mountains.

The Early Church historian, Eusebius ("Hist. Eccl." Iii.5) records that in 68 A.D. the Christians in and around Jerusalem and Judea fled the area upon hearing "a certain oracle." Was it the circulation of Jesus' teaching from the Olivet Discourse here in Matthew 24? Perhaps, but it could also have been a prophetic message, a warning from a dream. Many went far away, including some who were recorded going to the city of Pella in northern Greece. Jewish historian, Josephus, also noted that *"many of the more conspicuous citizens fled from the city, as men abandon a sinking ship*" ("Wars", iv. 9, 1; v. 20, 1). The mountains of the Gilead range, east of the Jordan region were sought for more immediate refuge (Ellicott's commentary).

The warning of Jesus was that if these signs were present, the wise thing to do was to flee. This was a specific instruction for believers to survive the upcoming Judean struggle with Rome and the destruction of Jerusalem. Indeed, it makes sense to flee when the specific signs and warnings given by God are present. Being prepared and vigilant are important character qualities to develop, balanced with the Apostle Paul's teaching:

Do not be anxious about anything, but in every situation, by prayer and petition, with thanksgiving, present your requests to God. (Philippians 4:6-7)

B. "Up on the roof" (17)

17 Let no one on the housetop go down to take anything out of the house.

Hurricane Harvey, in August of 2017, flooded many square miles of residential and urban areas. Rescues involved people being brought out of their homes or vehicles by boat or helicopter. With over 50 inches of rain in a few days, the effect was overwhelming. People had to leave their homes with only the essentials. One mother had to swim a mile while helping her 4-year-old son, they survived and she praised God for the strength and eventual help she received. When the floods of water, or invading armies, rise (as in the case of Jerusalem), the priority is your life. The flat-topped houses of Judea had stairs on the side for easy access and escape. For protection people might try to lock themselves in and close the windows and block the doors. But this would be no match for battering rams and torches. Forget the stuff that could hinder your survival, let it stay below. Keep your focus on the moment to flee and the future ahead. Don't be like Lot's wife who looked back to see Sodom and Gomorrah's destruction, and then became paralyzed, turning to "salt". The paralysis of not letting go and trusting God is the issue.

C. "Out Standing in your field" (18)

18 Let no one in the field go back to get their cloak.

Jesus thought of many circumstances and professions of work. Farmers and shepherds wouldn't have time to go to their homes, they would need to flee from where they were. If the "legions of doom" were marching into your town or city, and you were on the outside watching them come in, would this be the time to go back in and be confronted or killed? This would be particularly difficult to watch, and not to try a rescue, if your family and friends were there.

In the times we live in, people carry their smart phones around as a "life-line", for a sense of "security". These marvelous tools of communication and information have given people a false sense of well-being, protection and connectivity. Already, with GPS (Global Positioning Satellites), our electronic devices are emitting information that is being used for driving commerce and increasing surveillance. What happens when our communication devices are useless during a power outage? What happens when these devices start radically (even negatively) affecting our brains and our behaviors? Worse, what happens if these devices are used against us by a sinister enemy to track us down? We could all learn from the lesson of the Farmer or Shepherd who does not run to get "their cloak" (their shroud of security – a smart phone) when the danger is imminent. Don't get caught texting or looking at YouTube when the time to drop your phone, respond and run, is "now"! The distractions and security "cloaks" of this world will not always help you be alert and nimble. What is a suitcase of clothing when survival is at hand? The outer garment can be lost; however, the soul is of far greater worth and must be saved.

III. Jesus speaks of Days of Dread with a call for prayer (19-20)

19 How dreadful it will be in those days for pregnant women and nursing mothers! 20 Pray that your flight will not take place in winter or on the Sabbath.

A. Jesus' concern for life and compassion for the vulnerable (19)

19 How dreadful it will be in those days for pregnant women and nursing mothers!

Jesus expressed compassion, tenderness and concern for those most vulnerable. He was concerned for the preservation of future generations and placed great importance for the role of mothers and the nurture of infants and children. Jesus is "pro-life" in every respect. The "days of dread" coming for the Jews and Christians in Judea, following Jesus' time of ministry, would require upholding the priority of protecting women and children. Jesus led the way to show us the value of all human life; He also revealed the heart of God to protect and shield people, to give warning. The time of Jerusalem's siege and destruction by the Romans was horrendous, even involving the death of women and infants who were present in the city.

Throughout history, the worst atrocities have involved such evil deeds. Jesus spoke with warning as His heart was filled with pain at the consideration of future suffering, genocides and war. During World War II, in the Philippines, Japanese soldiers raided cities and villages. One woman recalled surviving an invasion as a child, as she hid she witnessed soldiers throwing babies into the air and spearing them with their bayonets. The dreadful conduct of wartime upon the innocent was upon Jesus' thoughts as He sought to warn them, but also as He prepared Himself for why He needed to go to the cross. Paul was inspired to comment on why Jesus humbled Himself for humanity's salvation:

"God made him who had no sin to be sin for us, so that in him we might become the righteousness of God." - 2 Corinthians 5:21.

How will God bring about justice, as God also is contending for our reconciliation and redemption? God's compassion is for the vulnerable. Jesus came for salvation. God will not tolerate the inhumanity of evil forever, and the dreadfulness of sin.

B. Jesus' call for people to pray and be prepared (20)
20 Pray that your flight will not take place in winter or on the Sabbath.

Jesus was concerned about the practicalities, the logistics and timing of their flight from Judea. Our Lord knew people too well, how we are prone to procrastination, denial or strict adherence to religious or behavioral rituals. There are times in life when people must abandon the known path for the alternative, in a path that would lead them away from doom and to a new life. The dreadful day of destruction would come for the Judean Christians and Jews, it was essential that they put their prayers into action.

Preparation is an act of faith, a work of hope and obedience. How prepared are we for what God may allow to happen in our part of the world or universe? Wars and conflicts will arise and they can be devastating, leaving many people to become refugees. There are natural disasters, floods, earthquakes, infestations, occasional meteors, famines and plagues to name a few (alien or zombie invasions are a bit of a stretch, but one never knows). The fact is, we live in a dynamic world and universe with forces beyond our control. God wants people to be prepared, adaptable. Jesus calls people to be ready to respond, to have a plan of action or escape. The most important preparation is to be right with God and to be at peace through doing God's will and being persons who serve God and others with love, grace, truth and goodness. (More on this later with the Parables in Matthew 25).

IV. Jesus foretells the coming of the Great Tribulation (21)

21 For then there will be great distress, unequaled from the beginning of the world until now—and never to be equaled again.

> **A. Great distress (21a)** *21 For then there will be great distress,*

    Here in this sentence (v.21a), there was a transcendent shift in Jesus' warning that extended from what would soon happen in Judea to a climactic future time with even greater magnitude. Jesus transitions with *"for then"* to warn of a time for all of humanity, not just Judea. That future time of great distress would be an era of unparalleled conflict, danger, persecution and suffering. This event has often been referred to as the "Great Tribulation". Jesus has once again referred to the vision which was given to the prophet Daniel centuries prior (and may we not forget that Jesus was there at the right hand of the throne of God the Father as this vision was given to Daniel) :

> *"There will be a time of distress such as has not happened from the beginning of nations until then. But at that time your people—everyone whose name is found written in the book—will be delivered. 2 Multitudes who sleep in the dust of the earth will awake: some to everlasting life, others to shame and everlasting contempt. 3 Those who are wise will shine like the brightness of the heavens, and those who lead many to righteousness, like the stars for ever and ever. 4 But you, Daniel, roll up and seal the words of the scroll until the time of the end. Many will go here and there to increase knowledge." (Daniel 12:1-4)*

We will come back to this passage again, but for now we note the words *"time of distress"* as Jesus repeated verbatim a portion of what was spoken to Daniel. In Daniel's vision, the good news is that the people of God, those whose names are found in the "Book of Life", will make it through trials and tribulations and be delivered for everlasting life. The bad news for those without faith, who choose denial and alienation from God, is that they will not be found in the "Book of Life". Hence, their judgment will be shame, separation and consequential death; the "second death" being that of the "soul". We listen carefully to Christ's words, that shall come in future judgment to those who would be cowardly, unbelieving, vile, murderous, immoral, deceptive, idolatrous and hypocritical: *"They will be consigned to the fiery lake of burning sulfur. This is the second death"* (Revelation 21:8).

B. Worse than any other time in history (21b)
unequaled from the beginning of the world until now

The time of great distress that took place in Jerusalem in 70 A.D. was awful. However, does the event of Jerusalem's destruction fit the criteria of being unequaled in history up to that point of time? A case in point for debate was the flood of Noah's time, that was a worldwide cataclysmic event with even graver consequences. The great flood was God's cleansing judgment upon corrupted humanity, it was a divine act of consequence to sinfulness.

The great distress of A.D. 70, soon to happen in Jerusalem, was recorded by the historian Josephus as the worst conflict he had witnessed of human violence and suffering. Without going through all of history to that point, one may reasonably say that while the destruction of Jerusalem and the Temple was a very dark moment in history, there were many equally dark times. The point Jesus was making involves His knowledge of how awful this impending doom would be. He needed to state how bad it would be to help them prepare. Jesus was also looking forward to another future time that would be worse, of even more unequaled distress. The event of

Jerusalem's destruction may in some way signal the beginning of the era of the "end times", which is marked by waves of distress that will culminate in such an *"unequaled"* time of distress.

C. Never to be equaled again (21c)
—and never to be equaled again.

Therefore, the future time of great distress Jesus referred to will be even worse than the destruction of Jerusalem in 70 A.D., for there have been wars, genocides, and natural disasters even larger and more extensive since then. Consideration must also be given to the scale of global development and the increase of the world's population; in the end times this will be increased by the intensity and magnitude of war, conflict, oppression, natural disasters, climate change, political chaos, economic disparity, racism, religious apostacy and persecution of the faithful. The signs given by Jesus offer the faithful a realistic assessment and awareness of what to prepare for. May each of us be faithful and of good cheer, even as the day draws nearer to the Lord's appointed return and ultimate judgment of all humanity. For while the time draws near, and it can be overwhelming, we are promised God's abundant and sufficient grace in Jesus Christ. By faith in Christ, we shall make it through the storms, and we shall reach the finish line. Reliance is not upon our own ability, but on the all-sufficient grace, mercy, justice, peace and love of God that stands as our foundation and strength.

V. Jesus gives a glimmer of hope (22)
22 "If those days had not been cut short, no one would survive, but for the sake of the elect those days will be shortened.

A. Some will survive the "Great Tribulation" (22a)
22 "If those days had not been cut short, no one would survive,

While the times of trial seem long, and those who will go through a portion of the Great Tribulation will find it overwhelming, the promise of Jesus is that the days will be *"cut short"*. The implication of Jesus is that the "last part" of the "worst part" of the tribulation will be a matter of *"days"*, not years. The other meaning Jesus gives in *"cut short"* may also refer to the "Rapture", the time when the Lord will send His angels to gather up the elect on the earth to spare them the suffering of the Great Tribulation.

There are three points of view on this, some who maintain a "pre-tribulation" rapture, others who believe in a "mid-tribulation" rapture, some who believe in a "post-tribulation" rapture which is a way of saying that there will be no rapture at all before the glorious coming judgment and reign of Jesus Christ. Based on this passage, the indication of participation in some form of tribulation that all people will go through is supported. Whether believers will go through none, part, or all, of the Great Tribulation, is a matter of debate. This statement of inclusion by Jesus of *"if those days"* (of tribulation) *"were not cut short, no one would survive"*, tells us that the mercy of God is operative at some level for all humanity. Even if a person's name is not in the Book of Life, God still has a heart of compassion, and God will extend salvation and suspend judgment amidst tribulation and to its conclusion. God's message spoken through Ezekiel is appropriate here:

> *23 Do I take any pleasure in the death of the wicked? declares the Sovereign Lord. Rather, am I not pleased when they turn from their ways and live?-* Ezekiel 18:23

B. God will extend mercy and grace to the remnant elect (22b)

> *but for the sake of the elect those days will be shortened.*

This clarification of Jesus, that the *"days will be shortened"*, is now spoken specifically for the sake of *"the elect"*, that is, for reconciled believers. Jesus may also be giving an indication that there would be a faithful remnant in the days of the intensified tribulation. In any event, how long "Christians/Jews/the elect" would suffer within the world during a time of great tribulation is a matter of God's plan of grace. As stated in this chapter's introduction, there are three essential scenarios for how *"the elect"* may experience and even glorify God in tribulation.

1). "PRE-TRIBULATION": The "elect", whose belief will be rewarded by God's grace and mercy, may be spared from the whole of the Great Tribulation. If this is the scenario, involving a "pre-tribulation" rapture, then it should be noted that "the elect" are already part of the common tribulation of humanity. God knows how much we could endure, and is merciful and just; keeping His people from the time of intense suffering and tribulation; this administration of mercy is a matter of God's gracious favor.

2. "MID-TRIBULATION": This scenario would involve "the elect" experiencing a portion of the time of Great Tribulation, then being raptured to Heaven amid faithfulness of witness to the world from their trial and testimony. Because of their faith and obedience, God would use their testimony as a final witness to bring others to faith and salvation. This scenario has much credibility, for God often strengthens His people to shine brightly through adversity.

3.) "POST-TRIBULATION": There is also the possibility that all living believers will be preserved until the time of judgment as a witness to unbelievers throughout the time of great tribulation; these believers would faithfully represent God. While this is not a popular point of view, there is something to be said for God giving believers courage, and God cutting the days of the Great Tribulation short for both believers and non-believers. This scenario still involves the coming of God's Kingdom through the return of Jesus, as the triumphant Christ, to reign and administer justice and judgment.

Each view leaves open many questions that shall only be answered as God determines to extend mercy and grace, and the final days of earth reveal the details of God's plan of salvation and judgment.

CONCLUDING THOUGHTS:

The idea of "Temple" (given by God for the benefit of people), a temporary dwelling place to focus upon and experience God, has both individual and corporate application. For each person, the holy place, or holy temple to care for is the seat of the soul – the body. Paul writes: *"Do you not know that your bodies are temples of the Holy Spirit, who is in you, whom you have received from God?"* (1 Corinthians 6:19). Paul, a faithful Jew and converted follower of Jesus Christ, also understood another important spiritual reality about how we are joined together in Christ:

> *19 Consequently, you are no longer foreigners and strangers, but fellow citizens with God's people and also members of his household, 20 built on the foundation of the apostles and prophets, with Christ Jesus himself as the chief cornerstone. 21 In him the whole building is joined together and rises to become a holy temple in the Lord. 22 And in him you too are being built together to become a dwelling in which God lives by his Spirit.* - Ephesians 2:19-22

Paul's theology emanates from the Lord's Supper, the tradition and communion of Passover, where Jesus identified with the "bread of shared suffering" and the "cup of affliction".

> *"Take and eat; this is my body"* (Matthew 26:26); *"Drink from it, all of you. This is my blood of the covenant, which is poured out for many for the forgiveness of sins."* (Matthew 26:27-28).

Consider the spiritual conflict and tension Jesus faced with people's sin and hypocrisy and His own ministry of holiness and forgiveness. People then and today struggle with conceiving of God being Sovereign Creator while God is patiently enduring and sacrificing for His children who are rebellious and have often gone astray from that which is right and good. The idea and design of the Temple for the Jewish people, and for all nations that were to be blessed by the Covenant of Abraham, was that God is seated on the throne (the Ark of the Covenant) within the Temple. The Ark of the Covenant was lost after the Babylonian captivity and destruction of the first Temple. Nonetheless, the belief was that God was in the Temple even if the Ark was not. In Sovereign mercy, God will forgive; in Sovereign justice, God holds all people into account. The Temple was intended to be the place to worship God in closest proximity, to bring sacrifices of a contrite heart and offerings of thanksgiving and praise.

Therefore, the Temple of Jerusalem represented the location of the mercy seat of the One True Sovereign God, the holy place set aside for the people of Israel (and for all nations) to worship Yahweh. This was to be the very center of the heart and soul of their community (and all the world in potential). The people of God were to be a *"light unto the nations"* (Isaiah 51:4), a *"city set upon a hill"* (Matthew 5:14). However, since the Temple of Jerusalem had become so infected with the rebellious spirit of the people, their sin and abomination (along with the Roman occupier's idolatry), this awful mess precipitated the just and inevitable consequence of "desolation", complete destruction.

Whatever trials and tribulations people may face, the call of God's Son is both a warning and an invitation. *"Repent, for the Kingdom of God is at hand"*, said Jesus as He walked along the sea of Galilee announcing the season of God's grace before the eventual judgment of God. The invitation of the Gospel would continue to be extended; those who have come to faith have experienced a transformation of their hearts and minds in devotion, life and worship. The Apostle Paul, who had once persecuted Christians, came to a vital relationship with the living, saving, Lord

Jesus Christ. His word to the persecuted church in Rome helped them to consider that their bodies could be a temple for the Holy Spirit, and that their lives are a witness to God's grace and Sovereignty:

> *1 Therefore, I urge you, brothers and sisters, in view of God's mercy, to offer your bodies as a living sacrifice, holy and pleasing to God—this is your true and proper worship. 2 Do not conform to the pattern of this world, but be transformed by the renewing of your mind. Then you will be able to test and approve what God's will is—his good, pleasing and perfect will.* - Romans 12:1-2

Questions:

1. Why does a parent give warning to their children?

2. The upcoming destruction of the temple, and the destruction and devastation of Jerusalem, would be a horrendous event. Why was it important for Jesus to give specific words of warning regarding this?

3. What were the disciples to do with this information? What are we to do with this information?

4. How is Jesus calling people today to be alert, vigilant and ready?

5. If we are living in the "end times", what might we expect, according to Jesus (Matthew 24:15-22)?

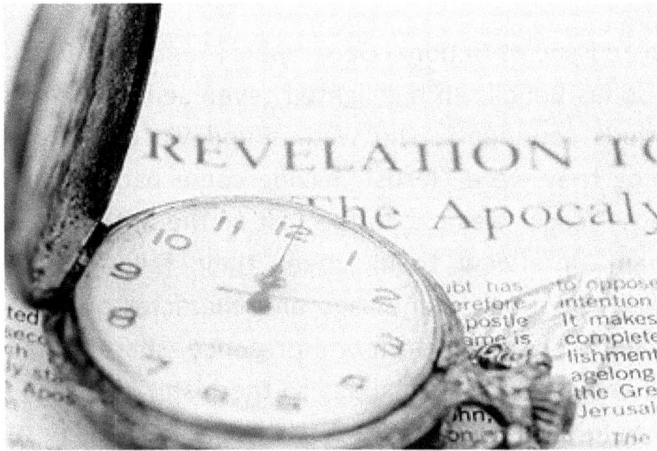

Part 4: "False messiahs"
(Addressing false hopes and claims)
Matthew 24:23-28

23 At that time if anyone says to you, 'Look, here is the Messiah!' or, 'There he is!' do not believe it. 24 For false messiahs and false prophets will appear and perform great signs and wonders to deceive, if possible, even the elect. 25 See, I have told you ahead of time. 26 "So if anyone tells you, 'There he is, out in the wilderness,' do not go out; or, 'Here he is, in the inner rooms,' do not believe it. 27 For as lightning that comes from the east is visible even in the west, so will be the coming of the Son of Man. 28 Wherever there is a carcass, there the vultures will gather.   - Matthew 24:23-28

Introduction: Guard against gullibility.

(Be discerning)

In an issue of National Geographic (August 2017, p. 87-93), a story by Jonas Bendiksen highlighted seven self-proclaimed Christs from various continents who were found via the internet, each proclaiming they were "Jesus", having come back to finish God's work. Each "Jesus" was put to the test as the author took time to meet them, interview them, meet their followers and make observations about their message and character qualities. These men all exhibited a positive moral presence, shared a message of love, and showed similar qualities to the historic Jesus. From this, Bendiksen formed a few observations and then postulated a question:

> "I know a lot of people will dismiss these men as fakers or lunatics. But I've always thought that a fundamental part of the Abrahamic religions – Judaism, Christianity, Islam – involves the coming of a messiah. Those faiths may disagree about identity and timing, but I think they agree on the basic premise. So, if one accepts that, why couldn't it be one of these guys?" (Jonas Bendiksen, National Geographic. 8/2017. P. 86)

Jesus was fully aware that there would be imposters after Him. People were drawn to Jesus, and there is something very good about following Jesus in faith, devotion and example. Yet only Jesus could be the Savior, and only Jesus is the Messiah, the One and Only Begotten Son of God in the original and truest sense. In this passage from Matthew 24:23-28, Jesus gave fair warning that there would be false messiahs and false prophets. Appearances and actions can be deceiving. However, Jesus gave them a clear vision that His return would be magnificent and unmistakable for all the earth at the same time. While Jesus came first as an infant child, His second coming will be as the glorified Son of God in full display of God's power and glory. Let's explore what it means to be discerning and not gullible, as it pertains to guarding people from following "false messiahs" or "false prophets". History has been riddled with people making such claims and deceiving people. What does Jesus teach His disciples so that they and we may discern and avoid deception?

OUTLINE of Matthew 24:23-28

I. Jesus knows that Fakes will come to deceive (v.23)
    A. In the time of Jerusalem's fall there were false Messiahs (23a)
    B. Do not believe those who deceive with false hope (23b)

II. The deceptions of false messiahs and false prophets (v.24-25)
    A. Appearances can be deceiving (24a)
    B. The signs can mislead you (24b)
    C. Wonders are not always wonderful (24c)
    D. The "Elect" can be deceived (belief misplaced) (24d)
    E. Jesus calls for discernment (be skeptical) (25)

III. Jesus warns believers that they can be misdirected (26)
    A. Escapism as a cult of deception (26a)
    B. Teaching and meditation as a cult of deception (26b)

IV. Jesus explains that His Second Coming will be distinctive (27-28)
    A. Example of lightning (Power and Visibility) (27)
    B. Example of gathering vultures (28)

V. Thoughts – Why was it important that Jesus warned people?

Study on Matthew 24:23-28

I. Jesus knows that Fakes will come to deceive (v.23)

23 At that time if anyone says to you, 'Look, here is the Messiah!' or, 'There he is!' do not believe it.

A. In the time of Jerusalem's fall there were false Messiahs (23a)

23 At that time if anyone says to you, 'Look, here is the Messiah!' or, 'There he is!'

Jesus would fulfill His primary ministry, and accomplish the righteous work and will of His Heavenly Father through His passion, crucifixion, death and resurrection. Jesus ascended to Heaven in the sight of His disciples. He shall return as He has promised, in His Heavenly Father's timing. Until then, Jesus warned people specifically that they must be weary and watchful of deceivers claiming to be Him, or telling them that He was "here" or "there". Charlatans are often narcissistic or opportunistic, and they manipulate people through deceptive claims and/or subtle charm. People looking for an immediate solution, some tangible hope, often commit to their deceptive or vain causes. Jesus foretold not only the appearance of those who would be imposters, He gave specific words of warning about what they might say and how they would gain a following. One false messiah, known as Jonathan, came to deceive the people of Jerusalem just a few years (68 A.D.) before the destruction of Jerusalem, and then reappeared again after the Temple's destruction:

> *.. before the destruction of Jerusalem; and a little after, one Jonathan, a weaver, persuaded many to follow him into the desert, most or all of whom were slain or made*

prisoners, and he himself taken and burned alive, by order of Vespasian. As several of these impostors thus conducted their followers into the desert, so did others into the secret chambers, or places of security. (Benson's Commentary. Bible Hub.)

The Jewish historian Josephus mentions that just prior to the Temple's destruction, a different (nameless) false messiah came and *"declared to the people in the city, that God commanded them to go up into the temple, and there they should receive the signs of deliverance"* (Josephus, by Bell. Vii.11.3). Men, women and children followed their "messiah", and soon afterward the Romans set their meeting place on fire, and over six thousand people perished tragically. There were other false messiahs prior to the destruction of the Second Temple and soon afterward. For close to 2000 years after Jesus gave this warning, a string of false messiahs and false prophets have misled millions. One must take the warning of Jesus seriously, and realize that when Jesus comes again, it will be known by all. Don't settle for an imitator, a fake, a "wolf in sheep's clothing".

B. Do not believe those who deceive with false hope (23b)   *do not believe it.*

One wonders why people are so inclined to believe false teachings or follow messiah-like figures. At our core, and from our infancy, we were designed to operate based on trust, faith, hope and love. False messiahs and prophets first gain people's trust and faith, then they manipulate people's hopes and affections to suit their presumptuous, or hidden, agendas. Their mode of deception operates from a pretense of stating their own higher moral ground, an assertion of divinity or infallibility. Because adherents long for direction, inspirational presence and leadership, they are willing to believe, follow, and be taken in.

In 1977, Jim Jones was a leader of a growing cult, the People's Temple. They had begun in California and had formed a commune in Guyana, South America. The movement began with seemingly good intentions, a caring community that was developing sustainable life outside the ills of society through a secure environment, faith in God, shared work, organic gardening and family support systems. Jones, however, began to abuse his authority to manipulate others for his plans. An investigation by Congressman Leo Ryan and a crew from NBC news in mid-November of 1978 was sent for a fact-finding mission to verify or dismiss reported concerns of human rights violations. When Ryan and the news crew tried to leave and take 15 people along, the congressman, two reporters, a cameraman and one defector of the People's Temple in Jonestown, Guyana were shot dead. With mounting pressure, Jones demonized the outside world, and began to prepare his community for a mass suicide. On November 18th, 1978, he led a worship service that involved drinking "punch" that was spiked with deadly poison. Over 900 followers died, knowing that they were committing suicide. Here is what Jones recorded, just before the event he was about to lead and participate in:

> *"We committed an act of revolutionary suicide protesting the conditions of an inhumane world."* (Jim Jones, "Death Tape" 1978)

What a horrid moment. The problem of spiritual deception is often a matter of psychology mixed with evil. People are trained and influenced to think in ways that are pounded into them through repetition, reinforcement and intensity. This differs from God's intent for a Covenant of Faith. True believers are not meant to be brought into bondage, but freedom and dignity through Christ. The "spirit of evil" is within people's behaviors of bondage and resulting systems of racism and oppression. Sadly, people are drawn into deadly deceptions within cults and religions of bondage.

II. The deceptions of false messiahs and false prophets (v.24-25)

. 24 For false messiahs and false prophets will appear and perform great signs and wonders to deceive, if possible, even the elect. 25 See, I have told you ahead of time.

A. Appearances can be deceiving (24a)
24 For false messiahs and false prophets will appear

One would think that people would learn lessons from history, yet just fifteen years after Jonestown another false prophet, David Koresh, led the "Branch Davidians", to a standoff with U.S. federal authorities that resulted in a defiant death by fire of Koresh and 75 of his followers in Waco, Texas in 1993. Koresh was quoted as saying: *"If the Bible is true, then I'm Christ."* He also stated: *"I am more than willing to come out when I get my message from my commander"*. Koresh shows the split personality of many cult leaders. On one hand, they claim to be in control as "Christ" and yet they gain followers with the appearance of being led by God amid confusion, chaos and deceptive practices. Another example is Sun Myung Moon, the leader of the Unification Church. He describes the requirement of members:

> *"A member must say that he is a member of the Unification Church and that he is the follower of Sun Myung Moon. If he doesn't have the courage to say it, he is not worthy of me."*

Manipulation, mind control, crushing social pressure in a peer group, behavioral repetition, legalistic requirements, focus on exclusive loyalty to a human figure, denial of individuality, justification of breaking ties with family, rationalization of unconscionable behavior, exclusive teachings that don't allow for discussion or debate; these are the warning signs of cults, false religions and false messiahs. For people who are fooled by false messiahs and false teachers, they often tend to seek an authority figure who will provide direction, stability, acceptance and security. The initial illusion blinds people from seeing the deception beneath the surface.

There are also false messiahs and false teachers who are not as obviously heinous or hideous. The "self-help" gurus who sell happiness, the tele-evangelists who tell people they can "buy a miracle" with their donation, the fitness fanatic who promises happiness in following the right training and regimen. Then there are the politicians who give false hope and promises they can't fulfill, building a base of support on people's fears and anxieties. As long as mankind is fallen and corrupt, and until God makes all things new, there will be deceivers; Satan poisons and pollutes the minds and souls of people. Yes, there are still many good people who are seeking to help others and provide responsible leadership in their fields of service, education, medicine, business, governance, research, and human service; however, the overwhelming bent of sin is still pervasive, cancerous. Humanity needs salvation.

B. The signs can mislead you (24b)
and perform great signs

The ability to perform great signs or miracles in Jesus' day was thought to have one of two origins (as we consider people's responses to Jesus' ministry). Jesus was either of divine origin and authority, or, He was of demonic inspiration and deluding people for evil purposes and self-glory. The people who witnessed Jesus' ministry and the miracles of healing were torn by what they had been taught by the Pharisees and what they saw in person. In one instance, Jesus confronted the Pharisees in a teachable moment following the driving out of a demon:

> 22 Then they brought him a demon-possessed man who was blind and mute, and Jesus healed him, so that he could both talk and see. 23 All the people were astonished and said, "Could this be the Son of David?" 24 But when the Pharisees heard this, they said, "It is only by Beelzebul, the prince of demons, that this fellow drives out demons." 25 Jesus knew their thoughts and said to them, "Every kingdom divided against itself will be ruined, and every city or household divided against itself will not stand. 26 If Satan drives out Satan, he is divided against himself. How then can his kingdom stand? 27 And if I drive out demons by Beelzebul, by whom do your people drive them out? So then, they will be your judges. 28 But if it is by the Spirit of God that I drive out demons, then the kingdom of God has come upon you. - Matthew 12:22-28

The concern of the Pharisees was not unreasonable, had Jesus been just another imposter for being "God". The outcry of the Pharisees, however, had little to do with theology and more to do with their concern for losing power. Their cry of hypocrisy and apostacy was a cover up for not discerning, and listening to discover, if Jesus had authenticity and truly was the Messiah. Jesus performed these signs so that people would open their hearts to God, not that their hearts would become captive to a strict religious bondage. Great signs, as understood by the Pharisees, might have been an indication of supernatural activity that was of Satan. Jesus did not dismiss their concern. He answered in a way that acknowledged that such evil deception existed, but that this was not applicable to Him. Jesus clarified His Godly nature and motives by pointing out that *"every kingdom divided against itself will be ruined.. If Satan drives out Satan, he is divided against himself."* Jesus came with a different purpose, to bring and build up the Kingdom of God. Satan loses every time someone is liberated from demonic oppression and the bondage of sin or disease.

Jesus continued His reasoning with a proposition for them to ponder: *"If it is by the Spirit of God that I drive out demons, then the kingdom of God has come upon you."* Jesus invited their analysis, their perception, their skepticism, questioning and free-will to decide. He did not dismiss their concerns. Indeed, Jesus' logic gave an objective ground of evidence, a revelation of God's mercy, for people to weigh over the facts and then come to faith.

Related to Jesus' warning in Matthew 24:24b, those who perform great signs with narcissism, selfish political ambition, ulterior motives, utopian intent, or blind ambition may not realize the danger that lurks in gaining power. Those who present themselves to be "Messiah", "Emperor", "Fuhrer" or "Divine Teacher" often impose their agenda and will upon others. They don't normally invite thinking, often the exchange of ideas is stifled. They don't encourage discussion, they try to restrict it. They don't encourage the will, they try to suppress and oppress it. This differs significantly from Jesus, who encouraged people to ask and seek. The pulpit commentary notes qualities of false messiahs and errant religions:

> *"Without assuming the name of Christ, many impostors shall be found who, professing to be inspired or lawful teachers, shall lead hearers into false doctrine, or claim to possess a new revelation, or something additional and supplemental to the eternal gospel. Such was Mohammed; such were the founders of Buddhism, Mormonism, and other so-called religions, who based their views on special revelation given from heaven for the purpose of improving the existing faith or introducing a new*

one… Two usual terms for miracles, the former regarding rather the evidence afforded by them, the latter the element of the marvelous inherent in them.. That such men did work actual miracles, or what were regarded as such, cannot be reasonably doubted. Satan was on their side, and, as far as he was permitted, confirmed their teaching by supernatural assistance. St. Paul testifies that such should be the action of the antichrist, "whose coming is after the working of Satan, with all power and signs and lying wonders" (The Pulpit Commentary, Matthew 24:24)

C. Wonders are not always wonderful (24c)
and wonders

Deception doesn't have to be obvious or heinous, many times the snare of wealth and success can lead people into moral or spiritual sleep, or pleasant and comfortable lies. The apocalypse may indeed look beautiful and serene to those who are comfortable in their possessions, social position and false gates of security. All too often, people will be wooed by the wonder of technology, or the allure and addictions of human creations. Civilization has a temporal charm and deceptive draw. The wonder of humanity, and the beauty of people in their capabilities, is not to be divorced from our Creator and Heavenly Father. God's plan is for healthy relationships that are in harmony with God's design and creation. Humanity, however, is broken and alienated from this ideal because of sin. Amidst the wonders of life that are all around, God is ever present. Replacement of worship (what we ultimately "give worth to") is, however, what has led us to exchange a relationship with God for believing lies that deny God, and God's revelation. The Apostle Paul put it this way:

28 Furthermore, just as they did not think it worthwhile to retain the knowledge of God, so God gave them over to a depraved mind, so that they do what ought not to be done. 29 They have become filled with every kind of wickedness, evil, greed and depravity. They are full of envy, murder, strife, deceit and malice. They are gossips, 30 slanderers, God-haters, insolent, arrogant and boastful; they invent ways of doing evil; they disobey their parents; 31 they have no understanding, no fidelity, no love, no mercy. 32 Although they know God's righteous decree that those who do such things deserve death, they not only continue to do these very things but also approve of those who practice them. You, therefore, have no excuse, you who pass judgment on someone else, for at whatever point you judge another, you are condemning yourself, because you who pass judgment do the same things. Romans 1:28-32 – 2:1

D. The "Elect" can be deceived (belief misplaced) (24d)

to deceive, if possible, even the elect.

Here is a sobering and challenging statement by Jesus. Deception is possible among those who are "the elect". This lightning bolt from Jesus sends shivers up the spines of those who assume that "believers", the "elect" (people within the Jewish or Christian context of faith), cannot be deceived. Historically, there have been ample examples of when "good people" foolishly followed monarchs or went head-long into violent and/or politically motivated crusades. The "elect" can be fooled by those who would manipulate issues of faith to steer people in a way that may redirect or misdirect their concern or compassion. The religious moral compass is a good thing, but when that compass is redirected and compromised, people become caught up in diversions that can move their focus away from God's will. Those who call themselves "Christians" are not necessarily followers of Jesus Christ. Those who claim the principles of the Bible are not necessarily being led by the Word of God. The "elect" can become like "tools" or "slaves". People go onboard the "Partisan-Ship" and discover later that it is bound for a stormy wreck, or the vessel breaks down and everyone waits onboard for a rescue (all the while dealing with the stench of systemic decay). People ride the "band-wagon" only to realize that they have been hijacked. The problem continues as people are often too proud to admit that they should jump ship or step out. Justification for continuance is given by the leader or group that continues to point at their moral issue while denying their own deceptive and manipulative practices that continue the lie/exploitation. One doesn't have to look far back in history, this is a present reality in the world of politics, economic injustice, social oppression and racism.

In Jesus' time, people followed several different competing camps of ideology. There were the pragmatic Sadducees who taught that alliance with Roman rule could be a means to maintain peace and stability. There were the philosophical Pharisees who taught the adherence to the Law and Commandments could be maintained alongside Roman rule and oppression. There were the Zealots who wanted to make Israel great again by using violence and force to establish God's Kingdom.

In the history of the Church there have been crusaders and colonizers, many of whom were corrupted by a bent toward conquest, not good will, peace and salvation by grace and truth. Overwhelmingly, when the Church institutionalized its partnership with merchants, governance and politics, the result was mostly heretical, abusive, violent and exploitive, an antithesis of the Gospel and life of Jesus Christ. The warning of Jesus in Matthew 24:24 is that Christians are to be faithful to the will of God, wise and discerning in matters of teaching and practice. Jesus was concerned about discernment and the future life and witness of the Church when He said:

> "Do not give dogs what is sacred; do not throw your pearls to pigs. If you do, they may trample them under their feet, and turn and tear you to pieces." Matthew 7:6

In the future, as the intensity of the signs increase, and a time of great tribulation comes, the deception of "the elect" will manifest itself even more. People of faith will be looking for someone in politics, business, or the entertainment/media world to come forth and present a vision that will match their hopes or assuage their anxieties. Those persons (or an individual) with the "spirit of Anti-Christ" (an agenda that is to glorify self/man above God and Jesus Christ) will come and deceive *"even the elect"*. They will allude to the name of "Jesus" or "God" to give the impression (illusion) of sincerity of faith. One has only to look at history to realize that the "naming of God" is not the proof, and therefore Jesus warned the disciples about the future and what they needed to know regarding false messiahs and false teachers. One time when Jesus confronted the hypocrisy of the Pharisees, as they were upset with Jesus that His disciples did not always wash their hands before eating, the Lord quoted the prophet Isaiah:

> 8 *"'These people honor me with their lips, but their hearts are far from me. 9 They worship me in vain; their teachings are merely human rules." 10 Jesus called the crowd to him and said, "Listen and understand. 11 What goes into someone's mouth does not defile them, but what comes out of their mouth, that is what defiles them."* Matthew 15:7-11

People must carefully consider what they hear and whether it is of God. There was a pastor of a large Mega-Church from Chicago who was asked to attend a gathering of evangelical leaders in New York City during the presidential election of the United States in the Fall of 2016. A large table was filled with people who were well known church leaders and pastors. The host had not arrived, but they decided to have a few minutes of prayer. Finally, the host arrived and took his seat at the head of the table. A well-known leader, an evangelist whose father was also an evangelist, spoke up and said: *"Sir, we are praying for you."* The presidential candidate replied, *"Thank you, but I don't need your prayers. I need your votes."* The response of the pastor, who was now reporting what happened to his congregation, was to tell them of his surprise and concern. The pastor told the thousands listening (many of whom were interested in supporting this candidate): *"I don't see anything of God in this man."* (I share this story from directly hearing this pastor on a Sunday morning in Chicago when I was visiting family). I respected the pastor for his discernment and candor, and I could hear his concern for the Church, "the elect", that they not be fooled or misdirected.

The deception of non-believers is expected, but Jesus makes it clear that believers may also be deceived, and this is of equal concern. What must one do? Guard your heart and mind from those who would seek to steal it. Keep your focus and hope on the Lord Jesus Christ, and accept no other substitute. Do not allow anyone else to pre-empt the honor, glory and praise that is due only to God and to His Son Jesus Christ. Rely upon the wisdom and discernment from Jesus and God's Holy Spirit, also find wisdom among Christ's true believers and humble shepherds who care for the flock above themselves.

E. Jesus calls for discernment (be skeptical) (25)

25 See, I have told you ahead of time.

Jesus had a vision that included near and distant future events and leaders. His warning was both immediate and far reaching. Jesus, the teacher, the good shepherd, wanted His disciples (and all of God's children) to be aware and skeptical, to stay sharp and vigilant to discern truth from error. A parent will try to warn their child of danger. Jesus also spoke to warn His disciples of the dangers that they would face, near term and long term. The teachable moment was His "leaving the Temple". His upcoming Passion, as "the Good Shepherd who would lay down His life", embodied all that Jesus had taught them. By the goodness of God's grace, the final word was not in the hands of those who would deny or crucify God's Son, and it wasn't in the coercion of those who would mislead the crowds. The final word was in God's presence, God's power to forgive people and give new life. Christ was victorious over evil by the power of love, and the Father raising Him over death. Truth triumphed over deception, and judgment issued grace over condemnation to those who repent and believe.

III. Jesus warns believers that they can be misdirected (26)

26 "So if anyone tells you, 'There he is, out in the wilderness,' do not go out; or, 'Here he is, in the inner rooms,' do not believe it.

A. Escapism as a cult of deception (26a)

26 "So if anyone tells you, 'There he is, out in the wilderness,' do not go out;

John the Baptist had been an essential part of God's plan to prepare the way for Jesus. Here Jesus is warning that there will be imposters who will claim to be the Messiah, and will gather people in the wilderness much as John the Baptist did. The key difference was that John the Baptist had already finished the work of preparation, and Jesus was the fulfillment of God's plan for a Messiah. The disciples were being warned that others would try to replicate either John the Baptist or Himself, but their means of gaining followers would be violent and their end, destruction. One such person was Simon, son of Gioras, who gathered multitudes in the desert of Tekoah around 68 A.D. as they prepared to battle the Romans for Jerusalem. This charismatic warrior was extremely strong and had many followers who believed in the forceful overthrow of the Romans, and though he outwitted the Romans in the battle of Jerusalem (70 A.D.) by hiding in subterranean tunnels, he came out due to hunger and was captured. When brought to Rome as a trophy to Titus, he was dragged through the streets and then hurled 80 feet over the Tarpeian Rock to his death (Josephus. "B.J." vii 2, 1; vii 5, 6, 7 & 8.).

There have also been peaceful attempts for utopian societies led by voices calling people to the wilderness. During the late 1960's, when the "hippie movement" could not sustain itself economically within mainstream society and cities, some tried to develop alternative societies or communes. The ideology was that the system was so broken and messed up that the only hope was to escape, to start anew. To do this, people were lured to follow charismatic leaders and then try to develop alternative utopian ideals together out of their own good will. One behavioral psychologist with much credibility, B.F. Skinner, believed that a community could develop in which positive behavior is rewarded through positive reinforcement, and negative behavior could be modified also through careful positive reinforcement. A novel that he wrote in 1948, "Walden II", became popular in the late 60's and early 70's. In it he imagined a society where people could use behavioral techniques and humanistic philosophy to create a more sustainable and peaceful society. Several attempts were made to replicate and apply his ideas, but only a few attempts with very limited success did thrive or survive. B.F. Skinner noted in 1976:

> *Either we do nothing and allow a miserable and probably catastrophic future to overtake us, or we use our knowledge about human behavior to create a social environment in which we shall live productive and creative lives and do so without jeopardizing the chances that those who follow us will be able to do the same.* (Skinner B.F. Walden two. New York: Macmillan; 1976. Preface. pp. v–xvi.)

Skinner was focused on a "humanistic", solution. The logic goes: "Man is the measure of all things. If the problems or behavior of man need to change, then man must find ways through inherent better nature to make the changes." A harkening back to nature, to a form of naturalism, has an appeal. Henry David Thoreau, who wrote "Walden" from his time of meditation and escape to discover himself in solitude, noted:

> *"However mean your life is, meet it and live it; do not shun it and call it hard names. It is not so bad as you are. It looks poorest when you are richest. The fault-finder will find faults even in paradise. Love your life, poor as it is. You may perhaps have some pleasant, thrilling, glorious hours, even in a poorhouse. The setting sun is reflected from the*

windows of the almshouse as brightly as from the rich man's abode; the snow melts before its door as early in the spring. I do not see but a quiet mind may live as contentedly there, and have as cheering thoughts, as in a palace." (H.D. Thoreau. Walden. 1854).

Thoreau, was an advocate for deep thinking and discovery within the context of humility and faith, sparked by the general revelation of God in nature. *"Profession is to be always on the alert to find God in nature—to know his lurking places",* wrote Thoreau. Yet even in nature he could not absent himself from reminders of the ills of society, the ants who warred with one another were a reminder of the wars of mankind. The slant of history in a civil war, where slavery meted injustice, meant that isolation was not a long-term option. Thoreau reminds humanity that we are designed for deeper thinking, and to know the Origin and Genius of that which may draw us both earthward and heavenward at the same time. Moreover, Thoreau also exemplifies the reality that internal harmony is temporal because the world itself is not at peace; the wild is but a respite to renew the soul and point it to the greater reality and purpose of God the Creator/Redeemer. The Apostle Paul once reflected:

19 For the creation waits in eager expectation for the children of God to be revealed. 20 For the creation was subjected to frustration, not by its own choice, but by the will of the one who subjected it, in hope 21 that the creation itself will be liberated from its bondage to decay and brought into the freedom and glory of the children of God. 22 We know that the whole creation has been groaning as in the pains of childbirth right up to the present time. 23 Not only so, but we ourselves, who have the firstfruits of the Spirit, groan inwardly as we wait eagerly for our adoption to sonship, the redemption of our bodies. - Romans 8:19-24

B. Teaching and meditation as a cult of deception
(26b) *or, 'Here he is, in the inner rooms,' do not believe it.*

The words *"here he is"* give importance to the idea that the Messiah will be announced and presented by people. When Christ Jesus comes in glory, no headline will be necessary. The announcement will be from the trumpet blast and heavenly host of angels. You will not have to search for the Messiah, He will be revealed in God's glory as He comes on the clouds.

While there is a need for teaching and discipleship, the coming of Jesus for instruction has already occurred in His first coming. His return will be to consummate the work of the Church and the work of God's salvation. The word for "inner room" here is the same used by Jesus in Matthew 6:6:

> But when you pray, go into your **"room"** close the door and pray to your Father, who is unseen. Then your Father, who sees what is done in secret, will reward you. 7 And when you pray, do not keep on babbling like pagans, for they think they will be heard because of their many words. - Matthew 6:6-7

The modern equivalent for this type of "room" is that of a "closet" or "secret place". The concern Jesus had was not a matter of one's act of prayer, but that of the focus and intent of prayer. If a person is looking within for the answer, and not to God, the result will be spiritual deficiency or spiritual deviancy (either from their imperfect context of life or from the presence of demonic influence). The disciple Peter wrote that Satan is prowling around looking for ways to deceive and devour those who approach their spiritual deficit without direction and faith in God.

> 8 Be alert and of sober mind. Your enemy the devil prowls around like a roaring lion looking for someone to devour. - 1 Peter 5:8

Marshall Applewhite had a near death experience in 1972 that convinced him to explore his spiritual nature. Sadly, instead of discovering the revelation of God in the Scriptures where he could discover God's story of grace and truth in Jesus, Applegate formed a philosophy and religion on his own. The "Heaven's Gate" cult formed in 1975 and was based on the premise of Applegate that they could capture the attention of extraterrestrials to rescue them from their "containers" (bodies) and bring their released souls to a higher physical existence.

Following an anonymous tip, police entered a mansion in Rancho Santa Fe, an exclusive suburb of San Diego, California, and discovered thirty-nine victims of a mass suicide. The deceased, twenty-one women and eighteen men of varying ages—were all found lying peaceably in matching dark clothes and Nike sneakers and had no noticeable signs of blood or trauma. It was later revealed that the men and women were members of the "Heaven's Gate" religious cult, whose leaders preached that suicide would allow them to leave their bodily "containers" and enter an alien spacecraft hidden behind the Hale-Bopp comet. In 1997, as part of its 4,000-year orbit of the sun, the comet Hale-Bopp passed near Earth in one of the most impressive astronomical events of the 20th century. In late March 1997, as Hale-Bopp reached its closest distance to Earth, Applewhite and thirty-eight of his followers drank a lethal mixture of phenobarbital and vodka and then lay down to die, hoping to leave their bodily containers, enter the alien spacecraft, and pass through Heaven's Gate into a higher existence. (History.com, This Day in History, March 26, 1997).

This is but one of many instances in which human philosophies have sought to take on a "truth" of their own apart from God's revealed truth in creation or Scripture. There are many people who believe the solution to overcome sin and brokenness is found through meditation and imagination, and through this, a means of peace or escape is their hoped for "Nirvana". Jesus prayed to the Heavenly Father for His disciples:

15 My prayer is not that you take them out of the world but that you protect them from the evil one. 16 They are not of the world, even as I am not of it. 17 Sanctify them by the truth; your word is truth. 18 As you sent me into the world, I have sent them into the world. (John 17:15-18)

IV. Jesus explains that His Second Coming will be distinctive (27-28)

27 For as lightning that comes from the east is visible even in the west, so will be the coming of the Son of Man. 28 Wherever there is a carcass, there the vultures will gather.

A. Example of lightning (Power and Visibility) (27)

27 For as lightning that comes from the east is visible even in the west, so will be the coming of the Son of Man.

Jesus used an example from nature (lightning) to talk about His second coming. His return will be powerful, quick and extensively visible. When lightning flashes across the sky, it can be seen from all angles on the earth below. The speed of the light is 671 million miles an hour (299,792,458 meters/second). Of course, the speed of how the molecules from the earth to the clouds form a current to create lightning is not as fast (220 million miles per hour – 1/3 the speed of light), but this is still blazing fast! The speed of sound, in which one hears the thunder, is 750 miles per hour. Whether people see or hear this event, the speed and immediacy of the moment will catch people by surprise. How long people will have to respond and react is a mystery. Another mystery of debate pertains to what comes after Christ's gathering up of "the elect" at that time. Will it involve a great tribulation for a brief period prior to His final return to bring the Kingdom of God to earth (spoken of in Revelation 21)? The teaching of Jesus favors a time of harvest, followed by a time of greater tribulation, followed by Christ's return to give final judgment (Matthew 25:31-46) and bring in the Kingdom of Heaven to a transformed earth. The more important matter of verse 27 is how extensive, powerful and profound this event of Christ's return for the gathering up of God's people will be.

William Barclay, in his book "The King and the Kingdom", wrote:

> The Jews were convinced that this Day of the Lord would descend on the world without any warning whatever. This is an idea which we find re-echoed in the New Testament. "The Day of the Lord will come like a thief in the night (I Thessalonians 5:2). But the Day of the Lord will come like a thief (2 Peter 3:10). They believed that the day when god intervened and broke into history would come suddenly upon men. This was a very wise and very valuable note to sound, because it means that always we have to be in readiness for the coming of God. (William Barclay, The King and the Kingdom, Westminster Press, Philadelphia, 1968. p. 115)

In contrast to the powerful, swift, and unmistakable event of Christ Jesus's return, there will be imposters and those who come as "wolves in sheep's clothing".

> "Watch out for false prophets. They come to you in sheep's clothing, but inwardly they are ferocious wolves. (Matthew 7:15).

The state of technology in the world today now allows for almost instant transmission of information through satellites and relay towers throughout much of the earth. The spread of news, true or not, is rapid. Stories, news, data and information is delivered almost instantly and the term used for a high level of interest is that it "goes viral". The infrastructure is in place for various groups or individuals to communicate their message globally, and in many cases, it can be streamed live. Still, there is a delay of seconds for streaming between when an event happens and when it can be viewed through television or the internet on a device or computer.

False Christ's will use the internet and people's mobile devices to deceive. The hacking of information raises the concern of what one can trust. Politically charged groups and religious zealots will slant information or tell outright lies to suit their agendas or tear others down. Do people have enough time, wisdom and discernment to sift through the errors and have an accurate and truthful grasp on what is going on? There is good reason to raise the shields for security, be more informed and skeptical.

Even when Jesus does come, consider this: Jesus said that He shall come again like lightning. Could the event of His return be captured on video? Could it be simply retransmitted and repeated for the sake of deciding matters of faith? Readiness is ultimately a matter of having faith prior to Christ's moment of return. When He does come, the description given by our Lord supports a *"taking up"* or *"rapture"* of God's redeemed, perhaps as fast as a flash of lightning. The point here is that those of genuine faith, who trust in the Lord Jesus completely, will be taken up quickly prior to the time of greater tribulation and God's cleansing wrath. There are still many questions that remain a mystery. Be wary of anyone who claims to have it all figured out.

How then are people to be ready? Jesus taught that readiness is more a matter of how we live, not how we wait. Even the technology we develop can't prepare us for the lightning quick rapture of our Lord to be implemented at the rescue of His own from the destruction to come. The best way to be ready is to simply be faithful, and be like Jesus out of genuine care and kindness; do the will of God in reaching out to the neighbor, the stranger, your family and friends and anyone the Lord places in your path or guides you to serve (we shall examine this later in the parables of Matthew 25).

B. Example of gathering vultures (28)

28 Wherever there is a carcass, there the vultures will gather.

Jesus gave another illustration from nature, "the carcass" and the "vultures", to refer to signs of the end times.   Jesus' metaphor here is commonly experienced in the wild, but the application remains a bit of a mystery for interpretation. Scholars have noted that the word for "vulture" is the same used for other raptors such as "eagles". Some disagreement exists between those who would apply the Roman symbol of the eagle on their standards and shields as applying to the siege and destruction of Jerusalem that Jesus was foretelling. There may be some parallel to this, but the context of Jesus' metaphor here is pertaining to a time of finality, the coming of the "Son of Man" in power and extensive glory. The destruction of Jerusalem would occur, but the end of times, the judgment of the nations, fits more closely to what Jesus had just been speaking about. Furthermore, the reference to the "vultures/eagles" could be more clearly interpreted as symbolic of God's "clean-up crew", or the angels that will be involved in the final battle. They will devour and remove the "carcasses" of those destroyed and punished by God during the time of greater tribulation and after the final judgment. Jesus had already taught that the Kingdom of God was like a field with good seed and bad seed coexisting, but that eventually a harvest day of judgment would come, and that involving the host of angels sent by Jesus:

> 38 The field is the world, and the good seed stands for the people of the kingdom. The weeds are the people of the evil one, 39 and the enemy who sows them is the devil. The harvest is the end of the age, and the harvesters are angels. 40 "As the weeds are pulled up and burned in the fire, so it will be at the end of the age. 41 The Son of Man will send out his angels, and they will weed out of his kingdom everything that causes sin and all who do evil. 42 They will throw them into the blazing furnace, where there will be weeping and gnashing of teeth. (Matthew 13:38-43)

This "weeding out" by the angels, combined with Jesus' image of the vultures gathering to clean up as part of the Judgment, is foreboding of God's righteous indignation of evil. When Jesus was betrayed by Judas and taken into custody by the Temple guards of the Sanhedrin in the Garden of Gethsemane, He could have chosen to defend Himself. Jesus, however, did not call on angelic armies to defend Him. Instead, He continued with God's plan of salvation and His ministry to "root out" sin by becoming the target, the lamb of God who came to take away the sins of the world on the cross. Jesus was fully aware that He had this choice, which was a temptation, to call upon Heaven's strength. Jesus chose mercy instead of wrath:

> 53 Do you think I cannot call on my Father, and he will at once put at my disposal more than twelve legions of angels? 54 But how then would the Scriptures be fulfilled that say it must happen in this way?" Matthew 26:53-54

Jesus had Divine awareness and Heaven's authority to call upon His Heavenly Father and the angels at any given time to intervene. Jesus chose to continue, however, to be obedient to the will of His Heavenly Father that would fulfill the Scriptures. Jesus is, after all, the Word of God made flesh. (John 1:14). Jesus did not come to prove His identity and authority, He came to serve and save humanity through His perfect sacrifice for our sins. A display of power would have been impressive, but it would have been premature. The plan of God's salvation is invitational, not a matter of God's imposition. God opened the way for people to come to faith in Him, and be saved by grace in the gift of Jesus His Son, who first rooted out sin and conquered it by His death and resurrection.

Regarding the angels, we note in biblical history that they have been active in matters pertaining to salvation, ministry and judgment. Angels have been authorized to announce or speak on God's behalf; they have also been called upon to minister to people. The angels ministered to Jesus in the wilderness following His forty days and nights of fasting and temptation (Matthew 4:11). Jesus refers to angels again as He was betrayed by Judas and arrested prior to His passion. Instead of calling upon a multitude of angels, Jesus went forward to fulfill God's plan of forgiveness through His willing suffering work and perfect sacrifice that culminated in a victory over sin at the cross. Jesus came to accomplish salvation first, for all who believe in Him, repent of their sin, and receive the gift of God's grace giving the second birth of the Holy Spirit for reconciliation and new life. Christ's victory was first to be for our redemption. Finally, in the Second Coming, Jesus will indeed come accompanied by an incredibly vast and powerful host of heavenly angels. God's righteous wrath will conclude with cleansing, a removal process.

V. <u>Thoughts – Why was it important that Jesus warned people?</u>

God loves people! That is why God sent Jesus to be our Savior. That is why God's Son Jesus not only invites people to believe and have new life, but Jesus also warns people about God's eventual plan of judgment in which the earth shall be cleansed for a new beginning. If we as human beings had not chosen disobedience in our Genesis, represented by the Garden of Eden, then our state of being would not have been corrupted. However, the problem of evil is real, and the effect of willful rebellion to God has charged the condition of humanity with brokenness, chaos, sin. The condition of the human spirit and mind has been corrupted; a combination of chronic and aggressive diseases have put humanity at risk and peril.

The parallel can be made to the earth and its people having what might medically be described as a chronic type of "cancer". The thing about a chronic cancer, such as certain types of Leukemia or Lymphoma, is that they can grow slowly in the body for years going unnoticed. However, once a Chronic cancer takes over vital organs, or affects the production of healthy blood cells in the bone marrow, it becomes life threatening. Doctors Fintel and McDermott articulate that there are four types of events that can trigger the development of cancer: 1) The Invasion of a Virus, 2) The rearrangement of genes, 3) Loss of a suppressor gene, and 4)

Redundant duplication of a chromosome (Cancer, by William Fintel and Gerald McDermott, Baker Books, 2004. P.14-21). Evil can invade like a virus, Infection taking over without the suppression of a shield or defense of immunity. Chaos results and involves rearrangements that are not beneficial. For the human body, soul or society, people may be infected with deception that can take over when people lose the ability to suppress erroneous information. This is true on many levels, be it cellular, communal or spiritual. The spread of false teaching involves redundant duplication of unhealthy cells that reproduce in ways that "take away" and "choke out" life from the body, whereas healthy cells duplicate in harmony and are life giving/sustaining to the body. One then can make the case that the cancer of sin, devised by Satan, has pervasively infected and affected humanity. The application of the damaging reality of "duplication of erroneous information" is rampant and pronounced in a hypermedia world and culture.

Why then was it important for Jesus to warn people about the future? Since Jesus was fully aware of how messed-up humanity was, He needed to prepare His disciples, and future generations of humanity, for three essential matters: 1) His upcoming passion and work on the cross, followed by His resurrection and ascension, (2) the challenges yet ahead for people in the Age of the Church both proximate and long term, and (3) the need to prepare people for what to expect realistically for God's work, this involving patient endurance and vigilance for a long time-frame prior to His eventual supernatural return that shall be unmistakable.

Questions for Discussion:

1. What are some examples of modern-day "false messiahs" or "false teachers"? What is it that they are telling people to believe or trust in?

2. What are some specific warning signs, or examples of deception, that Jesus teaches His disciples? Are these signs relevant for people today? In what ways?

3. How do you relate to the thought that the "Chronic" condition of humanity involves a corruption, like cancer, in the body? What are some of the social sins and personal sins that beset people?

4. How are you discovering the peace of God and the presence of Jesus to help you "stand" and be a faithful, loving and truthful witness and servant of the Gospel?

Part 5: "Christ Comes in Great Power and Glory"
(Unmistakable Cosmic Entrance)
Matthew 24:29-36

29 "Immediately after the distress of those days "'the sun will be darkened, and the moon will not give its light; the stars will fall from the sky, and the heavenly bodies will be shaken.' 30 "Then will appear the sign of the Son of Man in heaven. And then all the peoples of the earth will mourn when they see the Son of Man coming on the clouds of heaven, with power and great glory. 31 And he will send his angels with a loud trumpet call, and they will gather his elect from the four winds, from one end of the heavens to the other. 32 "Now learn this lesson from the fig tree: As soon as its twigs get tender and its leaves come out, you know that summer is near. 33 Even so, when you see all these things, you know that it

is near, right at the door. 34 Truly I tell you, this generation will certainly not pass away until all these things have happened. 35 Heaven and earth will pass away, but my words will never pass away. 36 "But about that day or hour no one knows, not even the angels in heaven, nor the Son, but only the Father."
- Matthew 24:29-36

Introduction: When the Time comes...
Everyone will know it

Jesus continued teaching about what to be prepared for, what the signs will be at the very time of His cosmic entrance. Here, Jesus described the remarkable vision of the "Day of the Lord". One can imagine His voice resounding as a trumpet of truth, explaining what would happen after the time of extreme distress. Wonder and awe awoke in the disciples, Jesus unveiled the eventual signs of His glorious reappearance. This event would include astronomical events. Was Jesus describing eclipses, or the blocking out of the moon and the darkening of the sun due to smoke, dust or disturbance to the earth's atmosphere? Jesus also poetically described a shakeup of the earth, the moon and its atmosphere unlike anything ever recorded in human history. Most importantly, the *"Son of Man"*, Jesus Himself, will come and appear *"on the clouds of heaven with power and glory"*. The Angel of the Lord will blow the trumpet and the rapture of the "elect" will bring about the harvest of God's people, and God's final steps of judgment will commence.

Jesus then concluded His oracle, this prophetic vision, by using a metaphor from nature as a broad summation.   The illustration of the "fig tree" changing color, as it is laden with fruit, visibly displays a near harvest. In masterful application, Jesus revealed how God's plan of salvation and judgment shall mature and then become ripe. Ultimately, the harvest of people for God's magnificent and triumphant Kingdom is on a timetable, the season will draw nigh for Jesus Christ's return.

Finally, Jesus clarifies in this teaching that the exact timing of this great and awesome "Day of the Lord" is a mystery, reserved only to God the Heavenly Father's exclusive knowledge and prerogative. Even Jesus Himself, and the Angels in Heaven, do not know exactly when this shall happen. Yet when it does happen, everyone will know it.

In writing this book, there have been events of great significance and concern from August 2017 into September 2017. There was a solar eclipse that ran its course across the United States of America on August 21, 2017. People were moved by this event, and spoke of it as a monumental experience, almost spiritual. Just a few days later, however, hurricane Harvey gathered speed, direction and momentum to dump a record amount of rain in much of Texas. Many thousands of people in Houston were flooded out of their homes with rainfall of over 50 inches and the rise of rivers and lakes that has never been seen before. On September 7th, 2017, hurricane Irma, category five (with winds of 185 mph), came and devastated the Caribbean Islands and Florida. It was called the largest and most powerful hurricane to ever develop in the Atlantic Ocean. Satellite images also showed two other hurricanes developing east and west of Irma (Jose and Katia). By the grace of God, Jose curled out into the Atlantic (It was even larger than Irma), and Katia fizzled out as it drenched Central America. However, soon afterward hurricane Maria came and devastated Puerto Rico, leaving millions of people without clean water, power, safe homes and roads. The destruction of trees, roofs and walls of homes being torn off, and vehicles strewn about, was unparalleled. The relief efforts, cost, and consequence of health from all these hurricanes are overwhelming.

Besides the hurricanes, there were also two large earthquakes in Mexico during September, with many buildings collapsing on people in Mexico City. There was also a large earthquake in Japan. On the west coast of the United States, in Los Angeles, California and Oregon, large wildfires burned and blocked out the sun with smoke. Climate change was not only swirling in the tropical storms, it was fueling brush and forest fires and destroying many homes.

Amid all this, the president of North Korea, Kim Jun Un, has been escalating his threats to the United States, South Korea, Japan and the world. North Korea successfully tested a nuclear hydrogen bomb underground and is threatening to use it on an inter-continental missile. President Trump warned that there may be no other solution than to respond to the threat with a powerful military strike. The response of North Korea was to state that the United States was declaring war, and so they announced that millions more of their citizens have joined their army in preparation. Insanity!

Meanwhile, the United States, Britain and other countries are going through tumultuous internal conflicts and a crisis in leadership stability. What will happen in America and the world for the next seven years until the next full solar eclipse tracks its way from the state of Texas to the state of Maine? Of course, the world is not just about North America and the United States. Perhaps this is precisely the point of why God is allowing these things to happen; and in history God has allowed things to happen to nations whose pride and arrogance had become intolerable. There is a mystery to suffering and grief, and those of faith recognize that God allows adversity. God is present to teach humility, and to give peace and strength through hardship. God is sovereign, just, and merciful. The Day of Judgment is close at hand. For the "elect" of genuine faith, their hope is that the redemption and re-creation of this corrupt and cancerous world draws ever so nearer.

Outline of Matthew 24:29-36

I. The Great Tribulation, and Jesus Christ comes (v.29-30)
   A. Distressful days conclude with cosmic events (29)
      1. The sun will be darkened
      2. The moon will not give its light
      3. Stars will fall from the sky (meteorites?)
      4. Heavenly bodies are shaken (planets?)

   B. All People will mourn when Jesus appears (30)
      1. People will see the sign of the Son of Man in heaven
      2. People will see the Son of Man coming on the clouds
         a. with power
         b. with glory

II. Jesus gathers God's elect (v.31)

   A. Angels are sent out with a loud trumpet call
   B. Angels will gather God's elect from among the nations
   C. Angels will gather God's elect from areas beyond our knowledge

III. Awareness of the signs (v.32-33)

   A. Learning from the Fig Tree (32)
   B. Nearness and urgency (33)

IV. The church age will culminate in fulfillment (34)

V. The words of Jesus are faithful and constant (35)

VI. The exact time of Jesus Christ's Second Coming is unknown. (36)

   A. No human can know
   B. Angels do not know
   C. Jesus the Son does not know
   D. Only God the Father knows

Study on Matthew 24:29-36

I. The Great Tribulation, and Jesus Christ comes (v.29-30)

29 "Immediately after the distress of those days "'the sun will be darkened, and the moon will not give its light; the stars will fall from the sky, and the heavenly bodies will be shaken.' 30 "Then will appear the sign of the Son of Man in heaven. And then all the peoples of the earth will mourn when they see the Son of Man coming on the clouds of heaven, with power and great glory.

A. Distressful days conclude with cosmic events (29)

29 "Immediately after the distress of those days "'the sun will be darkened, and the moon will not give its light; the stars will fall from the sky, and the heavenly bodies will be shaken.'

Upon deep consideration of this passage, the reader is struck by the uniqueness of this interruptive future event that Jesus has revealed. Continuing with Jesus' reference to the *"birth pains"* of the Kingdom of God, this cessation of *"distress"* will be a time for something new, beautiful and awesome from God to arrive and break forth. The dawn of a new era commences while God's Judgment brings a conclusion to the previous era. Those who will behold this shall be like the prophet Isaiah, who saw the Lord enthroned in heaven:

> *"Woe to me!" I cried. "I am ruined! For I am a man of unclean lips, and I live among a people of unclean lips, and my eyes have seen the King, the Lord Almighty."* Isaiah 6:5

To understand the signs that will accompany the Day of Judgment, let's take a closer look at the description Jesus gives in Matthew 24:29.

1. The sun will be darkened

29 "Immediately after the distress of those days "'the sun will be darkened,

The cosmic occurrences of the future, revealed by Jesus, are both poetic and scientific. God speaks through Jesus' words to begin to describe the cataclysmic changes coming. Even though speculation and theorization is about all we can muster about the future, Jesus' message is that God is still in control. Nonetheless, God wants us to ask questions, to ponder and analyze with the tools of observation and science in astronomy, mathematics and physics. How could the sun be darkened in a way that would also involve the darkening of the moon, the obscuration of the stars and the shaking of the planets?

One hypothesis is that our moon or one of the solar system's planets might be hit by a large asteroid. The result could be a debris field so large that it would eventually affect the earth's atmosphere. On March 17, 2016, an earth-sized asteroid hit the planet Jupiter (NASA). The effect on Jupiter was visible to earth and was initially recorded by an amateur astronomer. Because of Jupiter's immense size, no debris field had likely left its atmosphere. The fact is, Jupiter has acted as a large gravitational magnet for objects in our solar system. If not for Jupiter, which absorbs about 6 large meteors a year, earth would not be as well protected and would not have developed a sustainable ecosystem for life. Nevertheless, some meteors have burned up in the earth's atmosphere. Jupiter and the other planets have not caught them all. A few large asteroids and meteors to hit the earth have been recorded in history, such as that which brought about the destruction of dinosaurs and initiated an ice age. Craters can be seen on the earth and on the moon. In Jesus' description, there will be a significant, earth changing, cosmic event. Indeed, if a large asteroid hit our moon or a more proximate planet like Venus or Mars, the effect would be dramatic.

The likelihood of the earth or one of our smaller planet neighbors being hit by a large meteor may be improbable, especially compared to Jupiter being hit by a meteor. It would be as if you threw a baseball out the window of your car and it hit another baseball being hit by a batter over the right field fence as you drove past. There is greater likelihood that your car would be struck by the batter's home run, and it would be less likely that your thrown ball would be hit. However, the possibility exists. Over enough time, with enough activity, it could truly happen. However, what if it is not simply a matter of probability, but of providence. Think about it, is there not an element of timing in life that is not simply circumstantial or coincidental. If one believes in the existence, providence and sovereignty of God, the impossible is possible. When Paul Simon wrote the song "So beautiful, or so what?", he appealed to the questions of existence, meaning and faith. We may believe that beauty is from God, life is from God, awesome events are in God's planning; the alternative is to say "so what?", "it's all simply chance", "there is no originality to intelligence in the universe."

The good news of the Gospel of Jesus, is that this human existence is not doomed for destruction amid a dynamic universe. There will be suns that expand or explode, meteors that collide with planets or moons. There are black holes, worm holes and sink holes. However, there is also a loving Creator God who is working out a plan of redemption, and this plan considers all the big events of cosmic significance that will affect life on earth. The sun being darkened is the first sign of this cosmic event.

3. The moon will not give its light
and the moon will not give its light;

Looking up into the night sky, one is wooed by the light of the moon. The seasons and times are well ordered by the lunar cycle of the earth's shadow upon its face. Without the moon's light, the nights are darker and the people and creatures of the earth are left in the shadow of chaos at night. The moon reflects the sun, but it cannot do so if the light of the sun is blocked, altered or diminished. The blocking of light described by Jesus would either be between the earth and the moon, or between the moon and the sun. In either case, the scenario is serious. Jesus seems to indicate that the moon would not be destroyed.

4. Stars will fall from the sky (meteorites?)
the stars will fall from the sky,

On January 9th, 2017 at 7:47am EST, a large asteroid (between 36-111 feet in diameter) was spotted (2017 AG13) going between the earth and its moon (126,461 miles away) with a relative velocity of over 35,100 mph. First spotted by the Catalina Sky Survey, it came close to the earth without prior detection. Later in 2017, NASA prepared a proposal for Near-Earth Object Preparedness, and the effect of a meteor like "2017 AG13" was determined:

> *"In the case of 2017 AG13, the asteroid would likely have exploded high in the atmosphere with the force of 700 kilotons. The Nagasaki bomb was 20 kilotons."* (NASA, as noted by www.thesun.co.uk)

Jesus' poetic words, "falling stars", may refer to meteorites, or a field of asteroids going through the solar system with some breaking up in the earth's atmosphere. People in the time of Jesus looked up into the starry night sky and paid notice, they would observe meteorite showers and remember larger explosive events. Spectacular recent sightings of larger asteroid or smaller meteorite events are recorded involving a bright trail of blinding light and loud explosions upon the object(s) burning up and sometimes making impact. Jesus may be describing an event involving a significant asteroid or meteorite event; or perhaps even the debris from another heavenly body, moon, or proximate planet raining upon the earth. This third sign of a cosmic event, happening prior to Christ's glorious appearance, will be beautiful and breathtaking while also being powerful and potentially destructive. One could picture the Harvest of God's people coming before the time of greater tribulation that would occur because of such cosmic events and their consequence. The key point here is that God has a timetable. There is a designated event of cosmic significance, and it will be God's way of heralding a change that shall involve judgment.

5. <u>Heavenly bodies are shaken (planets?)</u>
and the heavenly bodies will be shaken.'

One wonders how the heavenly bodies might be shaken or moved. Studies and a proposal in 2001, by Dr. Greg Laughlin, Don Korycansky and Fred Adams of the Nasa Ames Research Center in California, have suggested one remedy for the earth's global warming problem. The idea they have postulated is to deflect an asteroid or comet to initiate a closer flyby of that object nearer to earth for beneficial results. The object's magnetic pull in close orbit would theoretically spin the earth faster, spinning the earth further out in its orbit from the sun. The earth would then be slightly cooler and we could save the planet from global warming.

> *"It involves the same techniques that people now suggest could be used to deflect asteroids or comets heading towards Earth. We don't need raw power to move Earth, we just require delicacy of planning and maneuvering'... 'Earth's orbital speed would increase as a result and we would move*

to a higher orbit away from the Sun,' Laughlin said. "All you have to do is strap a chemical rocket to an asteroid or comet and fire it at just the right time."
- (Theguardian.com/environment/2001).

The delicacy and potential danger of such a plan is considerable, as the strike of a large meteor of even a 100 kilometer object upon the earth would sterilize the biosphere and threaten life's survival down to the level of bacteria. *"The danger cannot be overemphasized"*, said Laughlin. The potential for planets being moved from their orbit, however, is real. The impact of asteroids and comets is a proven part of geologic record and planetary history.

The belief that the universe was a random occurrence and we are mere specks amid the dust storms of space, is based upon assumptions of non-personal or unintelligent design. What if we were to envision that God is involved in the universe and specific details pertinent to life on earth? What if God really does have a plan, with a deep concern for humanity, His children, who are created in His image? The hypothesis of a shakeup in the solar system around the earth, that would be ultimately beneficial for mankind, has merit. God's intervention will be necessary prior to a new era in which the earth may be reclaimed and redeemed. After the time of distress (some of which is already occurring), involving man-made conditions of ruin and other natural and supernatural forces, Jesus indicates the coming of a great day of "shakeup" involving astronomic events.

The Creator has a clock that involves location and changes of space, matter and energy; the "heavenly bodies" spoken of by Jesus. How presumptuous for us to think that Jesus, the very Son of God, would not be cognitive of these very big events at some level. What did Jesus know? He knew much more than people gave Him credit for. This prophecy invites God's Spirit, Jesus Himself, to knock at our door, expand our thinking, broaden our vision and direct our faith to God the Heavenly Father. Will we believe and put our trust in God? Will we trust the foreknowledge of Jesus, and have faith that He is the Son of the Living God (the Messiah)? Or, will we simply dismiss Jesus as a lunatic or a liar? Will we react in disbelief, as if Jesus never lived or spoke of such important matters? We are invited to have faith in the One who can move mountains and knows about the movements of planets, meteors, asteroids and comets.

B. All People will mourn when Jesus appears (30)

30 "Then will appear the sign of the Son of Man in heaven. And then all the peoples of the earth will mourn when they see the Son of Man coming on the clouds of heaven, with power and great glory.

Conjecture is not necessary as to what the "sign" of the "Son of Man" in heaven will be. The sign will be the "Son of Man" Himself appearing and coming. The bright and glorious presence of Jesus will be like that experienced by John who beheld Him in Revelation chapter 1:

12 I turned around to see the voice that was speaking to me. And when I turned I saw seven golden lampstands, 13 and among the lampstands was someone like a son of man, dressed in a robe reaching down to his feet and with a golden sash around his chest. 14 The hair on his head was white like wool, as white as snow, and his eyes were like blazing fire. 15 His feet were like bronze glowing in a furnace, and his voice was like the sound of rushing waters. 16 In his right hand he held seven stars, and coming out of his mouth was a sharp, double-edged sword. His face was like the sun shining in all its brilliance. - Revelation 1:12-16

Saul, before He was given the name Paul by the risen Lord, had this experience:

3 As he neared Damascus on his journey, suddenly a light from heaven flashed around him. 4 He fell to the ground and heard a voice say to him, "Saul, Saul, why do you persecute me?" 5 "Who are you, Lord?" Saul asked. "I am Jesus, whom you are persecuting," he replied. 6 "Now get up and go into the city, and you will be told what you must do."
- Acts 9:3-6

These are just a few of many biblically recorded encounters that people had with Christ in His Glory. Since then, there have been countless others who have experienced the comforting and guiding presence of Jesus. Some have beheld the brilliant light of Jesus, the "Son of Man", in His glorious state since the New Testament accounts.

Testimony of Jesus (a personal encounter)

I would be remiss not to mention my own experience of a direct encounter with Jesus, a transformative time of prayer following a diagnosis of having stage four cancer (Non-Hodgkin's Lymphoma). One night in January 2002, the beautiful and bright light of Jesus entered our bedroom as I prayed, my wife Marilyn was fast asleep. Much to my surprise, while praying, and praising God in my heart, Jesus appeared in resplendent glory. At first, all I saw was a flood of glorious light, unlike anything I had experienced. From this light, and with great warmth and joy in my heart, I saw Jesus as the one from whom the light came from. He came to me and the brightness increased. Jesus then placed His hands upon my head and shoulders. Within me, I felt something beautiful and powerful, something healing to my core. Jesus touched and filled me with the healing power of God's love, a life-giving and healing energy that flowed into me as I have never felt before or since. After the Lord left me, the joy I felt did not dissipate. After at least a half an hour of silent gratitude, I could then speak to tell my wife.

Half asleep, she said: "Oh, that's nice", and continued sleeping. The next morning, I asked her if she remembered me waking her up, and she did. (Further details of this story are in "Soul Fruit: Bearing Blessings through Cancer").

The result and proof of this encounter was that several days later, after a CT scan, my doctor, Rizwan Danish, reported that my cancer was "all gone". He wanted to know what happened, and so I told him how Jesus came to me in brightness and glory as I prayed, and then Jesus touched me. Being a Muslim, he said: "You Christians are different." Now, over 15 years later, I am still cancer free and serving joyfully for the Savior and Lord who saved my soul and healed my body.

1. People will see the sign of the Son of Man in heaven
30 "Then will appear the sign of the Son of Man in heaven.

In the New Testament, when Jesus appeared after His ascension (Acts 1:9) into heaven, the experience was that of brightness, glory and awe. The *"sign"* of Jesus return is also the subject of what *"two men dressed in white"* told the disciples at the ascension of Jesus into Heaven at Galilee. The disciples were caught gawking and starring, looking up into the clouds intently, to see where Jesus had gone.

> *10 They were looking intently up into the sky as he was going, when suddenly two men dressed in white stood beside them. 11 "Men of Galilee," they said, "why do you stand here looking into the sky? This same Jesus, who has been taken from you into heaven, will come back in the same way you have seen him go into heaven." –*
> Acts 1:10-11

The latter part of verse 11 indicates, according to these "angelic" messengers, that Jesus will return from above, from the skies, from Heaven in a visible way. Of course, when they saw Him go up, it was prior to His being fully clothed with Heavenly Glory as His Father would clothe Him with upon His return to the right hand of His Heavenly Father's throne. When Jesus does return in God's timing and glory, as Jesus indicated about His return in Matthew 24:30, it will be direct, personal and profound.

2. People will see the Son of Man coming on the clouds

And then all the peoples of the earth will mourn when they see the Son of Man coming on the clouds of heaven, with power and great glory.

The response of people in this part of Matthew 24:30 is deep emotion, a mix of feelings that will move all people on earth to weeping. For people who are right with God, there is overwhelming joy mixed with concern, even compassionate heartache. The mourning involves both realized joy and consummated grief in letting go, praying for loved ones and trusting God in a final departure in leaving and a preparatory cleansing. For people without faith, who are filled with anxiety, dread and shame; the moment of revealing will involve panic; some will repent, and others will choose denial or destructive woe. This kind of mourning will involve fear in confusion, a hopelessness that is the result of having no spiritual ground in relationship to God. The vision of Jesus will evoke many things from people, and by the grace of God, there will be last minute conversions and confessions.

Jesus, in this oracle, may have also been referring to the same event in the vision given to the prophet Daniel: (*"In my vision at night I looked, and there before me was one like a son of man, coming with the clouds of heaven"* (Daniel 7:13). Jesus is congruent with Daniel's vision of His reappearance to earth revealing both His power and glory.

a. with power -   For the disciples of Jesus, who hoped Jesus would immediately use His power to establish the Kingdom of

God, they trusted this promise of Christ's power. The full work of God's Kingdom, however, involved a timeframe that was quite different from what they had hoped for or assumed. The timing of God, the very ways God, are higher than we can presume. Jesus would eventually return, according to God's plan, to fulfill the prophetic vision given by the Lord to Daniel (in 553 B.C.):

14 He was given authority, glory and sovereign power; all nations and peoples of every language worshiped him. - Daniel 7:14a

The eventual reign of Jesus Christ over the earth shall come, in God's good time and way; it shall involve His Son's just and redemptive use of authority, wisdom and power. While there are people from most every nation who believe in Jesus, and worship Him in the Holy Spirit with God the Father; the return of Jesus will lead to even greater participation of people of every language and nationality, worshipping Christ Jesus as Lord, being filled and set free by God's Holy Spirit. Christ's coming with authority and power shall bring hope, healing and liberation.

b. with glory - God's Kingdom, as it shall come to fulfillment in Jesus Christ, will engage people in genuine worship. Healing reconciliation and justice shall be administered to all the peoples of the world. For Christ's Kingdom to be established, an essential time of judgment shall occur involving "a sifting" that accompanies a harvest. All of this shall lead to the gracious and righteous governance of Christ. Jesus shall renew and fulfill the call of responsible stewardship and dominion first given to Adam and Eve. In Christ, the positive use of shared knowledge, resources and talents will be administered. From Christ's Divine governance of God's Kingdom, under the Sovereignty of God the Father, there shall be a Kingdom whose reign and peace shall have no end. This is stated in the second part of Daniel 7:14:

His dominion is an everlasting dominion that will not pass away, and his kingdom is one that will never be destroyed.
   - Daniel 7:14b

II. Jesus gathers God's elect (v.31)

31 And he will send his angels with a loud trumpet call, and they will gather his elect from the four winds, from one end of the heavens to the other.

What will Jesus do when He returns in power and glory?

There are three things Jesus shall do upon His return from His own words in verse 31:   (1) Angels are sent out by His commission, (2) the angels are given authority to gather Christ's *"elect"* from among the known nations, and then (3) the angels have the responsibility and authority to go out to nations and places unknown and gather the "elect" there too. The knowledge of Jesus about people in far off places, yet known to his immediate disciples, is amazing. The Lord is also aware of people yet born of generations to come.

A. Angels are sent out with a loud trumpet call
31 And he will send his angels with a loud trumpet call,

The first thing Jesus shall initiate is a monumental *"trumpet call"* through the trumpeting command of the archangel (I Thess. 4:16). This would then be followed by a loud and clear, attention getting, heavenly tone, sounded for all the world to hear. Even the deaf shall feel the vibrations. Everyone will know that a momentous event is happening. The dispatch of many angels *"to the four winds"* gives the perspective of global coordination and coverage by God's heralds.
   When Jesus was born, the angels appeared to the shepherds while they watched their sheep by night, and *"the Glory of the Lord*

shown around them". The angels praised God and proclaimed: "*Glory to God in the highest, peace on earth, good will to mankind*" (Luke 2). The angels will again be summoned, this time to sound the fulfillment of God's plan of peace everywhere on earth, as Jesus the Christ returns.

The Apostle Paul writes about the triumphant return of Christ, and the role of angels, to the Church in Thessalonica:

> *16 For the Lord himself will come down from heaven, with a loud command, with the voice of the archangel and with the trumpet call of God, and the dead in Christ will rise first. 17 After that, we who are still alive and are left will be caught up together with them in the clouds to meet the Lord in the air. And so we will be with the Lord forever.*
>
> I Thessalonians 4:16-17

The "*voice of the archangel*" is a unique feature of Paul's prophecy, and "*raising the dead in Christ*" poses some debate about what happens to people when they die. The man on the right of Jesus on the cross, believed, then Jesus stated: "I tell you, this day you will be with me in paradise!" Yet Paul describes a situation where believers are raised from the ground and are brought up into Heaven by the angels just prior to all those "*still alive*" who are brought up at this event of Christ's return. This is a mystery that is not worth splitting hairs over. God is the author and finisher of the believer's salvation, whether it involves a quick exit of the soul to Heaven or a sleepy vacation of rest for the soul before going to Heaven. The taking up of Elijah is noteworthy in the Old Testament (2 Kings 2:12), and the raising of Lazarus (John 11:43) by Jesus stimulates faith, thought and questions too. Perhaps the way Jesus resurrects people is best left for His and the Father God's discretion and may involve people's varying spiritual and physical conditions. The preference of many is to think of the believer as being taken into Heaven immediately by Jesus upon their death, as He promised in John 14:2-3:

> *2 My Father's house has many rooms; if that were not so, would I have told you that I am going there to prepare a*

place for you? 3 And if I go and prepare a place for you, I will come back and take you to be with me that you also may be where I am. John 14:2-4

This promise by Jesus can, however, be interpreted two ways: One, to refer to immediate occupancy by the soul into a new body in Heaven, or two, that there is a delayed occupancy in which Jesus is preparing the place of Heaven for each and all (raised or living) to arrive at the same time. The issue of man's time and God's time is what makes all this beyond our comprehension. What is striking, if one looks carefully at the direct invitation and promise of the Lord, is that it is deeply personal. *"I will come back and take you"*. This promise, in which Jesus addresses the disciples gathered, is direct and personal, also *"you"* is both individual and corporate. My own faith and practical application is to trust and believe that those whose bodies "die in the Lord" do enter God's care in Heaven without delay and precede those who of faith who are living or who are yet born who shall come to faith. If, however, there is a time of "sleep" until the Lord comes for Judgment, then this should be of no consequence for division of essential belief in Jesus Christ and His Second Coming. This point is not of ultimate concern for salvation, because the greater concern now is belief that is evidenced in how we live. Faith with service prepares for, gives witness to, and anticipates God's eternal kingdom. How Christ's return to earth may initiate another chapter, involving both those who will be in Heaven already or those in a state of spiritual sleep (both perspectives comprising the dead in Christ) and those who shall be alive upon the earth and caught up with the host of Heaven at Christ's return, is a very daunting mystery to try to perceive or understand.

Perhaps it is just as well that the Lord left this promise as either, and that He did not try to give us all the details. Faith and trust in the resurrection power and authority of Jesus Christ is essential. He will come back in whatever time and way is necessary, both personally and powerfully, in the time of our judgment (be that upon death or upon His return in Glory). According to the

Apostle Paul, who tried to encourage the young Church in these mysteries, the important point for believers in Christ is that they are not to grieve, or be without hope, like the rest of mankind.

> *13 Brothers and sisters, we do not want you to be uninformed about those who sleep in death, so that you do not grieve like the rest of mankind, who have no hope.*
>
> I Thessalonians 4:13

B. Angels will gather God's elect from among the nations

and they will gather his elect from the four winds,

Gathering takes place when people chose to respond and come, but also as people are brought together. This gathering involves both willingness and necessity. The "elect" need to be ready to drop what they're doing and respond to the great invitation. "Gather" is the verb that describes how the angels shall bring in God's harvest. The collection by the angels is met by the reciprocal response of faith and joy of "the elect". Once again, this gathering is referred to as the *"rapture"*. The *"four winds"* refer to *"every quarter of the universe"* (Pulpit Commentary).

"The "four winds" may actually be interpreted with two essential meanings: One, as a poetic reference to East, West, North and South, which gives a wholeness and totality to God's gathering of souls for Christ's Kingdom. Two, as a reference to God's Holy Spirit that intersects with the whole of nature in the Lord's appearance. The announcement will be made globally, and the gathering will occur globally. (Some interpreters would even say this is an event involving more than the earth itself, extending out to the universe. For now, we won't get carried that far away.)

The work of God's angels to gather the redeemed, "the elect", will be complete as people also respond in faith to God's call. The signs accompanying Christ's appearance in the clouds, and the glory of Christ Jesus Himself, will be unmistakable. His appearance, the trumpet call, the great host of angels, will be far different from the imposters who did not come with such power, extensiveness or authenticity from God and the great host of Heaven.

C. Angels will gather God's elect from areas beyond our knowledge
from one end of the heavens to the other.

Jesus reinforced the global nature of His appearance, and He gives assurance of the comprehensive rescue work of the angels for the "elect". The vision of Jesus is beautiful and dreadful, inviting and magnificent. While Jesus uses "wide open" language for scope to enlarge the hearts and minds of those who are called to share the Gospel of His Kingdom. Decisions of faith still need to be made, and the response of people is to trust God and move in faith to meet Christ. The angels shall be ready to give assistance.

The repetition of a phrase with slight variation was a literary tool among Israel's teachers and prophets. Jesus enlarged the vision and imagination of His disciples. The Kingdom of God, and those referred to as "the elect" involved places and peoples that were unknown to Jesus' disciples. The Kingdom of God is not to be defined with human parameters, it is expansive and extensive, reaching even far beyond our earth: *"From one end of the heavens to the other"*. We don't have to wait for Christ's return to have our vision enlarged, begin in your heart and mind to see the spectrum of people invited to partake in God's Kingdom.

III. Being prepared and observe the signs (v.32-33)

32 "Now learn this lesson from the fig tree: As soon as its twigs get tender and its leaves come out, you know that summer is near. 33 Even so, when you see all these things, you know that it is near, right at the door.

A. Learning from the Fig Tree (32)

32 "Now learn this lesson from the fig tree: As soon as its twigs get tender and its leaves come out, you know that summer is near.

Jesus brought up a beautiful and simple metaphor. What are we to learn from the fig tree that Jesus referred to? There on the Mount of Olives, where He was teaching them, fig trees also grew. The fig tree symbolized Israel as a symbol of hope and fruitfulness.

Fig trees have fruit blossoms with initial tender twigs of fruit that arrive before the leaves, this explains why Jesus says: "*as soon as its twigs get tender and its leaves come out*". While Jesus refers to this natural process, He is making a statement about the process of God's unfolding Kingdom. With all the amazing things Jesus had just revealed to the disciples through prophetic discourse, He now condenses it all by pointing at the fig tree and opening their eyes to have faith that this natural process is like the supernatural work of God.

The next phrase by Jesus is packed with meaning: "*you know that summer is near*". One interpretation is that the growth of the Kingdom of God is at hand for the disciples, the work of the church in the great commission will soon begin. They are the "first fruits", the "*tender twigs*" of the fig tree's new growth. The Church is therefore the fruitful new life and extension of God's covenant that began with Abraham and is fulfilled in Christ for the expansion of God's Kingdom. This New Covenant in Christ is for Gentiles (all people) as well as for fulfillment and salvation for the Jews (who God chose to begin His Covenant with).

The context of this passage, coming right after Jesus' reference to the signs of the end times and His return, has sometimes been directly applied to "*summer is near*". Those who follow this line of interpretation will identify the future summertime as arriving upon Christ's return.

This perspective, however, falls short, it is inconsistent with the return of Christ, and the angels, being at a time of harvest. Jesus refers to summertime to give the disciples a perspective of the urgency of the work in front of them. The opportune time for God's Kingdom work was now "sprouting" like a fig tree before them. Therefore, the Gospel was to go out to the nations, a harvest would begin and sprout upon other branches on the fig tree of humanity. The blossoms will give way to leaves that will support the growth of God's Kingdom through the Church (the Body of Christ).

Therefore, the most accurate and biblical interpretation of *"the summer is near"* is that this refers to the work of the Church that had just begun. Jesus was simply bringing His disciples back to their responsibilities. Jesus knew that they had been caught up in the awesomeness of what He had just presented to them. Now they needed to come back to earth, to a visible reminder, a framework for envisioning their calling.

B. Nearness and urgency (33)

33 Even so, when you see all these things, you know that it is near, right at the door.

Faith gives light to vision, and vision opens the heart to truth, and truth inspires motivation for action. Even before Jesus began His ministry, John the Baptist was preparing and motivating people with vision and truth by saying: *"Repent, for the Kingdom of Heaven has come near"* (Matthew 3:2). Jesus, after His baptism by John and His temptation in the wilderness, came to walk along the sea of Galilee, calling *"Repent, for the Kingdom of Heaven has come near"* (Matthew 4:17). John was preparing people to get ready for the Christ, Jesus was calling people to discipleship and service because He was the Christ that John prepared for.

Jesus led His disciples as they dropped fishing nets (Peter, James, John and Andrew), stepped out of tax booths (Matthew), left their shade trees of contemplation (Nathaniel) and followed Him. Jesus not only taught them the great truths of God, He gave them a message to share and a ministry to perform. The work of the Kingdom was at hand, right in front of them, so near. One of the first missions was to go to people's doors and share the good news of God's saving grace to all who will open their hearts, repent and believe. Jesus told them:

> *"When you enter a town and are welcomed, eat what is offered to you. 9 Heal the sick who are there and tell them, 'The kingdom of God has come near to you.'"* (Luke 10:8-9)

Note how Jesus gave them a role and responsibility to minister to people's needs as the first act of care before they would share the message of the Gospel. The matter of faith for the disciples meant traveling light, and trusting that God's Spirit would go before them and be involved in the hospitality of those they reached out to. The disciples discovered that God was doing something new, and this involved a "summertime" of grace. People would not only welcome them, they would offer hospitality and listen because the Spirit of God was at work to open their hearts. Since the time of Jesus, the tendency for the Church is to get this evangelism perspective mixed up. Instead, the Church often "imposes" itself when it should "present" itself.

Jesus calls the disciples to have full dependence upon God, and to trust that God will open the way outside of the comforts of our tradition, buildings and programs. We are to go simply, lightly and confidently in the moving of God's Holy Spirit. God will open the way for us to listen and learn how to minister to others; God will then open the way for us to share the Gospel of the Kingdom of God. By being present and available, we discover the way in which the message of Jesus is at work to bring people into the light of God's grace and truth. The work of the Kingdom is near, right at the door.

Of course, this verse also applies to the time of harvest, when the ripening season comes to its conclusion. Then, the work of the Kingdom in the summertime will have run its course. Jesus will come again as the "land owner" of the garden and supervise the workers as they harvest its fig trees, vineyards, wheat and various crops (Matthew 13:24-29). For now, people are to work with the eventual harvest in mind. It is not so far away. In fact, the

Lord even gave indication that we have initial harvests for the kingdom while we await the greater harvest:

> "The harvest is plentiful, but the workers are few. Ask the Lord of the harvest, therefore, to send out workers into his harvest field." Luke 10:2-3

The purpose of Jesus vision was to give them urgency, to inspire the service of His disciples then and into the future.

IV. The Church Age will culminate in fulfillment (34)

34 *Truly I tell you, this generation will certainly not pass away until all these things have happened.*

The "Church Age" is a term for the period between Jesus' call to ministry and the fulfillment of God's Kingdom work in the great harvest at Christ's return. Currently, we are living in the "Church Age". The *"generation"* being referred to by Jesus is broader than the immediate generation of the inaugural twelve disciples; He is referring to the Church Age in a covenantal sense of God's working. While it is true that some of the disciples would live long enough to see the destruction of much of Jerusalem and the entire Temple of Herod in 70 A.D., Jesus was referring to the whole of *"all these things"*, not just a portion of His prophecy. Here in Matthew 24:34, Jesus issues a promise of God's protection for believers who will compose the "generation" of the Church Age. Jesus gives purpose and continuity to His Church's ministry; He assures them that their work will continue until the final harvest is ready and the Church's work shall be completed. The previous verses in Matthew 24, and the whole of Jesus' teaching of the Kingdom of God, make it clear that patient endurance is necessary, and that eventually there will be an incredible finale.

V. The words and Jesus are faithful and constant (35)

35 Heaven and earth will pass away, but my words will never pass away.

Jesus spoke with authority. Jesus could do so because of His origin and identity as: *"the Word that was with God.. He was with God from the beginning, ... Jesus is the very Word of God made flesh"* (John 1:1-2,14). The apostle John was inspired to write of Jesus:

> *3 Through him all things were made; without him nothing was made that has been made. 4 In him was life, and that life was the light of all mankind"* (John 1:3-4).

In Matthew 24:35, all people are invited to trust in the Word of Jesus. Those who do believe are encouraged in the steadfast nature and promise of Jesus as the everlasting Word, co-eternal with God the Father. The call is to enter into a communion of belief wherein life is safe within His Word and promise that shall not perish (this was not just another passing human philosophy or teaching). The Word of Jesus was life and light, coming from God's Son. While the disciples would all experience physical death, the Word of Jesus had brought them life eternal within their souls, born of God's Holy Spirit. Their hope, and God's revealed Word of promise, would be complete through Christ's resurrection and their belief and receipt of God's gift of saving, redeeming, grace.

The earth will experience dynamic changes in which continents rise and fall into the sea, and life as we know it passes away upon new forms of life. To *"pass away"* involves not just death, but change that has a purpose. The *"good seed"* of the Gospel is for a Kingdom that shall replace the old systems and fallen nature of mankind. Since God spoke creation into being, as we note in Genesis chapter 1: "God said: *"Let there be…"*; God also speaks redemption and new life for the creation, and for mankind, through His Son, Jesus, the Living Word.

VI. The exact time of Jesus Christ's Second Coming is unknown. (36)

36 *"But about that day or hour no one knows, not even the angels in heaven, nor the Son, but only the Father."*

A. No human can know

But about that day or hour no one knows,

God holds the compass of time as it stretches out to draw a large circle. The beginning of God's work shall have a length of completion. The *"day or hour"* of the *"Son's"* (the Christ's) return is something that only God the Creator/Father knows. The work of God's reconciliation and redemption, starting from the Garden of Eden's fall to the seed of Abraham and extending in Christ Jesus to all people, is a work that shall culminate in a specific and determined way. Fortunately, only God the Father knows exactly when. If we did know, we would be unmotivated to serve God and tend toward irresponsibility. Procrastination would become prevalent and not preparation. Be thankful that God has time in His hands and that God holds back knowledge that could burden, spoil or hinder our growth and service. Until we are completely transformed, our knowledge will be in part.

B. Angels do not know

not even the angels in heaven

God even keeps heavenly angels, His agency of heaven, in the same state of alertness through thoughtful ignorance and reasoned innocence; this is necessary for vigilance until Christ's return. This is fascinating, because there is a spiritual warfare and conflict among the rank of God's "winged" angelic servants. Some angels have fallen and rebelled. We are told of angelic wars in the heavens, of Michael fighting against Satan and his ranks.

> *Then war broke out in heaven. Michael and his angels fought against the dragon, and the dragon and his angels fought back. 8 But he was not strong enough, and they lost their place in heaven. 9 The great dragon was hurled down—that ancient serpent called the devil, or Satan, who leads the whole world astray. He was hurled to the earth, and his angels with him.* (Revelation 12:7-9)

Given this mysterious reality, Jesus included the detail of how *"not even the angels in heaven"* know either. The reason, like that of humankind, may be that it also pertains to their free will. They, like humans, are beings who may choose. Angels may have faith or give way to doubt. The faithful angels trust and obey God, the rebellious ones have chosen to disobey God. Speculation about the origin and nature of angels may vary. Scripture teaches that they are servants of God, sent to minister and communicate God's purposes from Heaven.

Scripture also suggests that angels may be mixed in with other intelligent creatures on earth and throughout the universe. This mystery has sometimes been tied to the Genesis account of the Nephilim, the *"sons of the gods"* who appeared on earth and had relations with the *"daughters of men"* just prior to the flood of Noah. God was not pleased with their behavior and its effect on humanity (see Genesis 6:2-4). Speculation can abound on this topic, and it wise not to read too much in to Scripture on the topic of alien life forms. Essentially, considering Jesus' discretion and economy of words; we are reminded that knowledge itself is not the goal, faith is what connects us to God in Christ. It's alright to admit that there is much we do not, or should not, know.

The key point of Matthew 24:36 is that God withholds the date of His Son Jesus's return to earth; it shall come about in accordance to our Heavenly Father's discernment. The mysteries of existence, of the universe, and life throughout the depths of the universe, the heavens, are still unfolding to our knowledge.

C. Jesus the Son does not know

nor the Son,

Jesus knew much more about God and the mysteries of the universe than we were ready to receive. He also understood how much to reveal and what was in His Father's exclusive knowledge. Jesus admits, in admirable humility, that even He does not know the exact day or hour of His return. Jesus confirms His Sonship, that is unique, to God the Father. The authenticity of Jesus, and the transmission of His teaching here in the Gospel of Matthew, is reinforced. Jesus did not state or fake omniscience, at least He could not do so in His human form, within the limits of His human mind. Jesus was given the knowledge necessary to work within His human condition. Perhaps His previous state of knowledge has resumed upon His return to the right hand of the throne of God. Even then, if Jesus in His glorified position also waits in a state of readiness (and partial knowledge) for this day of His return, when the Father sends Him from Heaven to Earth for the consummation of salvation, judgment and redemption; Jesus has risen and He is glorious as the Son of God. Jesus' role currently, is to intercede with His Word before God the Father on behalf of those who pray in His Name.

D. Only God the Father knows

but only the Father."

God is wise in sovereignty, and due all praise, honor and glory. God is the *"Ancient of Days"* as noted in Daniel's vision. Intimately, Jesus refers to God as *"Abba"* (Mark 14:36, translated:

"Daddy"). At a time when the Pharisees were ready to stone Jesus in Jerusalem because He did not deny His Divinity or Sonship, Jesus said, *"I and the Father are One* (John 10:38)." To Moses, God reveals as *"I am that I am"* from the burning bush (Exodus 3:14) . This name God gave Moses is an invitation for personal discovery, for existential reality within seeking, and for growth of relationship with God through faith, love and respect. The holiness of God is what reminds us of the otherness, freedom, and uncontainable personality of God. The holiness of God defies those who would create definitions and limitations for God. The risk of religion is that people create a "god" as an idol. To exchange the liberating and dynamic truth about the Living God for a lie of our own design, is to imagine a god that doesn't exist. God desires that we enter into a reconciled and redemptive relationship with Him, and this through faith in His Son, the Savior, Jesus the Christ.

Jesus spoke intimately and joyfully about His union with God His Father, and about completing the work of His Heavenly Father on earth. Throughout the time in the Upper Room at Passover, in the 14th to 17th chapters of the Gospel of John, Jesus had much to say on behalf of His Heavenly Father. Jesus was also expressive about His love for God the Father and the Father's love for Him. Before His Passion, Jesus then revealed more clearly that there is a Third Person who will bind Father, Son and people together, the Holy Spirit.

> *"I have much more to say to you, more than you can now bear. But when he, the Spirit of truth, comes, he will guide you into all the truth. He will not speak on his own; he will speak only what he hears, and he will tell you what is yet to come. He will glorify me because it is from me that he will receive what he will make known to you. All that belongs to the Father is mine. That is why I said the Spirit will receive from me what he will make known to you."* Jesus went on to say, *"In a little while you will see me no more, and then after a little while you will see me."* John 16:12-16

Jesus came to reveal God the Father and prepare the way for the Holy Spirit. Jesus would go to the cross, through the valley of the shadow of death and then to Heaven to intercede for people. Jesus would send the Holy Spirit to counsel and empower the disciples to continue the work of the Church. The Holy Spirit would call to mind the things Jesus did and the very words Jesus spoke. Jesus and God the Father knew that the disciples would feel grief and that they would need the help of the Holy Spirit following Jesus' earthly ministry. The wisdom and comfort of the Holy Spirit was especially powerful in its transformative presence as the disciples prayed following Jesus ascension from the upper room in Jerusalem to the Day of Pentecost and beyond. Jesus had their incubation and maturity as spirit-filled disciples in mind. Jesus also had in mind the totality of the Church Age, and how the Holy Spirit would fill and direct future disciples to preach and give testimony to the Gospel of the Kingdom of God.

The Church is the Bride, preparing for the Groom, Christ. What remains essential, in Matthew 24:36 is that Jesus will faithfully and lovingly act and speak on the Father's behalf. This is what leads Jesus to pray to the Father for them, Himself and for many others into the future. The key role of intercession is heard from our Savior's blessed heart and words:

> After Jesus said this, he looked toward heaven and prayed: "Father, the hour has come. Glorify your Son, that your Son may glorify you. For you granted him authority over all people that he might give eternal life to all those you have given him. Now this is eternal life: that they know you, the only true God, and Jesus Christ, whom you have sent. I have brought you glory on earth by finishing the work you gave me to do. And now, Father, glorify me in your presence with the glory I had with you before the world began."
> John 17:1-5

The Heavenly Father, the Ancient of Days, sent His Son Jesus with a plan, a purpose, a ministry of reconciliation. Jesus would finish the work of sacrificial atonement on the cross. Jesus walked through the "valley of the shadow of death", taking on our cares, sins and burdens in accordance with His Heavenly Father's heart and mission of love. Jesus triumphed over sin and death. The glory that Jesus once had was then to be restored to Him in His resurrection. This previous glory was once seen by Daniel in His vision of the One who could approach the Ancient of Days (God):

> 13 *"In my vision at night I looked, and there before me was one like a son of man, coming with the clouds of heaven. He approached the Ancient of Days and was led into his presence."* Daniel 7:13.

Concluding Thoughts:

There are some things that are far above and beyond our comprehension, and that's more than alright, it's very good. God shall reveal and fulfill His plan according to what is needed and timely. As children need to understand only what they need to know at various stages of development, so too, humanity is going through spiritual and existential development. The limited awareness of humanity does not diminish the plan and vision of God. The one who has placed the stars and planets is also capable of sending meteors that can spin the earth to a better orbit. Dictators can play God but can never be God. Scientists can study how things work in the world, but their greatest inventions are inspired and guided by what already exists.

God holds the compass and draws to the circumference, far beyond human comprehension, knowing what will be best. The pivot point of creation is firm in God's strength and it holds fast while God's hand of providence and design stretches out ever wider and more beautiful. The qualities of God's character, the fruit of the

Spirit, are manifest within God's handiwork and in humanity, who are created in God's image. The depth of the span of grace and truth are evident within creation, and within God's interactions spoken and recorded in God's Scriptures and revealed within our daily walk of faith. We are given all this from God so that we may have life, abundant and free. God has not only revealed the big picture in Christ Jesus, the Spirit of God helps us to discover the fine lines and details of God's intimate work alongside us in the journey of faith.

While there is a spiritual battle between God and the forces of rebellion in Satan and the fallen angels, which has also involved human beings who have exchanged the truth of God for a lie; God has built healing and redemption into creation by making all things through His Only Begotten Son. In the coming of His Son Jesus, God ministers to us by being with us. The incarnation and intervening work of Jesus was in God's plan, a forethought for humanity's redemption.

God shall continue to complete His Kingdom work in a way that combines the administration of justice and mercy. Justice is evident in the allowance of how we may learn through the freedom of responsibility and the verdict of consequence. While discipline from the Heavenly Father may seem harsh to some who would only see God as gracious. In fact, God is forgiving and gives room for repentance, reconciliation and renewal. God's mercy shall be extended through deliverance to people who heed God's warning and seek the Lord's rescue and redemption. The call for people of faith is to be prepared by service in the name, character and discipleship of Jesus. There is no limit to the measure and variation of God's gift of life and light, goodness and righteousness, that leads willing and intelligent beings into a relationship of righteousness through faith. The author of Hebrews wrote this about those whose faith was genuine, among the Hebrew people:

39 These were all commended for their faith, yet none of them received what had been promised, 40 since God had planned something better for us so that only together with us would they be made perfect. 1 Therefore, since we are surrounded by such a great cloud of witnesses, let us throw off everything that hinders and the sin that so easily entangles. And let us run with perseverance the race marked out for us, 2 fixing our eyes on Jesus, the pioneer and perfecter of faith. For the joy set before him he endured the cross, scorning its shame, and sat down at the right hand of the throne of God. 3 Consider him who endured such opposition from sinners, so that you will not grow weary and lose heart. - Hebrews 11:39 - 12:3

Questions for Discussion:

1. How does much of the world view the Scriptural prophecy of Jesus about the end times, judgment and His coming that will bring in the Kingdom of God?

2. In the things Jesus taught in Matthew 24:25-36, what did Jesus teach that gives you hope for the future? What did He teach that is troubling?

3. What are some examples of what makes it difficult to "stand firm" in the faith?

4. Does it give you hope that Jesus has knowledge about future events involving a big change for the earth and its peoples?

5. Why is it essential for the development of our faith that we trust God our Heavenly Father's time for Jesus' return?

Part 6: "Keep Watch, Faithful and Wise Servants" (God's Timing)

Matthew 24:36-51

36 "But about that day or hour no one knows, not even the angels in heaven, nor the Son, but only the Father. 37 As it was in the days of Noah, so it will be at the coming of the Son of Man. 38 For in the days before the flood, people were eating and drinking, marrying and giving in marriage, up to the day Noah entered the ark; 39 and they knew nothing about what would happen until the flood came and took them all away. That is how it will be at the coming of the Son of Man. 40 Two men will be in the field; one will be taken and the other left. 41 Two women will be grinding with a hand mill; one will be taken and the other left. 42 "Therefore keep watch, because you do not know on what day your Lord will come. 43 But understand this: If the owner of the house had known at what time of night the thief was coming, he would have kept watch and would not have let his house be broken into. 44 So you also must be ready, because the Son of Man will come at an hour when you do not expect him. 45 "Who then is the faithful and wise servant, whom the master has put in charge of the servants in his household to give them their food at the proper time? 46 It will be good for that servant whose master finds him doing so when he returns. 47 Truly I tell you, he will put him in charge of all his possessions. 48 But suppose that servant is wicked and says to himself, 'My master is staying away a long time,' 49 and he then begins to beat his fellow servants and to eat and drink with drunkards. 50 The master of that servant will come on a day when he does not expect him and at an hour he is not aware of. 51 He will cut him to pieces and assign him a place with the hypocrites, where there will be weeping and gnashing of teeth.

- Matthew 24:36-51

Introduction: Each generation is to keep watch

Being a pastor and chaplain has made me acutely aware that God's timing is different from our human sense of timing. Being present with people in times of waiting is a discipline of love and respect, be it illness, suffering and pain; or hopeful waiting that involves joyful anticipation, liberation, healing and celebration. From belief, we may embrace the tension that defines our current existence, that there is *"a time for every purpose under heaven"* (Ecclesiastes 3:1-8). Solomon wrote this, and surmised:

I have seen the burden God has laid on the human race. He has made everything beautiful in its time. He has also set eternity in the human heart; yet no one can fathom what God has done from beginning to end.

- (Ecclesiastes 3:10-11)

In life, throughout the seasons, burdens and beauty, there is something to discover in recognizing the presence of God, even if we cannot fathom all mysteries. If there is a lack of knowledge it does not necessitate a lack of faith. In fact, our hearts have eternity planted within, even if our lack of knowledge humbles or disappoints us. The key to life and love is faith, sharing and experiencing the care of presence, being with one another, and being comforted and transformed by the presence of God's Spirit.

Discovery of the power of God's presence is vital. Life in the Spirit is found by listening to the presence of God and the leading of God's voice, wisdom and word. Furthermore, there is meaning found in carefully listening to others that also helps us to discover God's presence in them. God's call is for us to be attentive to Christ's work in others and to then be present and respond accordingly. Sacrifice of self is essential to be truly watchful, ready and available. Holding the hand of a loved one who is going through sickness, loss, grief or anxiety is a calling, an opportunity to partake in the good work of God's Kingdom. Being present is the first step. Being responsive is the follow-through of how people become helpful and then bear fruit in caring actions.

A chaplain from England, Steve Nolan, described spiritual care as involving four types of presence: *Evocative presence, Accompanying presence, Comforting presence and Hopeful presence* (Steve Nolan, "Spiritual Care at the End of Life", John Knox Publishers, London 2012). First, there are times that a chaplain evokes people's transference, either positive or negative, about God, relationships and matters of faith. Secondly, when being with others, chaplains can also provide companionship, friendship and strength simply by presence. Third, in difficult moments of pain, loss or grief, the chaplain provides comfort by being the representative and manifestation of God's presence. Fourth, and most essential, hope is then built through being present, by caring as Christ Jesus cared, and by learning to rely upon the Spirit of God being both present and powerfully healing. This kind of healing is not based upon a "cure" but upon people being present and responsive in community and support. When people know that they are not alone, they discover hope in the realization of God's presence, power and faithful promises. In this respect, the Church, the people of God, are the evocative, accompanying, comforting and hopeful presence of God, and of Jesus Christ, in the world.

This passage in Matthew 24:36-51 continues by also being a prophetic word of warning. Jesus teaches that there will be either positive or negative consequences that depend upon one's ultimate state of faithfulness or foolishness. While all have sinned and fallen short of the Glory of God, the saving factor is faith in God's grace and the way of God's love shown through actions that are unselfish and true to God's Spirit in Christ.

What shall people do, therefore, with the warning signs from the Lord that are to lead us to repentance? The concluding verse from the previous section, is the starting verse, or pivot point, for this section: verse 36, "about the day or hour no one knows".

To explain this further, Jesus compares His return to the days of Noah, the time before the flood. Once the Son of Man comes on the clouds, the time of harvest will be swift, with no immediate warning. While there shall be times of distress, and signs that will accompany a general awareness that the return of the Lord is imminent, the moment of Christ's unveiling cannot (and should not) be predicted. He will come like a "thief in the night".

Therefore, each generation is to keep watch and be ready. How can people do this? The answer of Jesus involves being prepared by constant vigilance and faithful stewardship. He gave an analogy of home security, but also a parable about faithful and foolish servants. The result of one's life, in the final analysis with God, is that your destiny and reward will depend upon whether one's faith was genuine or fake, whether a person used their life or wasted their life. Faithfulness involves action, living life intentionally, being present, using one's time, applying talents and being resourceful. God calls us to use what we are given, and by the impartation and application of wisdom and grace, we may become a blessing to others. The fruit we bear depends upon the seeds we sow and cultivate; therefore, we are to respond to the opportunities God grants us. God's Holy Spirit is more than sufficient to lead and equip us. To live and serve as Jesus inspires, as God ordains and entrusts, is the way to find true joy, hope and peace. To be prepared for Christ's return, faithful service is the path of Jesus for those who believe.

Outline of Matthew 24:36-51

I.   No one knows the day or hour (v.36)

II.   Comparison to the days of Noah (v. 37-39)
       A. Similar situation and severity (37)
       B. Similar lack of listening (38)
       C. Similar surprise (39)

III.   Rapture of God's elect (v.40-41)
       A. Two men in a field (v.40)
       B. Two women grinding at the mill (v.41)

IV.   Preparation is made through faithful service (42-47)
       A. Keep watchful and vigilant (42)
       B. Analogy of the thief in the night (43-44)
       C. Analogy of food preparation (45-46)
       D. Reward to the faithful (47)

V.   Judgment will come to the wicked and irresponsible (48-51)
       A. God sees injustice and abuse (48-49)
       B. Jesus the master will come and judge humanity (50)
       C. Judgment of the wicked (cut off from God) (51)

Study on Matthew 24:36-51

I. No one knows the day or hour (v.36)

36 *"But about that day or hour no one knows, not even the angels in heaven, nor the Son, but only the Father.*

Starting where we concluded last chapter, verse 36 is a bridge between the section of Jesus' teaching on the signs and nature of His appearance and humanity's need to be prepared and faithful. The knowledge of the exact time of Christ's return is not as important at the fact that it shall occur. When a baby is conceived, no one knows the exact time of birth, but the process that leads to birth will come and is inevitable. The pains associated with pregnancy and birthing give awareness, warning and alert for vigilance, especially as specific pains (associated with muscle contractions and dilation) increase in frequency and intensity. Still, the exact hour and minute remain a matter of patience and preparation.

The matter of patience in waiting may also be experienced in hospice care, as a loved one is going through the last days of a terminal illness. The prognosis is that a person will die, and their family and caregivers seek to understand the factors, sometimes multiple, that will cause their vital organs to cease. When asked, "How long will it be?", medical professionals and experienced caregivers can only estimate based on experience with certain signs. However, the exact day, hour or minute remains a mystery. What is needed is compassion, presence, assistance, patient endurance, support and permission to ultimately trust in God's care, keeping and deliverance. "No one knows the day or the hour." At the "end of days", for this chapter of human history to conclude at Christ's return, no one knows the day or the hour other than our Heavenly Father. Jesus will come as He has promised.

II. Comparison to the days of Noah (v. 37-39)

37 As it was in the days of Noah, so it will be at the coming of the Son of Man. 38 For in the days before the flood, people were eating and drinking, marrying and giving in marriage, up to the day Noah entered the ark; 39 and they knew nothing about what would happen until the flood came and took them all away. That is how it will be at the coming of the Son of Man.

A. Similar situation and severity (37)

37 As it was in the days of Noah, so it will be at the coming of the Son of Man.

The activities of humanity will not let up prior to the coming of Christ, the "Son of Man", the King of Heaven's Glory. If anything, the people of these modern times will be even more absorbed in themselves than the people of Noah's time before the flood. Take, for example, the explosion of information technologies and media production and distribution. Never in known history has there been a time of such creativity and intercultural sharing. Much of it is amazing and breathtaking, a credit to the mind and design God has given for human creativity. There is certainly a witness to God within the culture and creative expressions of humanity. However, there is also another side to all that people have made, a shadow side. Like the people of Noah's time, people create images to worship in place of God. People become lovers of self and negligent of spiritual and social responsibilities. Much of mankind's pursuits are vain, divergent, and lead to the exploitation and pollution of the earth, instead of positive maintenance, healthy limits and good stewardship. A summary of the time of Noah is comparable to the times of our twenty first century A.D.:

> *Now the earth was corrupt in God's sight and was full of violence. God saw how corrupt the earth had become, for all the people on earth had corrupted their ways.* Genesis 6:11-13

B. Similar lack of listening (38)

38 For in the days before the flood, people were eating and drinking, marrying and giving in marriage, up to the day Noah entered the ark;

Life was normal in many ways prior to the great flood. Still, as was indicated by the Genesis account, there were serious problems that were pervasive. In the time of Noah, the influence of the "sons of God" and the "Nephilim" were contributing and corrupting factors. It remains a mystery as to exactly who these beings were. How were they differentiated from mankind, yet similar physically? Were they like the "angels"? Whoever they were, even if they were completely human, we note that their influence had tipped the direction of mankind toward evil. We read in Genesis chapter six:

> *When human beings began to increase in number on the earth and daughters were born to them, the sons of God saw that the daughters of humans were beautiful, and they married any of them they chose. Then the Lord said, "My Spirit will not contend with humans forever, for they are mortal; their days will be a hundred and twenty years." The Nephilim were on the earth in those days—and also afterward—when the sons of God went to the daughters of humans and had children by them. They were the heroes of old, men of renown. The Lord saw how great the wickedness of the human race had become on the earth, and that every inclination of the thoughts of the human heart was only evil all the time.* - (Genesis 6:1-6)

The inclination of thought, and the affection of the human heart, moved away from God and toward wickedness, perversion and violence. This was the legacy of these "sons of God" and "Nephilim". Were they deceptive and boastful human leaders, fallen angels or corrupting aliens? This remains a mystery. In either case, God took decisive action to cleanse the earth and give humanity a new start.

Looking at life in the twenty first century, we see that many similar concerning conditions exist. On one hand, people are still going about good and normal activity, and the institutions of marriage and family are still valued. Yet if one looks closely, the earth is once again experiencing another type and level of wickedness. The effect of humanity's population growth and the stress placed on the earth's weather and ecosystems is seen in climate change. With stress and conflict, nuclear weapons are again proliferating and are threatened for use once again by those in political leadership. The sinister idea of "mutually assured destruction" has boomeranged back as a policy of defense and intimidation.

Evil continues to resurface and give rise to even more intense violence and corruption among the people of the earth. A lone shooter, Stephen Paddock, planned and carried out a mass killing of innocent people at a Country Music concert in Las Vegas. What was going through his mind for months of preparations? What kind of conscience can send thousands of deadly bullets into a crowd?

On the front of social evil, why are large corporations, media outlets and political entities getting away with manipulating people? "Towers of Babel" have been built that broadcast a spiraling increase in our bent toward foolish pride and corruption. Wickedness and evil must be named, confessed and repented of. Recent proceedings of women and men speaking out about the incidence and problem of sexual abuse by movie directors, actors, political leaders, district attorneys, congressmen and others indicate that sexual immorality is not a trivial or relativized concern.

One does not need look far, especially in the pervasive video driven media culture, to see that the internet, movies and television are used as tools in ways that are both good and evil. The battle ground itself may appear to be neutral; however, there is an addictive quality and deceptive influence within technology that gives people an illusion of control, pseudo-security, and a false sense of freedom. The temptation to keep eating from the modern equivalent to the *"Tree of the Knowledge of Good and Evil"* goes on and on, often without discernment or discretion. This is reinforced as repetitive and addictive behaviors create unknown results and a loss of genuine community, perhaps even giving rise to dire relational poverty.

Where people of ancient times had their heroic stories and myths, those influences and illusions that made some think of themselves more highly as "sons of God" with the pretense of divinity; so too, people today may also be absorbed in a world of man's heroic myths and legends. While the desire to aspire to greatness seems to be in our makeup, and this says something about our "being made in the image of God"; the problem of not being wise to handle knowledge and power is real. The average individual who uses a smart phone, tablet, smart television or computer has unlimited information and has the impression of being in charge. The reality, however, is that people are targets of intense marketing, personal tracking, and aggressive behavioral modification. Those who write software programs for applications will admit that they design electronic psychological triggers, using manipulative alerts and instant messages, to keep our attention. If Noah were alive to come and warn us of Christ's immanent return, would we notice or hear him over the clamor and distractions? When preachers and laypeople warn people to get ready, to serve and be faithful because Jesus is coming; do people listen and act? Much like Noah's day, people still turn a deaf ear and reject those who speak of Jesus' return as being fools under delusion.

C. Similar surprise (39)

39 and they knew nothing about what would happen until the flood came and took them all away. That is how it will be at the coming of the Son of Man.

Despite God's messengers giving warning, calling people to repentance, most people will be completely surprised when Jesus returns. Even with the teaching of Jesus here in Matthew 24, the alarming reality is that people just don't want to listen to the voice of truth, to the message of salvation, to the call of repentance and hope in God's Kingdom. Instead, people would rather live with denial or diversion. People would rather procrastinate in the matter of believing, trusting and serving God. The problem is not that God has been silent, or that the creation's dynamic forces cannot be observed. The problem is that people would prefer to live in ignorance and not listen. Have you ever had a conversation where someone was talking to you and suddenly you realized that you weren't catching a thing of what they said. First, you need to apologize for being distracted, and then, if you care, you will ask for the person to start again. If we care about the message of God, we must repent and listen. Even when God's Son Jesus came to earth full of truth and grace, and revealed God's heart of love and forgiveness, people still resisted. The moment of Christ's return will take many people by surprise.

III. Rapture of God's elect (v.40-41)

40 Two men will be in the field; one will be taken and the other left. 41 Two women will be grinding with a hand mill; one will be taken and the other left.

A. People at work (v.40-41)
40 Two men will be in the field; one will be taken and the other left

Jesus begins to describe the event of His "rapture" in a way that is alarming and disconcerting. There will be a sifting. The harvest of "the elect" of earth involves some going to heaven and others remaining on earth. Jesus describes a situation of two men working out in a field, side by side. One is *"taken"* and the other is *"left"* behind. If you have decided for Jesus, and are on Lord's side, it shall make all the difference.

This event of the "rapture" involves God's angels going forth to the corners of the earth to gather the redeemed community from the impending tribulations that will come to the earth. While there are differing perspectives regarding how much tribulation believers will endure, Christ's teaches the nearness of the Kingdom of God, and a time of angels coming for a harvest. The point of Jesus was that readiness is not a matter of looking up into the skies. Readiness comes through having already repented of sin and believing in a way that has led to acts of love and service, this being the very fruit and witness of those who are "born-again" of God's Spirit in Christ.

The decision of who will be taken up is ultimately up to God. Those included in the Book of Life will be those who have believed and served. The likelihood that people will receive a "text message" or "live video stream" of the event is not to be counted on as readiness. Alerts on your smart phone and breaking news on television will not save you. One must rely upon the gift of God's grace through faith in Jesus Christ.

Those to be "*taken up*" will be helped by the host of heaven; the angels shall extend to the corners of the earth for this harvest. Jesus's lightning appearance will be combined with a great angelic host who shall swiftly and personally usher God's people into the safety of Heaven's "*strong tower*" gates.

> *For you have been my refuge, a strong tower against the foe. 4 I long to dwell in your tent forever and take refuge in the shelter of your wings* - Psalm 61:3-4

Faith is required if one is to be written into the Book of Life, and to be included in the rapture when Jesus the Christ returns:

> *And without faith it is impossible to please God, because anyone who comes to him must believe that he exists and that he rewards those who earnestly seek him.* - Hebrews 11:6

B. Two women grinding at the mill (v.41)

41 Two women will be grinding with a hand mill; one will be taken and the other left.

Jesus reveals a second portrayal that tells of the rapture story. Work is common theme in these stories of the rapture. The idea conveyed is that people should go about their lives and keep working. Jesus did not include a scenario where people were reclining or fixated in a watchful position. Looking a bit deeper, one notes a connection between the two sets of workers. The image of fieldwork and millwork are together involved with the production of bread. The men in the field are growing the grain, the women at the mill are turning it into flour, or meal, which will be used to make the bread. The work of God's Kingdom is symbolized in these two steps that will lead to the eventual result. The harvest of God's elect will also lead to the eventual result of God's coming kingdom.

The ultimate concern of God and His people is to prepare for the Kingdom of Heaven, and this involves the work of the harvest leading to salvation. Even if people are at work or busy, the most important preparation is not the work itself, but in being ready in one's heart and soul. People can go through the motions of life and still miss the importance of a faith relationship with God.

IV. Preparation is made through faithful service (42-47)

42 "Therefore keep watch, because you do not know on what day your Lord will come. 43 But understand this: If the owner of the house had known at what time of night the thief was coming, he would have kept watch and would not have let his house be broken into. 44 So you also must be ready, because the Son of Man will come at an hour when you do not expect him. 45 "Who then is the faithful and wise servant, whom the master has put in charge of the servants in his household to give them their food at the proper time? 46 It will be good for that servant whose master finds him doing so when he returns. 47 Truly I tell you, he will put him in charge of all his possessions.

A. Keep watchful and vigilant (42)

42 "Therefore keep watch, because you do not know on what day your Lord will come.

Jesus is about to tell His disciples a series of analogies, each illustrating the reality of how people may or may not fulfill their call to have faith and be ready through obedient responsibility. In verse forty-two, Jesus summarizes His warning by reinforcing the matter of "not knowing" when the day of His return will occur. Vitally important, without this knowledge, people must be ready for God's coming Kingdom (in life and in death) at any time through ongoing faith and obedience. Jesus reveals several instances and dimensions of how people may ignore, fail to hear, or choose not to respond to God's message of warning. There are consequences for faithlessness. Nonetheless, the good news is that there is hope for believers, for the faithful. The "elect" can look forward to being rewarded in God's Kingdom. Jesus conveys this promise from God to those who shall trust and obey, as they prepare for His return.

B. Analogy of the thief in the night (43-44)

43 But understand this: If the owner of the house had known at what time of night the thief was coming, he would have kept watch and would not have let his house be broken into. 44 So you also must be ready, because the Son of Man will come at an hour when you do not expect him.

Having a house broken into is startling and disturbing. Security measures often include locks and alarm systems that have sensors or video surveillance. The issue here is that some people are not vigilant, they assume that theft will never happen to them. Jesus points out that a thief will surprise the homeowner, coming when they would least expect. The homeowner, in this analogy, will be wise by being more realistic, intentional and prepared. However, they neglected to consider the risk and take appropriate measures. So too, people can learn from Jesus that it is essential to be vigilant and informed about the coming of God's Kingdom.

On a recent December evening, two nights before Christmas, someone broke in to our home, which is a parsonage next to the church I pastor. We were away at a movie, and when we returned we found that the main door had been broken in, with glass everywhere on the floor. We called the police and decided to wait for them before disturbing the scene of the crime. We did bring our dog outside, and were glad that little Teddy was alright. While waiting outside, we wondered what could have been taken: electronics, jewelry, gifts, valuables... The police arrived and took fingerprints and upon further investigation, it appeared that the intruder did not take anything other than some food. They may have been looking for shelter, a bite to eat, and maybe some prescription medications. In any event, the police were stunned that nothing of value was gone. The lights and television were left on, and the person breaking in even used a dust pan to try and clean up some of the glass and mess they created.

Considering the desperation of the person who broke in, I started to think about the meaning of Christ's birth. What is of ultimate value and concern? What was the person looking for? What were their deeper needs that had gone unmet to precipitate their action? During our waiting and subsequent search inside, we all agreed that the material things could be replaced if they were stolen. On the other hand, if the dog had gotten loose and lost, that would have been an awful loss and heartache. Our prayers and hearts then considered the desperation of the soul who was looking for "room in the inn". Sadly, we weren't there when we could have been of help. I pray, in humility, that my heart would have been ready to serve. Upon application to verse 43, I was reminded of something else Jesus had once said:

> "Do not store up for yourselves treasures on earth, where moths and vermin destroy, and where thieves break in and steal. But store up for yourselves treasures in heaven, where

moths and vermin do not destroy, and where thieves do not break in and steal." - Matthew 6:19-20.

C. Analogy of food preparation (45-46)

45 "Who then is the faithful and wise servant, whom the master has put in charge of the servants in his household to give them their food at the proper time? 46 It will be good for that servant whose master finds him doing so when he returns.

Jesus now appeals to those who have the gift of hospitality, management or food preparation. What preparations would the head chef or dining hall manager make if they knew that a food critic or state restaurant inspector was coming? Better yet, what if the President was going to stay in their inn or dine at their table? Politics aside, they would prepare and try to make a good impression. But what if it was part of a chain of restaurants and the corporate boss arrived unexpected and undercover? Would the rooms be clean, the service friendly, and the meal be delicious? The best way for a manager (or servant) to function is to be faithful and consistently attentive and responsible. In Jesus' assessment, to motivate His disciples, He uses positive language by saying: *"It will be good for that servant"* if they are fulfilling their duties well. Instead of focusing on failure, Jesus focuses the disciples upon success, and a good work ethic, as indicative of what shall be appreciated and fruitful.

D. Reward to the faithful (47)

47 Truly I tell you, he will put him in charge of all his possessions.

Jesus not only focused on His disciples' efforts toward responsibility and success, He promises that there will be a reward for the faithful, a promotion with a bonus for their good work. When Jesus uses the word "truly", it is a verification of His word, something that the disciples may count on. He is not like the boss who manipulates workers through hollow promises and unsupported incentives. Indeed, Jesus gave them His Word (and His Word is a promise from God the Father), that they would be rewarded and promoted for their faithfulness. Their trustworthy character and excellent work will be matched by a commendation and advancement. The greatest goal, considering the message of Jesus, is to prepare for the Kingdom of God by living faithfully. The Word of the Lord will then greet us upon life's conclusion: "*Well done, good and faithful servant*".

The promise of Jesus is repeated in Revelation 21, this time to reassure believers in the Early Church to help them endure trials, suffering and persecution. The Lord wants them to keep the vision of His return in mind, so He says: "*Look, I am coming soon*". All that people shall go through, while standing firm in the hope and promises that Christ Jesus gave them from God the Father, will be worth it. Jesus gave His Word of God's Kingdom that shall come and the encouragement of Heaven's reward to those who would keep and share the faith:

"Look, I am coming soon! My reward is with me, and I will give to each person according to what they have done..." - Revelation 22:12

V. Judgment will come to the wicked and irresponsible (48-51)

48 But suppose that servant is wicked and says to himself, 'My master is staying away a long time,' 49 and he then begins to beat his fellow servants and to eat and drink with drunkards. 50 The master of that servant will come on a day when he does not expect him and at an hour he is not aware of. 51 He will cut him to pieces and assign him a place with the hypocrites, where there will be weeping and gnashing of teeth.

A. God sees injustice and abuse (48-49)

48 But suppose that servant is wicked and says to himself, 'My master is staying away a long time,' 49 and he then begins to beat his fellow servants and to eat and drink with drunkards.

Jesus takes this analogy to another level to illustrate the justice and fairness of God. The Lord anticipated the thoughts of His disciples: "Yes Lord, it's good that hard work and sacrifice are rewarded, but what about successful people who are corrupt, perverse, mean, abusive, or what about those who are irresponsible and lazy? What will be done about them?" Jesus understood how the disciples would wonder why certain wicked people seem to advance and gain status and wealth, while the faithful are not always treated with equity for their labors. It's just not fair!!

The brilliant imagination of Jesus takes them into the mindset of the wicked, and how they think. The first thing the "wicked servant" does is avoid accountability and speak to themselves as a means of rationalizing (justifying) their avoidance of responsibility. *"Hmm, my master is staying away..."*, so the wicked servant starts to abuse this freedom, coming in late, stealing things, wasting time. *"Hmm, he has been gone a long time..."*, the servant starts to bully their way around, put others down, spread gossip, and even becoming verbally or physically abusive. Perhaps they take on vices and squander their time, talents or treasure; they become addicted to alcohol and spend their money and free time at the bars or clubs. Will this unwise use of one's life and resources be pleasing to the Master?

Jesus wants His disciples to know that God sees all of this, and invites repentance. A day of accountability will come, but until then, the *"god of this world"* has blinded people (II Corinthians 4:4) and has clouded judgment and created havoc for social justice, economic integrity and personal responsibility. One must seek peace and justice and pursue it, but the ultimate hope is in God's sovereign plan. Alignment with, or rationalization of, "wicked" and hypocritical leaders/servants is deadly.

B. Jesus the master will come and judge humanity (50)

50 The master of that servant will come on a day when he does not expect him and at an hour he is not aware of.

While God desires that people repent of their wicked ways (II Chronicles 7:14), God will also hold all people into account. The Master will come again, and it will be on a day unannounced, at an hour without notice given. For those who want to be in control of their schedules, or for those who have something to hide, this is maddening. However, for those who recognize the importance of accountability and quality control, they understand this practice. The reality is that people are often less responsible if they know they can get away with the minimum, with less than what is best. Holding up a higher standard requires that someone will help keep that standard up, that certain competencies, procedures, protocol and measures of quality control are followed and evident. God is no less concerned about what we do, and how well we function as stewards of our lives, our work, our families, communities and this earth that we must care for.

A friend of mine was telling me about a recent vacation where he was visiting a small town in Pennsylvania. In the local newspaper, there was an article that went into detail about a large local restaurant that had violated many code violations upon inspection. In that small town, such a writeup did not go unnoticed, it was a measure of accountability that had to be reported and made known so that people would be informed and pressure for change in that establishment, and perhaps other restaurants, would occur.

C. Judgment of the wicked (cut off from God) (51)

51 He will cut him to pieces and assign him a place with the hypocrites, where there will be weeping and gnashing of teeth.

Now that God's quality control has been published by Jesus, and shall be upheld by Jesus in the fulness of time at His return; the truth of God being just and righteous has been established. What does this judgment of God look like? Jesus does not mince words, or try to paint a rosy, pretty, picture. The wicked will be cut down, piece by piece, and their remains will be sent to hell along with the hypocrites. Being cut off from God is the result of wickedness and unfaithfulness. The wicked are destroyed for their outright rebellion, the unfaithful are destroyed for their deceit or deficit; both rationalized hypocrisy through pride or self-righteousness. When all are brought before Christ, no amount of pride or works shall replace the need for faith, and rationalizations will not alter God's knowledgeable judgment at the "Great Inspection".

In Jesus ministry, there was a time that a Roman Centurion came to Him asking that Jesus would just say the word for his servant to be healed. Jesus was struck by the faith of the Roman, that this "Gentile" believed in His authority.

> Truly I tell you, I have not found anyone in Israel with such great faith. I say to you that many will come from the east and the west, and will take their places at the feast with Abraham, Isaac and Jacob in the kingdom of heaven. But the subjects of the kingdom will be thrown outside, into the darkness, where there will be weeping and gnashing of teeth." - (Matthew 8:10-12)

Jesus was, in part, foretelling the near judgment that would come upon Israel in the destruction of Jerusalem and the Temple in 70 A.D.. However, Jesus was also looking far into the future, the conclusion of the Church era, to the time of His return and the Day of Judgment. People in God's Kingdom will be from all nations. The feast will be attended by people of all nations and tribes who come to believe in Jesus as Savior, the Son of God. They shall sit alongside Abraham, Isaac and Jacob and those faithful within the Judaic covenant that Jesus was the fulfillment of. Outside, the unfaithful subjects of God's kingdom are cast out. They may have tried to fake their way in, dress in their own garments or robes of pride, but their sins have caught up with them. They are not acceptable because they have not humbled themselves to pray or have not sought the grace or mercy of God prior.

Jesus will mention this warning again and again, then finally we hear it pronounced and articulated in Revelation 22, where Jesus offers hope for the repentant and warning of condemnation for the wicked:

> 14 Blessed are those who wash their robes, that they may have the right to the tree of life and may go through the gates into the city. Outside are the dogs, those who practice magic arts, the sexually immoral, the murderers, the idolaters and everyone who loves and practices falsehood. "I, Jesus, have sent my angel to give you this testimony for the churches. I am the Root and the Offspring of David, and the bright Morning Star."   Revelation 22:14-16

Conclusion: God is watching.
Are we mindful and serving?

Jesus wants people to know that a day of inspection is coming. Already, the Lord is aware of how we are doing, and if we are faithful. When Jesus returns, those who are faithful, and those who have repented from their wicked ways and have begun to live faithfully, will be rewarded by being promoted into God's Kingdom of Heaven. Those who are unfaithful through hypocrisy or outright wickedness will be demoted, sent to hell for their punishment and eventual destruction.

Now there are people who would frown at such a vivid and "violent" view of God's judgment. They believe that a God of love could not also be of the mind to administer judgment or justice in such a strong and unforgiving way. The assumption of God's love being exempt from God's holiness and justice is not a biblical notion, but one of false and deceptive rationalization. Ultimately, there will be day of judgment, not all people or spiritual entities

(Satan and his demons included) will repent and turn to worship or serve God. A day of reckoning, a final surprise inspection, will be necessary.

What then is the church to do? How are we then to live in this time of tension in which it seems that the wicked thrive and are not yet held into account? How are God's servants to be present in the world, even though the world is corrupt, and people are not prone to repentance or responsibility?

Going back to the ministry of presence and of being faithful servants, it is essential for believers, the church, the "elect", to show up and be 'in the world, but not of the world' (John 17:15-18). Believers are to be present and responsible in the world to evoke God's truth and ambassador God's grace. Believers are to be present by accompanying the activities of our communities in a way that represents the character and love of God. Believers are to be present in the world by giving comfort to those who are hurt, sick, lonely or grieving. Believers are to be present in the world by giving hope to those who are hungry for truth and justice, thirsty for grace and righteousness, and desiring to know if God is real or that God may be known. The ministry of presence is exactly what Jesus modeled, it is what people are invited to participate in at many levels, using a variety of spiritual gifts and networks of relationships. Jesus prayed for His disciples to be representatives of God our Father, and of Him, the Son:

> Holy Father, protect them by the power of your name, the name you gave me, so that they may be one as we are one. While I was with them, I protected them and kept them safe by that name you gave me. None has been lost except the one doomed to destruction so that Scripture would be fulfilled. "I am coming to you now, but I say these things while I am still in the world, so that they may have the full measure of my joy within them. I have given them your word and the world has hated them, for they are not of the world any more than I am of the world. My prayer is not that you take them out of the world but that you protect them from the evil one. They are not of the world, even as I am not

of it. Sanctify them by the truth; your word is truth. As you sent me into the world, I have sent them into the world. For them I sanctify myself, that they too may be truly sanctified. My prayer is not for them alone. I pray also for those who will believe in me through their message, that all of them may be one, Father, just as you are in me and I am in you. May they also be in us so that the world may believe that you have sent me. – (John 17:11-22)

Jesus has called people, disciples, the Church, to be involved in ministry that often looks like chaplaincy, advocacy, friendship or the mercy of a medical care provider. This is especially needed in the end times as the stress of concern mounts with an increase in peoples' anxieties. People may even start to lose their faith, giving way to fear. Through the times of distress, believers are to be ambassadors of truth and hope to those whose focus is on temporal cures or momentary relief. Faith is essential in experiencing God's presence and ultimate power of salvation and redemption. God's gift of grace and ultimate transformation shall bring God's Kingdom within individuals, leading to a change of character, heart, behavior and thinking. Ultimately, this leads to a changing of our inner nature in the power of the Holy Spirit that will prepare us for our own resurrection and the very return of Christ. There awaits a great and revealing hope in the totality that culminates in God's work in the time of the coming New Heaven and Earth. Currently, our hope is not in fixing this world to our standards with our strength or manipulation; our hope is in the One who reconciles, redeems, resurrects and recreates while we are present and caring.

Healing is found in relationship to the eternal love, grace and truth of God. God will make all things new, the old world is fading and will pass away. The Gospel of the Kingdom of God in Jesus Christ is received in faith and sustained in being "hopeful" and "faithful" in active presence. The faithful are to trust in God's ongoing presence and power. In God's leading and timing we may participate in the very work God gives us to do. Eventually, this will culminate in God's Judgment, then the sunrise of a new beginning, a "*New Heaven and a New Earth*" (Revelation 21:1-4):

> *Then I saw "a new heaven and a new earth," for the first heaven and the first earth had passed away, and there was no longer any sea. I saw the Holy City, the new Jerusalem, coming down out of heaven from God, prepared as a bride beautifully dressed for her husband. And I heard a loud voice from the throne saying, "Look! God's dwelling place is now among the people, and he will dwell with them. They will be his people, and God himself will be with them and be their God. 'He will wipe every tear from their eyes. There will be no more death' or mourning or crying or pain, for the old order of things has passed away." -*
> (Revelation 21:1-4)

Questions for Discussion:

1. How are the days we live in similar to, or different from, the days of Noah before the flood?

2. Jesus will come on a day and hour that nobody but God the Heavenly Father knows. Why is this essential?

3. When Jesus comes, all people will know it, but most people will be caught by surprise. Can you describe the various feelings and thoughts that would run through your mind in that moment? What practical concerns would you need to let go of?

4. How is Jesus' "Second Coming", first involving the "Rapture of the elect", a bitter-sweet event?

5. How is the "Second Coming", a glorious and wonderful event?

Part 7: "Warning to the Church"
(Will you be wise or foolish?)
Matthew 25:1-13

1 "At that time the kingdom of heaven will be like ten virgins who took their lamps and went out to meet the bridegroom. 2 Five of them were foolish and five were wise. 3 The foolish ones took their lamps but did not take any oil with them. 4 The wise ones, however, took oil in jars along with their lamps. 5 The bridegroom was a long time in coming, and they all became drowsy and fell asleep. 6 "At midnight the cry rang out: 'Here's the bridegroom! Come out to meet him!' 7 "Then all the virgins woke up and trimmed their lamps. 8 The foolish ones said to the wise, 'Give us some of your oil; our lamps are going out.' 9 "'No,' they replied, 'there may not be enough for both us and you. Instead, go to those who sell oil and buy some for yourselves.' 10 "But while they were on their way to buy the oil, the bridegroom arrived. The virgins who were ready went in with him to the wedding banquet. And the door was shut. 11 "Later the others also came. 'Lord, Lord,' they said, 'open the door for us!' 12 "But he replied, 'Truly I tell you, I don't know you.' 13 "Therefore keep watch, because you do not know the day or the hour. Matthew 25:1-13

Introduction: The Wisdom of preparation.

Driving my old brown Mercedes 1979 coupe through the city of Boston, I noticed on a hot summer day that the temperature of the engine was rising above a safe level. Clearly, the fluid level was low, I had not refilled it that Spring. If I had the luxury of time to stop, let the engine cool down and put coolant in the radiator, I would have. However, I had an appointment to give counsel for someone back at my church. From previous experience I knew that I could not simply or safely open the radiator cap with all the heat and pressure and put fluid in. I remembered a temporary solution from another old car; switch on the heater to high and blow hot air to cool the engine. The trick, however, would be to keep the car moving, and not allow the car to sit still for long. Amidst traffic and maneuvering on roads that would sustain a steady rate of speed, without going too fast, became difficult, almost impossible (and all this at rush hour). The heat went down and up, down and up, with each intersection and traffic jam. The needle would rise to the red zone and then go down to acceptable levels with speed and air flow. This cycle continued until I arrived safely on time to home, church and the appointment.

While driving through this hour of city traffic I began to think about the parallel one could make to the journey of navigating through life. We are wise if we think ahead and take care of ourselves. With reasonable anticipation, we must expect that times of heat and pressure will develop. Without forethought, responsible care and planning, we may end up jeopardizing our journey. One could say that we live in the balance of things "heating up" or "cooling off" in the engine of human conflict. Global warming, political maneuvering, racial prejudice, economic disparity, and other matters of injustice will place people and our planet in precarious situations. Jesus reminds His Church, to all who look forward to His coming, that they should be ready and not caught unprepared for His return. Eventually a time shall come in which all the attempts toward cooling things down will fail, and the engine of humanity will break down. Before this happens, the Lord will come to rescue His Bride, the Redeemed, His Church, the Elect, in a rapture. Who will be ready by faith and faithfulness?

Outline of Matthew 25:1-13

I. Parable: Readiness for the Kingdom of Heaven (v.1)
    A. Ten virgins
    B. Lamps
    C. The Bridegroom

II. The Foolish and the Wise (v. 2-4)
    A. Setting the Stage (2)
    B. The problem of foolish assumptions (3)
    C. The wisdom of faith and hope (4)

III. God's preparations call for patience and perseverance (v.5)

IV. The Groom's midnight arrival and the symbol of the lamps (v.6-7)
    A. Midnight arrival (6a)
    B. Come to the Bridegroom (Heeding the Call) (6b)
    C. Waking up and trimming the lamps (7)

V. Readiness is a personal responsibility (8-10)
    A. Procrastination will leave you in the dark (8)
    B. People cannot solve everyone's problems (9)
    C. Vigilance will light the way into God's Kingdom (10a)
    D. Missed opportunity will keep doors shut. (10b)

VI. Not Knowing the Lord (11-12)
    A. Will mercy be extended? (11)
    B. Not knowing the Lord (12)

VII.   Be watchful and ready. (13)

Study on Matthew 25:1-13

I. Parable: Readiness for the Kingdom of Heaven (v.1)

1 "At that time the kingdom of heaven will be like ten virgins who took their lamps and went out to meet the bridegroom.

A. Ten virgins

The time Jesus is referring to is the "Parousia" (Greek for "presence" or "presence after absence"; see Bibletools.com). The Parousia is the moment of "Christ's coming" and "presence again" to the earth (*1 Corinthians 15:23; 1 Thessalonians 2:19; Thess. 3:13; Thess. 4:15; Thess. 5:23; 2 Thessalonians 2:1,8; James 5:7,8; 2 Peter 1:16; 3:4,12; 1 John 2:28*). The same word is also used once in the New Testament for the coming presence of the "Anti-Christ" (II Thessalonians 2:9). In Matthew 25:1-13, we will focus on Christ Jesus the Messiah who will come again to complete God's promise to Israel and to the Church (His "Bride"). The reference of Jesus' parable of the Ten Virgins is applicable to God's relationship with Israel as a covenant people, God's new covenant relationship with the Gentiles in Christ, and to details in the custom of Jewish wedding preparations and participation.

Ten is the number of perfection; such a number of persons was required to form a synagogue, and to be present at any office, ceremony, or formal benediction. Talmudic authorities affirm that the lamps used in bridal processions were usually ten. The "virgins" here are the friends of the bride, who are arranged to sally forth to meet the bridegroom as soon as his approach is signaled. "The Church, in her aggregate and ideal unity, is the bride; the members of the Church, as individually called, are guests; in their separation from the world, and expectation of the Lord's coming, they are his virgins" (Lange). The bride herself is not named in the parable, as she is not needed for illustration, and the virgins occupy her place. These virgins represent believers divided into two sections; evidently they are all supposed to hold the true faith, and to be pure and undefiled followers of the Lord (II Corinthians 11:2; Revelation 14:4), *to be waiting for his coming, and to love his appearing; but some fail for lack of grace or of perseverance, as is shown further on.* (Pulpit Commentary).

The mystery of who the ten virgins represent is left open by Jesus. If one believes that the Ten Virgins represent the Jewish people, then some will be prepared through belief and faithfulness to Yahweh, and others will be unprepared through disbelief and unfaithfulness. Those who are ready shall help to escort the Bridegroom (Jesus) and are called to be friends with the Bride (the Church). God has already sent His Son Jesus to be the one who will unite all humanity into the Covenant of God's grace (that began with Noah, Abraham and Moses). In this interpretation, the wedding is the consummation of Marriage, a New Covenant that unites old and new friends and guests, along with the Bride and Groom within God's Household (The Kingdom of God/Heaven). This interpretation has great merit.

Another interpretation is that the "virgins" represent either Jews or Gentiles, though some would restrict this specifically to one of these groups. Jesus' point is not to single out a group, but to illustrate the matter of readiness for God's coming Kingdom. Once again, for the virgins, their mission is to proceed with the Bridegroom to the Father of the Bridegroom's household, where the Bride awaits. At the Groom's Father's household (symbolically Heaven), the wedding proceedings have been prepared. All is ready. The Bride (the Church in Heaven) is ready, and the wedding guests are ready (everyone else in God's grace and favor). Within Jesus' illustration, the virgins represent those whom God has given a responsibility to, and in some measure, that pertains to all who will be living when Jesus returns. Who will be ready to accompany Christ into God's Kingdom upon His return? Let's investigate this parable of Jesus even further.

B. Lamps

The lamps represent the witness and life of the Spirit aglow in the hearts of those who are to journey in belief and obedience to God. These lamps are fueled by God's word and Holy Spirit that ignites and sustains our souls to shine.

In Jewish wedding proceedings, these lamps, some scholars say, were made especially for going out to meet the bridegroom, to then accompany Him to the Groom's home where he would then be reunited with the Bride.

They all made separate and personal, independent preparation for the meeting. These lamps (for they were not torches) were, as Dr. Edersheim notes, hollow cups or saucers, with a round receptacle for the wick, which was fed with pitch or oil. They were on these occasions fastened to a long wooden pole, and borne aloft in the procession. (Pulpit Commentary)

On a personal level (applying this to Christ's return or one's own death), the question will be that of faith or spiritual readiness. Shall the light of a person's soul be ready to shine, with the reserve and deposit of the "oil" of God's grace, forgiving love and truth? In the event of sleep, shall the jar of grace be filled or will it be empty or insufficiently low? The Lord, the One who can relights the wick of our souls is the One who raises the dead. Jesus the Risen Savior and Bridegroom shall return. Will our lamps be ready with trimmed wicks (through the forgiveness of our sins) and will our jars have sufficient oil (the deposit of God's Holy Spirit) filled with God's grace and truth?

C. The Bridegroom

God, the Father of the Groom, calls people to prepare the way for the Bridegroom and have our lamps working and in good order. The Bridegroom is Jesus Christ, and all our preparations will culminate in this special moment of His arrival and final procession as the Son of God. The faithful are called to accompany the groom with their lamps on the journey to His Kingdom's consummation. In Christ's return, there will be a great coming together in which Christ the Bridegroom leads the way to the great gathering, to the ceremony, celebration and feast with the Bride (the Church as it has already entered Heaven) and this amid the host of all included in God's Kingdom.

I must point out that there is still much that we can only point to and imagine within the symbolism of Jesus' parables, for a great mystery is contained in Christ's teaching. In a recent wedding that I officiated, the bride had a lacey white veil that hid almost all her face as she came down the aisle. We could only see a hint of her face until her father gave her away to the groom. Regarding the Bride of Christ, the Church, the Elect and the coming of the Bridegroom (Christ Himself), there is still much to be revealed about the Church, Jesus' return, the extension of God's redemption and the coming Kingdom of Heaven.

II. The Foolish and the Wise (v. 2-4)

2 Five of them were foolish and five were wise. 3 The foolish ones took their lamps but did not take any oil with them. 4 The wise ones, however, took oil in jars along with their lamps.

A. Setting the Stage (2)
2 Five of them were foolish and five were wise.

Wedding plans are often very optimistic, with joyful anticipation for every invited guest to come and be blessed. Sadly, people often do not appreciate the invitation, their priorities are absorbed or set elsewhere. In foolishness, regarding the Gospel invitation, people fail to respond or commit to God's invitation to new life, even though they are welcome based on grace.

God has established a covenant of faith in Christ. Jesus came to fulfill all righteousness, to fulfill the requirements of the law, to establish the fulness of this covenant between God and humanity in a way that is like marriage. The foolishness of many people, even people who profess to believe, is that of neglecting the important matters of: 1). Making the effort and giving priority to having time with God, and (2). Believing and coming into a relationship with God's Son, the Groom, Jesus Christ.

If people truly knew the Groom's Father, they would also care about the Son, the Bridegroom. They would not miss this moment or be unprepared. Wisdom, that comes by listening to God's Spirit, would tell them that being ready is of utmost priority.

Jesus gave us a story that reveals a split between people who will be ready for His return and those who will not be ready. In this parable of the virgins, half of the ten (the wise virgins) were ready and the other five (the foolish virgins) were not ready. The way to be ready is to seek after God, to come to a devoted life of faith in following and serving Jesus. To know and prepare for Jesus return is to be in communion with the One who gives life and strength to all who seek and receive this "oil of grace and truth" by the Holy Spirit.

B. The problem of foolish assumptions (3)

3 The foolish ones took their lamps but did not take any oil with them.

The foolish virgins may have had their lamps, but they had no oil as they had run out. They assumed wrong, thinking that the bridegroom would not come. Perhaps, they might have even thought that reliance upon the other virgin's supply of oil was sufficient. Essentially, the foolish virgins were unfocused and unfaithful. Like the servants who acted inappropriately, who had assumed that the master was going to be away a long time, these virgins lost their way by means of neglect and diversion. They had spent their oil for the wrong reasons, in selfish and unthinking ways that were indeed foolish. So too, people often don't think about how they will use their time and resources in life. When the Lord comes knocking, at His return or at their body's death, they are not ready; they have spent their oil in vain pursuits. Athletic trophies, Nobel prizes, degrees, titles, possessions, awards and accolades are indicators of great accomplishments, but it would all mean nothing at the Day of the Lord, if you are not ready spiritually/relationally with God. Some will be ready and shall proceed with the Bridegroom. Others will have assumed that the Lord was so long in coming that maybe it was not going to occur at all, and so, why wait? Why be prepared? Why pray? Why read the Bible? Why seek after the sustaining truth and saving grace of God? People have a million excuses.

C. The wisdom of faith and hope (4)

4 The wise ones, however, took oil in jars along with their lamps.

The light of the *"wise ones"* will shine, even after waiting a long time, because these genuine believers have maintained their hope and connection to God. Their spiritual "tanks" ("jars") are kept filled and ready, because they have chosen to believe and maintain their disciplines of prayer, meditation on God's word and service for God's Kingdom. Those who are not prepared have negated their duty of waiting. Those who are wise will take care of their spiritual supply.

III. God's preparations call for patience and perseverance (v.5)

5 *The bridegroom was a long time in coming, and they all became drowsy and fell asleep.*

The light of believers is to be maintained, and kept strong (especially in the night) and trimmed (not spent upon worldly pursuits); it is a discipline that allows the people of faith to shine when and where God calls them to shine, to be the very presence of love and grace within the waiting time of darkness. The reality of verse 5 indicates that all the virgins will have fallen asleep, and that it was a very long time of waiting. The implication is that human effort for all people has its limitations. This is understandable, considering God's big timeframe and our human frailty. In Gethsemane, when Jesus asked His disciples to wait and pray with Him, they failed to stay awake. Jesus observed:

> Then He said to them, "My soul is overwhelmed with sorrow to the point of death. Stay here and keep watch with me." Going a little farther, he fell with his face to the ground and prayed, "My Father, if it is possible, may this cup be taken from me. Yet not as I will, but as you will." Then he returned to his disciples and found them sleeping. "Couldn't you men keep watch with me for one hour?" he asked Peter. "Watch and pray so that you will not fall into temptation. The spirit is willing, but the flesh is weak." He went away a second time and prayed, "My Father, if it is not possible for this cup to be taken away unless I drink it, may your will be done." When he came back, he again found them sleeping, because their eyes were heavy. So he left them and went away once more and prayed the third time, saying the same thing. Then he returned to the disciples and said to them, "Are you still sleeping and resting? Look, the hour has come, and the Son of Man is delivered into the hands of sinners. Rise! Let us go! Here comes my betrayer! Matthew 26:38-46

Jesus' disciples were still in a position of faith without power. They wanted to be strong, but they had not yet received the Holy Spirit that would enable them to endure and thrive in fulfilling their call to live and share the Gospel. The Holy Spirit would come to them in the upper room when Jesus would reveal Himself to them after His death and resurrection, and it would come again through the mighty wind on the day of Pentecost in the same place. Until then, the disciples would find it difficult to be strong in the face of trial and perseverance; afterward, they found resolve, strength and deepened love and grace. The era of God's grace being outpoured to all who will repent, open their heart, and believe gives the elect a ministry that is urgent and constant until Christ comes. The gift of God's grace, the Gospel, is to be preached and believed, in season and out of season (even when it is less accepted by culture or society).

The idea of preparation is that waiting till the last minute is foolish. When it comes to faith, waiting till the last minute is foolish as it pertains to having "fuel" stored up in one's heart and soul through faith, acts of service and spiritual discipline.

IV. The Groom's midnight arrival and the symbol of the lamps (v.6-7)

6 "At midnight the cry rang out: 'Here's the bridegroom! Come out to meet him!' 7 "Then all the virgins woke up and trimmed their lamps.

A. Midnight arrival (6a)
6 "At midnight the cry rang out: 'Here's the bridegroom!

As mentioned before, the bridegroom would traditionally come to assemble his entourage, the virgins, and they would then join him to accompany his procession to the Bridegroom's Father's household to behold the Bride and celebrate the wedding and feast. The Bridegroom, in this case, was delayed many hours. If they had lit their lamps at twilight and allowed them to continue to burn until midnight, but did not have enough oil after that, their lack of foresight and preparation would now be a crisis as the arrival of the Bridegroom was heard by all, even as they were asleep at midnight. "*Here's the bridegroom!*".

The time of midnight would, by modern timekeeping, mean the beginning of a new day. However, the Jewish belief and practice is that the new day begins at sunset with the fading of twilight. Midnight would be many hours afterward. The time of midnight had significance historically for the Hebrew people as well. For we read in Exodus that the judgment of God came to the "*first born*" throughout Egypt at midnight.

> *So Moses said, "This is what the Lord says: 'About midnight I will go throughout Egypt. Every firstborn son in Egypt will die, from the firstborn son of Pharaoh, who sits on the throne, to the firstborn son of the female slave, who is at her hand mill,* – (Exodus 11:4-5)

Just as God had told Moses, so it happened that way. The judgment fell upon the firstborn of humans and livestock throughout Egypt, unless they were gathered in a home with the blood of the lamb applied upon all sides of the doorframe. Recent writings on this event acknowledge the importance of "midnight" in God's timing for judgment:

> *At midnight of 15 Nissan 2448 (1313 BCE), G-d broke the last manacle of Egyptian bondage by killing all Egyptian firstborn, and the nation of Israel was born as a free people. The time is significant: twice the Torah emphasizes that the event occurred exactly at midnight, and to this day, midnight is a factor in our annual re-experience of the Exodus at the Seder held each year on the eve of 15 Nissan. (Midnight is the deadline for the eating of the matzah and the bitter herbs, for the eating of the meat of the Passover offering, and for eating the afikoman which today represents the Passover offering at our Seder.)* – (Chabad.org)

To highlight why both *"twilight"* and *"midnight"* have significance, in "a beginning" and "a judgment"; consider that Jesus broke the bread and lifted the cup of Passover at twilight, the beginning of a new day. Furthermore, Christ was the Passover lamb; a new day of God's grace would begin in Him as the one who takes away the sins of the world. When Jesus hosted the Passover feast at the Upper Room in Jerusalem, He identified Himself with the Matzah, the bread of adversity, "this is my body which is broken for you". Then Jesus held up the cup of affliction, "this is my blood with is poured out for the remission of sins". God was at work in Jesus, in a new type of Passover. Midnight was coming, and a window of grace was offered by Jesus.

We read God's instruction to Moses and the people of Israel as to the process of choosing and sacrificing a Lamb at twilight on that first Passover:

> The animals you choose must be year-old males without defect, and you may take them from the sheep or the goats. Take care of them until the fourteenth day of the month, when all the members of the community of Israel must slaughter them at twilight. Then they are to take some of the blood and put it on the sides and tops of the doorframes of the houses where they eat the lambs. – (Exodus 12:5-7)

Throughout the Passover feast, the lamb would be eaten until it was fully consumed. The connection of Jesus being the lamb of God was given by John the Baptist at the beginning of Jesus' ministry:

> The next day John saw Jesus coming toward him and said, "Look, the Lamb of God, who takes away the sin of the world! This is the one I meant when I said, 'A man who comes after me has surpassed me because he was before me.' I myself did not know him, but the reason I came baptizing with water was that he might be revealed to Israel." -- (John 1:29-31)

God told Moses to instruct the people how to be protected and safe on Passover. God instructed them in the proper preparation of the Passover lamb as a sacrifice, the application of its blood upon the door posts, and their faithful and watchful waiting and prayers. For Moses and the people of Israel, midnight was coming on that first Passover. For Jesus and His disciples, in a few days after he told them this parable of the waiting virgins, a new twilight and midnight were coming with a new era, a new application of Passover in the Lord's Supper. The fulfillment of Passover for humanity's coming midnight of judgment is in Christ the Lamb of God and His blood that was shed to cover our sins. This new time of Passover, which is currently an open time window of God's grace, has remained open from the Twilight of Jesus' sacrifice. The gift of God's grace is available to anyone who repents of their sin, believes and receives the blood of Christ to cover the doorway of their heart. The offer of God's grace is available until a person dies in their natural lifetime or until the coming "midnight" arrival of Christ's future Judgment arrives. At that time, the open window of God's grace shall be closed.

The timing of midnight, that Jesus used in this parable of the bridegroom and virgins, (in the view of this author) is historically tied to the time of judgment on the first eve of Passover. In Jesus' parable, midnight symbolized the coming of the Judgment of God for the nations. Jesus, the groom, would need to present His Bride as spotless and pure. To accomplish this, to protect His bride, the groom offers Himself at twilight of Passover, in the bread and wine. This symbolic act would eventually be fulfilled in Jesus' perfect sacrifice as the *"Passover Lamb"* on the cross. In that sacrificial moment, Jesus made it possible for His Bride, the People of God, to be forgiven, and to have their sins "Passed over", forgiven and covered.

Midnight was the deadline to eat the Matzah's middle layer bread, called the "afikoman". This second layer (the "afikoman") is one of three layers of the Passover Matzah arrangement (three in one). The middle piece is traditionally broken (symbolizing Jesus in

His sacrifice), the Matzah is flat with stripes baked in along with pierced holes (Jesus' being scourged with a whip and pierced with nails).   After it was broken, a piece of the Afikoman was then hidden (death and burial). Later that evening it would be retrieved (the resurrection) by children who would look carefully to see where it was placed and celebrate finding the lost Matzah bread. It should be noted that most Jews see no connection of Passover to Jesus, and do not believe that the three layers of bread have any reference to Jesus as the Christ. There are, however, a growing number of Christians and Jews who make this connection of symbolism, and find continuity and congruity with Jesus as *"the Lamb of God who came to take away the sins of the world"*.

The beginning of the Passover feast was at twilight, a new day. The conclusion of the Passover feast was around Midnight. From twilight to midnight, people were welcome to come in and participate in the story of God's protection and salvation. Throughout the Passover feast, the matzah and the lamb are continually offered and eaten. This would go on until midnight, the time of judgment. Throughout Passover, there is a serious focus on trusting in the protection of God, while awaiting the coming judgment.

By coming at midnight, in the parable of the Bridegroom and waiting virgins, Jesus portrays His return as being delayed until the last hour of Passover, midnight. This may indeed represent the grace of God in Jesus Christ that is currently extended for people to receive salvation. The whole Passover feast connects Jesus' initial work of atonement on the cross to His eventual coming in power and triumph over evil. The meaning of Passover, in the Lord's supper, the Christian observance of Communion, expands God's grace from Israel to all people who believe in Christ Jesus for the forgiveness of sin and victory over death. This Passover in Christ comes by faith, believing that God honored His Son's perfect blood sacrifice. He was the Lamb of God, as identified by John the Baptist.

A window of grace was revealed at the Lord's Supper. Currently, we live in this period of God's grace available through faith in Jesus Christ. Someday, around "midnight", just before the time of judgment, the angel of the Lord will sound forth, a trumpet blast will rock the world. The great "Day of the Lord" will come. Jesus will bring forth His Host of witnesses, those bearing the lamps of their salvation. They shall come forth into the household of our Heavenly Father, with the Bridegroom and the Bride and all the guests for the Wedding Feast of Heaven.

Applied to Christ's Second Coming, the time of waiting is short in God's perspective of time, although it may seem long in our sense of time. From sunset to midnight seemed like a long time for the waiting virgins (one may remember how Jesus' disciples were also weary and fell asleep in their watch in the Garden of Gethsemane on the night He would was betrayed and arrested). It is vitally important that people not lose perspective and hope while awaiting Christ's Second Coming.

As the hour draws nearer, the time of waiting will conclude. Instead of seeing this time in a passive sense of waiting, believers are called to be active in their waiting. That is, they are to make the most of every opportunity to serve God, grow in faith and reach out in care for others. God will bring judgment to the earth, therefore, the important task of preparing people for the Wedding Feast, via faith and discipleship in Jesus Christ, the Bridegroom, is urgent.

Different from the Exodus of Moses and the Israelites out of Egypt, we are told that Jesus will lead the procession of virgins and His Bride (the Church) out from the world before the judgment. The overall message in both narratives is that the scope of salvation and the intervening power of God to deliver His people and lead them into His promised land will be complete and extensive. For the deliverance of the Church, the wise virgins and Bride of Christ, God's Kingdom procession (in Christ's return) will be global. Who will be spiritually ready?

B. Coming to the Bridegroom (Heeding the Call) (6b)
Come out to meet him!'

Therefore, a sure and swift response is needed by people if they are to be part of the Kingdom of God, and not be left behind to face the great tribulation and final judgment of God upon the unredeemed of earth. "Come out" involves leaving this world and all its cares and concerns, as well as all its pleasures and fancies. God has something better, something lasting, something uncorrupted, something beautiful, exactly what we were created for in a New Heaven and a New Earth. We are called to come out to the very Bridegroom, Jesus the Christ, the Messiah, the Son of the Living God, the Bright Morning Star, the Good Shepherd, the Alpha and the Omega, the Risen and Glorious King.

C. Waking up and trimming the lamps (7)
7 "Then all the virgins woke up and trimmed their lamps.

All the virgins wake up as the call of a sentinel is heard. The Bridegroom has arrived, it is time to accompany Him to the wedding. They *"trimmed their lamps"*, that is, they adjusted the wick so that it was clean and just the right length, this allows for the oil to flow better and burn at the right height (too low and it could go out, too high and it burns too quickly). If they had enough oil, they could join in and finish the procession.

An interesting parallel exists from this parable to the parable of the "seed and the soils". To summarize (from Matthew 13:1-9):
There were some seeds that fell on rocky ground and at once sprouted, but soon afterward dried up in the sun.

People may begin with enthusiasm, but then not continue with the disciplines that would give them life and protection. The good seed (the Gospel) may begin to grow, but then the cares of the world, which are like weeds, choke out people's faith. A parallel may be made to the oil or the wick of the virgins' lamps not being cared for, maintained or refilled. The cares and diversions of the world can contaminate the oil, even damage or burn up the wick. People must take care to be wise not to allow their priority to be diverted away from being true to God and God's Kingdom values.

The concern of each parable is care and maintenance. When the seed is not cared for, it has difficulty growing. If the virgins do not protect their oil, use it up frivolously, or leave the jar uncovered, it will be spent or dried up. If the virgins allow other oils or substances to get into their jars it will also affect the ability of the wick to burn correctly. When a wick is used incorrectly, burning too brightly, it can char up and harden. The result of improper use of the lamp is that it can be difficult to light and difficult to control. The lamp should be kept ready, as one's faith is to be cared for and maintained.

V. Readiness is a personal responsibility (8-10)

8 The foolish ones said to the wise, 'Give us some of your oil; our lamps are going out.' 9 "'No,' they replied, 'there may not be enough for both us and you. Instead, go to those who sell oil and buy some for yourselves.' 10 "But while they were on their way to buy the oil, the bridegroom arrived. The virgins who were ready went in with him to the wedding banquet. And the door was shut.

A. Procrastination will leave you in the dark (8)

The foolish ones said to the wise, 'Give us some of your oil; our lamps are going out.'

The parable of Jesus takes a dramatic turn, as it is evident some of the virgins did not take their waiting responsibilities seriously. Instead of having enough oil, they had already used their jar of oil for other purposes. Looking to the wise virgins, the foolish virgins demanded that the faithful ones be considerate and give them their oil. The clear issue at the time of Christ's return is that individuals are personally accountable for their own actions. The lack of decisive preparation is not the fault of those who are prepared. Personal faith is connected to one's accountability and preparedness before God. When it comes to spirituality, each soul must accept responsibility and discover personal faith, a relationship with God.

B. People cannot solve everyone's problems (9)

9 "'No,' they replied, 'there may not be enough for both us and you. Instead, go to those who sell oil and buy some for yourselves.'

The parable now features the response of those virgins who were wise enough to save enough oil for the procession. Truthfully, they only had enough oil for their own lamps for the journey. To give their oil to the foolish virgins would make it impossible for them to complete the journey to the Father of the Groom's home. The logic of the wise virgins, in presenting a potential solution, to *"go and buy some"* was a smart way for the wise to deflect the unreasonable demands of the foolish. As much as they wanted to help, the wise left judgment to the Bridegroom, and the foolish were soon to discover the consequence of their choices.

This response of the wise virgins is practical. We cannot save everyone. Heroic and helpful as we all want to be, there are limits and times when we cannot play the part of "Wonder Woman" or "Superman". Looking ahead to Jesus' teaching on "caring for the least of these" and discovering that "you cared for me" (Matthew 25:34-40), should be considered in counterbalance with this parable of wisdom.

C. Vigilance will light the way into God's Kingdom (10a)

10 "But while they were on their way to buy the oil, the bridegroom arrived. The virgins who were ready went in with him to the wedding banquet.

The consequence of the five foolish virgins' irresponsibility and misplaced priorities would now be experienced in being late. By the time they had their oil, and were trying to catch up in the dark of night, the wise virgins had already processed with Him into the Wedding Banquet Hall of the Bridegroom's Father. Their lack of faithfulness and preparation had put them at jeopardy of being included. For the wise and faithful, their vigilance would light the way into God's Kingdom. Such was not the case for the foolish ones.

D. Missed opportunity will keep doors shut. (10b)
And the door was shut.

The moment of opportunity had come, the time to respond was brief. Their lamps needed to be prepared and their jars filled with enough oil. The wise were ready and were now included in the great wedding banquet, but here the foolish find that the door has been shut and they are outside knocking, hoping to be let in. Sadly, and realistically, there are times when one can't catch the train or airplane that has left the terminal. One is reminded of Noah's ark, and how once the water started the rise, people on the outside must have realized that they missed their opportunity. The door of the ark was shut, the waters were rising. Noah wasn't such a fool after all!

Jesus continues to knock upon people's hearts. What is it that keeps people from letting Jesus in? Someday it will be too late, and the knocking will be replaced by a jolt of judgment. While there are doors that people keep shut to God and others, there is another great big door that God will someday shut. Make sure you are on the Wedding Feast side with the Bridegroom, the Bride and all who will be united in the Kingdom of Heaven.

VI. <u>Not Knowing the Lord</u> (11-12)
11 "Later the others also came. 'Lord, Lord,' they said, 'open the door for us!' 12 "But he replied, 'Truly I tell you, I don't know you.'

A. Will mercy be extended? (11)
11 "Later the others also came. 'Lord, Lord,' they said, 'open the door for us!'

The situation of the latecomers presents a predicament. All the preparations have been completed, the wedding hall door has been shut. Somehow, the late coming foolish virgins have persuaded the guards to call the Bridegroom to prove their worthiness of entry. The Bridegroom is not merciless, if indeed someone is to be included that has not quite made it. The continued assumption of entitlement by the foolish virgins is revealing itself again. This may be equivalent to those who feel "good enough" or "worthy" so as to be let into heaven by church membership, by means of genealogy, or by status and appearance of righteousness. We may recall the Wedding Banquet parable of Jesus, earlier in the Gospel of Matthew; one man was escorted out because His own robes of self-righteousness gave him away.

But when the king came in to see the guests, he noticed a man there who was not wearing wedding clothes. He asked, 'How did you get in here without wedding clothes, friend?' The man was speechless. "Then the king told the attendants, 'Tie him hand and foot, and throw him outside, into the darkness, where there will be weeping and gnashing of teeth.' "For many are invited, but few are chosen." (Matthew 22:11-14)

The problem for the late virgins turned out to be more than a problem of their oil, but of their actual state of heart, their lack of truly knowing what was important. If they did know the importance of this wedding, they would not have spent their oil on less important matters. If they had come and asked the Bridegroom to forgive them, it would have shown a heart of understanding and contrition. Perhaps then the Bridegroom would see that their repentance conveyed a desire for a relationship of reconciliation. Instead, their attitude had not changed, they demanded entrance on their own terms "open the door for us!" It was all about them, and not about the Bridegroom, the Bride and the Wedding. Their presence was not, therefore, welcome.

B. Not knowing the Lord (12)

12 "But he replied, 'Truly I tell you, I don't know you.'

The Bridegroom is aware of those virgins who didn't respond faithfully to His invitation, who didn't take their preparations seriously. He wasn't ignorant about who they were, its just that He did not "know" them as one "knows" a friend or close brother or sister. Even so, out of graciousness, the Bridegroom had given them an invitation. The issue is not identification, but identity. The concern is not for lack of an invitation, but of their lack of a faithful response. The truth is, they didn't care to know the Bridegroom when they could have developed a personal relationship of commitment, devotion and hope for His return.

Because a genuine relationship had not developed, even though the invitation had been offered, the response of the Bridegroom is fair, just and final. Later in Matthew 25, in the parable of the "Separation of the Sheep and the Goats", we will hear comparable words. However, in that parable, it will be the absence of preparation in the lack of service from the people who missed their opportunities of encountering the Lord when He was present, and knowable, within their lives.

'Lord, when did we see you hungry or thirsty or a stranger or needing clothes or sick or in prison, and did not help you?' "He will reply, 'Truly I tell you, whatever you did not do for one of the least of these, you did not do for me. (Matthew 25:44-45)

VII. <u>Be watchful and ready</u> (13)

13 "Therefore keep watch, because you do not know the day or the hour.

Jesus completes this parable by restating the premise and point of His prophetic teaching and warning. *"Therefore, keep watch!"* This is not a light suggestion, it is a clear command. The disciples, and those of coming generations, are to be ready by actively preparing for the Kingdom of Heaven. The point that Jesus has made before, *"no one knows the day or hour"*, is also reinforced, but this time with the personal pronoun: *"**you** do not know the day or the hour"*. Jesus has already indicated that only the Father God knows the day and the hour, so it is presumptuous for anyone to state exact knowledge. In this parable, Jesus reinforces the personal accountability each of His disciples are given for the care of their faith and relationship with Him. Therefore, as it pertains to being faithful to the Lord, it is essential that no one allows pride, entitlement or foolishness to divert or keep them from their appointed calling, service and priorities. Jesus prepares disciples, then and now, to be wise and ready by faithfully knowing and serving Him (this is seen in self-care and care for others).

Conclusion: God is watching. Are we mindful and serving?

Keeping watch necessitates being faithful, and this through preparations of the soul through a personal walk with God. One may indeed live into a vital and personal relationship of knowing God through faith, and this through receiving Jesus Christ. God has given His Son as Savior, and God's purpose is discovered by serving His Kingdom, and learning from His Son in His position of Lordship.

"Mindfulness", in the truest sense, is not only a great habit of thinking beyond oneself through techniques of meditative discipline; "mindfulness" in faith is being committed to walk with God in contemplation and meditation that leads to kind and thoughtful service. The best way to be watchful is to be faithfully active in the care of souls, your own and others. The Lord guides us as we listen, learn, share and trust in the power of God's presence. God's call of being present and available shall lead to shared Spirit-led blessings.

Recently, a few weeks into July, I looked out from my office window one morning and noticed a hummingbird peering in through the window as it hovered. Within less than 10 seconds it flew away. I then recalled a gift that someone had given us, a hummingbird feeder. It was still in the box, with the special feeding mix still in the bag. Some good that feeder and mix was going to be! I was reminded of the parable of the foolish virgins. I realized that if I didn't go ahead and set up the feeder, I would continue to miss further hummingbirds and forfeit a future in which the hummingbird would return, and an ongoing friendly relationship could develop.

Questions for Discussion:

1. The wise virgins saved enough oil and the foolish virgins did not. What meaning does this have as it pertains to people being ready or not for Christ's return?

2. The image of the bridegroom is given to Jesus, the virgins represent those called to accompany Jesus to the wedding. What does this parable teach about personal spiritual care and devotion to the Lord?

3. What areas of diversion, or loss of purpose, tend to sap our spiritual reserves if we are not careful?

4. In the end times, the coming of Jesus at midnight tells us that He will come in God's timing, and not ours. How do we keep awake, supported, steadfast and vigilant in readiness?

Part 8: "Accountability for All"
(Fulfilling your responsibilities)
Matthew 25:14-30

14 "Again, it will be like a man going on a journey, who called his servants and entrusted his wealth to them. 15 To one he gave five bags of gold, to another two bags, and to another one bag, each according to his ability. Then he went on his journey. 16 The man who had received five bags of gold went at once and put his money to work and gained five bags more. 17 So also, the one with two bags of gold gained two more. 18 But the man who had received one bag went off, dug a hole in the ground and hid his master's money. 19 "After a long time the master of those servants returned and settled accounts with them. 20 The man who had received five bags of gold brought the other five. 'Master,' he said, 'you entrusted me with five bags of gold. See, I have gained five more.'   21   "His master replied, 'Well done, good and faithful servant! You have been faithful with a few things; I will put you in charge of many things. Come and share your master's happiness!' 22 "The man with two bags of gold also came. 'Master,' he said, 'you entrusted me with two bags of gold; see, I have gained two more.'   23 "His master replied, 'Well done, good and faithful servant! You have been faithful with a few things; I will put you in charge of many things. Come and share your master's happiness!' 24 "Then the man who had received one bag of gold came. 'Master,' he said, 'I knew that you are a hard man, harvesting where you have not sown and gathering where you have not scattered seed. 25 So I was afraid and went out and hid your gold in the ground. See, here is what belongs to you.'   26 "His master replied, 'You wicked, lazy servant! So you knew that I harvest where I have not sown and gather where I have not scattered seed?   27 Well then, you should have put my money on deposit with the bankers, so that when I returned I would have received it back with interest.   28 "'So take the bag of gold from him and give it to the one who has ten bags. 29 For whoever has will be given more, and they will have an abundance. Whoever does not have, even what they have will be taken from them.   30 And throw that worthless servant outside, into the darkness, where there will be weeping and gnashing of teeth.'   - Matthew 25:14-30

Introduction: A way of living and bearing fruit.

Jesus was the ultimate story teller, His parables are simple and yet profound, structured and yet creative, symbolic and yet adaptable, purposeful in their time and yet applicable for all times. First, Jesus sets up the people and proceedings of the Parable of the Talents. It all began with a man who was going on a journey. This was no ordinary man, it was a man with land, fields, buildings and financial assets that all needed to be managed wisely while he was away. The "man going on a journey" may indeed be a projection of "the Son of Man", God's Son, the Lord Jesus, who holds authority and unity with God the Father. Christ's journey had brought Him to earth to give people the opportunity to participate in the work of God's Kingdom. Christ's journey away for a time gives the servants time to use their gifts fruitfully until He shall return.

One may scoff and ask, did Jesus really have lands, property and wealth? He did not, as such, have these earthly resources on paper or by law. Nonetheless, Jesus was the Son of God, and in a deeper sense, as being co-creator and Lord, He was indeed co-granter of all things with His Heavenly Father. In the story, Jesus is the man who will go on a journey, symbolically. The disciples and all of humanity, are represented by three servants, each of whom represent examples of responding to God's call and opportunity. The first two mentioned are motivated and active, enterprising and faithful. They are not overwhelmed by the opportunity given them, but are inspired to give honor and be a blessing to their master upon his return. The third servant, however, is indeed overwhelmed and anxious. His motivation is not faith, but fear, and the prospect of failure has gripped him. While the first two servants had five and two talents (bags of gold) respectively, the third was given one talent (bag of gold). What they each would do with their weight of responsibility and opportunity is how the story sets up, why they act differently is where the lesson comes in.

Twice, since I began writing this book, I have had a dream in which I climbed a ladder holding a modestly heavy medium-sized box in one arm and the ladder railing with the other hand as I climbed upward. Much to my surprise and wonder, each time I came near the top of the ladder, I began to look around to discover that I had arrived at the top of a super tall skyscraper at twilight. I would then take a deep breath, keep my cool, and step the last few rungs up the ladder unto the platform. Balancing myself from the ladder to the platform, I am aware of the height I have climbed and the potential danger. Still, the spectacular view fills me with awe, and despite my natural fear, I am comforted by a supernatural peace. The platform itself had no walls or guard rails, it is a small flat roof next to a transmission tower on top of this skyscraper. Then, after placing the box down, I would breath in the moment. Looking over the vast sparkling city below me, I appreciate the twilight's last array of colors, pink mixed with indigo blue. Instantly, I am aware of the beauty and danger of the place where I am standing. I marvel at the method of delivery of the package and how I had climbed there. I don't see who I am bringing this box to, but the import of the contents, I trust, are worth it. Whatever is contained within must be important, for I have brought the package up on a long and perilous journey. There is no wind, all is calm. For just a moment, time stands still as I stay for a moment on the platform overlooking the horizon with stars above and twinkling city lights below. Panic lightly whispers for a moment, but instead, I listen to the voice of calm, peace and reason. I take hold of the ladder and climb slowly down, my mission of delivery completed.

The meaning of parables, stories, dreams and visions can often point us to realizations of life's purpose and struggles. Each one of us are given a purpose, and are given varying degrees of talent and resource to work with. All of us are called to operate with faith, and not to let anxiety or fears keep us from achieving great things and climbing to great heights. I am still wondering what my dream was all about, but for sure I know that God has given each of us a package, talents, resources and responsibilities. If we let faith in God's presence and power lead us, we can overcome obstacles, trials and dangers. However, if we allow failure and worry to grip us, we won't be able to face the risks of life and overcome our fears. In view of the big picture of the end times and the dangers that the disciples would need to overcome, Jesus wanted His disciples to be wise and productive for God's Kingdom until He would return. The people being addressed were not simply the twelve disciples listening directly to the Lord on the Mount of Olives, Jesus message was for you and me, and for generations still to come.

Outline of Matthew 25:14-30

I. Parable: God entrusts people with resources and talents (v.14-15)
   A. The Master delegates resources and responsibility (14)
   B. The Master allocates various amounts to each person (15a)
   C. The Master gives freedom, space and time for stewardship (15b)

II. Project Implementation: What will they do? (v.16-18)
   A. Two servants were faithful and productive (16-17)
   B. One servant was unfaithful and unproductive (18)

III. The Master returns after a long time to settle accounts (v.19)

IV. Project Summary: Report of the Servants / Response of the Master (v.20-30)
   A. The first faithful servant (5 talents) (20-21)
   B. The second faithful servant (2 talents) (22-23)
   C. The third unfaithful servant (1 talent) (24-25)
      1. Negative assumptions about God (24)
      2. Fear of failure (25a)
      3. Avoidance and laziness (25b)
   D. The Master's response to the unfaithful servant (26-30)
      1. The Master confronts the servant's actions and motives (26)
      2. The Master confronts the servant's irresponsibility (27)
      3. The Master removes and reallocates his resources (28)
      4. The Master rewards & removes in accord to faithfulness (29)
      5. The Master will judge unfaithfulness with removal (30)

Study on Matthew 24:14-30

I. Parable: God entrusts people with resources and talents (v.14-15)

14 "Again, it will be like a man going on a journey, who called his servants and entrusted his wealth to them. 15 To one he gave five bags of gold, to another two bags, and to another one bag, each according to his ability. Then he went on his journey.

A. The Master delegates resources and responsibility (14)

14 "Again, it will be like a man going on a journey, who called his servants and entrusted his wealth to them.

Trust is essential for community to exist and be vital and fruitful. When trust is established and upheld, people can count on one another and work cooperatively with great results that bring forth blessings. When trust is broken, cooperation is strained and blessings are hindered by conflict, chaos and a loss of commitment.

The man going on a journey in this parable has great wealth and resources. He has faith that his servants can be given responsibility and be trusted. He knows their talents and capability. This man is not one to sit still as He is needed in another place for important business. He is wise and prudent, willing to risk leaving his estate to go on a journey. The master's faith to venture forth while trusting his servants with responsibility, even while he would be physically absent, tells us something about the change coming for Jesus and His disciples. They too would be physically separated, and the disciples would be given responsibilities. How well would they remain faithful, and would they be wise and fruitful in the use of their gifts.

The story also speaks to how God has entrusted all people with talents and resources of varying degrees, and that we are each given freedom, time and space to use what God has granted us. Will we be faithful and fruitful so we may please God? Will we seize the opportunity of life and bless God and others? The master, or man, has delegated resources and calls his servants to a higher level of responsibility, one in which their activity is not an obligation, but a calling involving personal governance and accountability without his direct oversight.

B. The Master allocates various amounts to each person (15a)

15 To one he gave five bags of gold, to another two bags, and to another one bag, each according to his ability.

The master already knows about the gifts, talents and personal characteristics of each servant. He gives each one the amount and type that they will be capable of handling. The amount of ability is not as important as using one's abilities. There are some people who have one primary ability that is genius level, amazing! When a specialist is needed, or a high level of competence in a specialization is required, this is the one you want to rely on. They may be a brain surgeon or a concert pianist, a court judge or a movie director. What they can do with a specialization, a focus, is a gift.

Then there are others who have multiple talents and abilities, and they juggle these talents with adaptability according to what is needed. They are often problem solvers and can bring people together in teamwork, or be good teammates. The issue in this parable is not about ability, but about willingness to work and be trusted. God gives us Spiritual gifts, talents, time, money and the opportunity to use these. When the Master returns, what will he find?

C. The Master gives freedom, space and time for stewardship (15b)

Then he went on his journey.

Jesus had His departure in mind, He indeed would be going on a journey. The metaphor of travel is used by the Lord as He refers to how this "man" would go away for a time. Jesus, the Master, had given instruction through His life in examples, direct teaching, and through experiences for the disciples to learn by. Now, the time had come for the Master to leave, and they would soon be on their own. Spiritually, they would not be without the help of the Holy Spirit or without the promise of Jesus' ultimate place at the right hand of the throne of God, where He intercedes for them. We are reminded that the same is true today for all people. We are each made with a purpose and God gives all of us the potential of development, growth and the hope of bearing good fruit, all this while seeking God's wisdom and the Holy Spirit in using our abilities and resources. Jesus gives each of us time to believe and space to serve. What will our response be? How well shall we fulfill our destiny and purpose?

II. Project Implementation: What would they do? (v.16-18)

16 The man who had received five bags of gold went at once and put his money to work and gained five bags more. 17 So also, the one with two bags of gold gained two more. 18 But the man who had received one bag went off, dug a hole in the ground and hid his master's money.

A. Two servants were faithful and productive (16-17)

16 The man who had received five bags of gold went at once and put his money to work and gained five bags more. 17 So also, the one with two bags of gold gained two more.

These two servants did not waste time getting busy. At once they put their money, and their wisdom and talents, to work. The result was that they doubled the initial amount they were given by the master. Faithfulness and productivity often complement each other. Of course, this is a parable that doesn't take various details of adversity and challenge into account. For a parable that illustrates adversity and competition, one might want to consider the parable of the different soils that the good seed is planted into (see Luke 8:4-15 about the rocky, shallow, weed-ridden and clean soils). For now, the idea is that hard work, intentionality, use of talents, will most often result in some form of an increase. This is an essential formula for work and success. How we define success and what constitutes healthy growth are another issue.

B. One servant was unfaithful and unproductive (18)

18 But the man who had received one bag went off, dug a hole in the ground and hid his master's money.

This third servant, however, did not go at once to work. The words "went off" suggest a bad start. Instead of getting right to it, the third servant delayed action and allowed anxiety to limit his actions and his options. The third servant made false assumptions of his capability and likelihood of failure. He presumed that the master would be so hard-nosed as to be concerned about getting back the amount he was given. Simply put, the third man was the victim of his own fears, and allowed *"stinkin' thinkin'"* to halt effort. He buried the master's money!

Although most of us would not want to admit it, we too bury or hide our talents. The need for someone to step forward and volunteer their talents, energies or time is often met with silence.

The need for people to give their money to help others in need during a catastrophe may be met by a fear of letting their resources go, just in case they personally might need it. The problem of digging holes, burying our talents and letting fear rule over faith keeps people from becoming their best. When people deny ownership of responsibility, there is a lack of initiative. All people are given some level of responsibility and opportunity. Faith helps us grow and bless others, fear disables our abilities and inhibits our potential.

III. The Master returns after a long time to settle accounts (v.19)

19 "After a long time the master of those servants returned and settled accounts with them.

Jesus will come again; the Master will return to settle accounts. Though people may think that Jesus will never come, His delay by God the Father is for a reason, for the extension of grace to more and more people. God offers the greatest gift, the greatest treasure, the Gospel of God's saving and redeeming love. In the final analysis, in account to God the Father and our Lord Jesus Christ, what will our report be? What will we do with the life and talents that we have been granted? Will we be faithful to share the good seed and truth of the Gospel? Will we bless people with love and grace through our gifts and abilities? Ultimately, will our lives reflect Christ's calling and presence and glorify God?

IV. Project Summary: Report of the Servants / Response of the Master (v.20-30)

20 The man who had received five bags of gold brought the other five. 'Master,' he said, 'you entrusted me with five bags of gold. See, I have gained five more.' 21 "His master replied, 'Well done, good and faithful servant! You have been faithful with a few things; I will put you in charge of many things. Come and share your master's happiness!' 22 "The man with two bags of gold also came. 'Master,' he said, 'you entrusted me with two bags of gold; see, I have gained two more.' 23 "His master replied, 'Well done, good and faithful servant! You have been faithful with a few things; I will put you in charge of many things. Come and share your master's happiness!' 24 "Then the man who had received one bag of gold came. 'Master,' he said, 'I knew that you are a hard man, harvesting where you have not sown and gathering where you have not scattered seed. 25 So I was afraid and went out and hid your gold in the ground. See, here is what belongs to you.' 26 "His master replied, 'You wicked, lazy servant! So you knew that I harvest where I have not sown and gather where I have not scattered seed? 27 Well then, you should have put my money on deposit with the bankers, so that when I returned I would have received it back with interest. 28 "'So take the bag of gold from him and give it to the one who has ten bags. 29 For whoever has will be given more, and they will have an abundance. Whoever does not have, even what they have will be taken from them. 30 And throw that worthless servant outside, into the darkness, where there will be weeping and gnashing of teeth.'

A. The first faithful servant (5 talents) (20-21)

20 The man who had received five bags of gold brought the other five. 'Master,' he said, 'you entrusted me with five bags of gold. See, I have gained five more.' 21 "His master replied, 'Well done, good and faithful servant! You have been faithful with a few things; I will put you in charge of many things. Come and share your master's happiness!'

The first servant's success is celebrated and rewarded by the Master. His reward was praise and appreciation initially, then added trust in a promotion of responsibility and influence. The added level of accomplishment was matched by an added level of leadership, trust and value. The master praised and rewarded him, inviting him to a party at His home. This is a foretelling of the servant's reward, for faithful believers, a reward for faithful service in God's Kingdom and the joy of being part of God's new work. Indeed, the happiness shall be celebrated in a party, the great reunion in heaven.

B. The second faithful servant (2 talents) (22-23)

22 "The man with two bags of gold also came. 'Master,' he said, 'you entrusted me with two bags of gold; see, I have gained two more.' 23 "His master replied, 'Well done, good and faithful servant! You have been faithful with a few things; I will put you in charge of many things. Come and share your master's happiness!'

This second servant has succeeded in the same way as the first. His reward will be the same. It is comforting to know that God is just and fair, not indiscriminate or prone to favoritism. God is full of praise for those who are faithful, and will use their gifts, talents and resources for His Kingdom.

C. The third unfaithful servant (1 talent) (24-25)

24 "Then the man who had received one bag of gold came. 'Master,' he said, 'I knew that you are a hard man, harvesting where you have not sown and gathering where you have not scattered seed. 25 So I was afraid and went out and hid your gold in the ground. See, here is what belongs to you.' 26 "His master replied, 'You wicked, lazy servant! So you knew that I harvest where I have not sown and gather where I have not scattered seed? 27 Well then, you should have put my money on deposit with the bankers, so that when I returned I would have received it back with interest. 28 "'So take the bag of gold from him and give it to the one who has ten bags. 29 For whoever has will be given more, and they will have an abundance. Whoever does not have, even what they have will be taken from them. 30 And throw that worthless servant outside, into the darkness, where there will be weeping and gnashing of teeth.'

For those who are unfaithful, what they have "sown" shall determine what they shall "reap". Already, we can sense what will happen to the third servant. Jesus has told the story in a way that the listener may identify with the master. The listener can anticipate what the just actions of the master may be. Hearing the rant and complaints of the unfaithful servant, one can also detect a self-defeating attitude that has led to his failure. The canvas of potential was open, either he did not trust his abilities (a lack of faith), or he let excuses prohibit action. Like many of us, he rationalized procrastination. The master repeats his own words back to him, which reflect the problems of laziness, a negative attitude, anxiety and fear. Instead of filling in the blank, he left the blank unfilled; his action was inaction. Instead of just doing something, and taking a minimal risk; He did nothing and took no risk. The result of not applying himself was not only disappointing, it would lead to discipline and the redistribution of his talent (bag of gold).

1. <u>Negative assumptions about God</u> (24)

   24 "Then the man who had received one bag of gold came. 'Master,' he said, 'I knew that you are a hard man, harvesting where you have not sown and gathering where you have not scattered seed.

Why is it that people allow their assumptions about God to hinder their faith or limit their initiative? If the third, unfaithful, servant thought he could appeal to God's mercy by means of cowering, of using his pretense of anxiety as a coverup for laziness, he would soon discover that the master was not gullible. The unfaithful servant should have focused upon his own responsibility. Instead, he was focused upon the master's use of position and power. The viewpoint of the servant was not a positive one, but a distorted perspective. Instead of appreciating the opportunity given to him, the servant resented the master's authority.

2. Fear of failure (25a)
25 So I was afraid and went out and hid your gold in the ground.

For fear of failure, and with an attitude of ingratitude, the servant rationalized His negative attitude. While he might be maneuvering for sympathy from the Master, the Master will recognize the foolishness of his inaction, and see the deeper issue; the foolish servant was projecting a mistrust in the kindness and generosity of the Master by hiding the gold in the ground. Ultimately, when people hide their gifts and do not risk serving, loving, or caring, the underlying issue is mistrust, fear and loss of faith in God and in one's abilities and potential.

3. Avoidance and laziness (25b)
See, here is what belongs to you.'

This moment of giving the bag of gold back to the Master, even without apology, with sarcasm intonated, was a verbal backhanded insult. This passive aggressive avoidance of responsibility was like the servant telling the master: "I know better than you what I am capable of". Underneath it all, the servant didn't respect his master's intent or trust his master's motivation. If the wicked servant had any decency and humility, he would have apologized and asked for another chance to prove himself. However, like a scene from a movie, one could imagine the servant throwing the bag of coins at the Master, saying: "Here, take your filthy, dirty, money!" The problem wasn't the money, but the way in which the money had been handled and the way the servant viewed the money. Instead of responding with faithfulness, the servant was infected with bitterness, his own teeth gnashing with contempt.

D. The Master's response to the unfaithful servant (26-30)

26 "His master replied, 'You wicked, lazy servant! So you knew that I harvest where I have not sown and gather where I have not scattered seed? 27 Well then, you should have put my money on deposit with the bankers, so that when I returned I would have received it back with interest. 28 "'So take the bag of gold from him and give it to the one who has ten bags. 29 For whoever has will be given more, and they will have an abundance. Whoever does not have, even what they have will be taken from them. 30 And throw that worthless servant outside, into the darkness, where there will be weeping and gnashing of teeth.'

What will the master do? What will he say? The master cuts through the false humility of the unfaithful servant. The servant was *"wicked"* and *"lazy"*. The master repeats the false assumption that was stated so shrewdly by the servant. *"Well then"*, gives us the warning that the master is not happy and has made a decision. Jesus teaches that there is consequence to inaction as much as there is consequence in acting foolishly and failing. The key difference is that inaction will always fail. In God's accounting, some sort of attempt is expected, and will yield at least a modest result. Indeed, through applied faith one will at least grow in "interest" and "knowledge" that can later be given another chance or opportunity.

1. The Master confronts the servant's actions and motives (26)

26 "His master replied, 'You wicked, lazy servant! So you knew that I harvest where I have not sown and gather where I have not scattered seed?

The Master confronts the servant for his loss of character and trust. At the root of his soul the servant is *"wicked"*, not willing to believe, obey or apply himself. The core problem of wickedness is then also coupled with *"laziness"*, a lack of motivation and purpose in life. Instead of embracing the opportunity to serve for the growth of the master's estate, and see his part in it; the servant resists by using the excuse of not meeting the expectations of the master. Within the servant's heart, there is a rebellious jealousy, a spirit of hostility, anger and resentment. The master has exposed the wicked servant's motives for inaction. Someday, God will expose people's sinful motives for inaction, disbelief and disobedience.

2. <u>The Master confronts the servant's irresponsibility</u> (27)
27 Well then, you should have put my money on deposit with the bankers, so that when I returned I would have received it back with interest.

The Master expected that his servant would have applied himself with the very minimum amount of care and responsibility. The very least he could have done is put the money in the bank for a return of interest. Someday, God will confront people about why they didn't take simple or basic steps of faith. Taking the money to the bank for investment is an honest way of letting others help you invest when you don't have an idea, or if you don't have a plan for starting or expanding a business. The foolish servant was unwilling to seek advice, too proud to let others help him. Putting the money in the ground, in fact, was itself even more risky and irresponsible.

3. <u>The Master removes and reallocates his resources</u> (28)
28 "'So take the bag of gold from him and give it to the one who has ten bags.

The Master will remove the servant's bag of gold, the talent that he had entrusted him to invest. Someday, God will remove and reallocate those unused (or unwisely used) resources and talents to those who are trustworthy. The world as we know it now is full of misappropriation and corruption. The problem of abuse of authority is also matched by the problem of lack of respect for authority.

4. The Master rewards & removes in accord to faithfulness (29)

29 For whoever has will be given more, and they will have an abundance. Whoever does not have, even what they have will be taken from them.

Ultimately, the coming reign of Christ will involve a big shakeup in who will be responsible for the management and development of the world's resources. For those who have been faithful and wise in the Master's service, they shall receive appreciation and promotion in accordance to their proven record and character. For those who have not been faithful, there shall be a time of reckoning, a time of discipline and demotion.

At first read, this sounds like a case for Christian capitalism, however, Jesus is referring to God's justice and the coming of His Kingdom. The reward and incentive of "more", referred to here, is that of increased participation in God's kingdom, not a personal and fleeting increase of wealth and financial gain. The abundance is also not simply material, it is an abundance of respect, joy, hope, purpose, fulfillment, friendships, goodness and grace; and this all within God's Kingdom. Anyone who uses this parable of the Kingdom of Heaven for leading people to toward a "gospel of prosperity", placing the love of money and wealth as a high priority, is on shaky sandy ground. Apostacy may fill one's bank account nicely, or allow one to build temporal wealth, but it doesn't impress Jesus. God the Father is looking for those who will worship in Spirit and in Truth. Jesus calls people to build up treasures in Heaven where moth and rust shall not destroy, to do this one follows Jesus with humility and service.

5. The Master will judge unfaithfulness with removal (30)
    30 And throw that worthless servant outside, into the darkness, where there will be weeping and gnashing of teeth.'

The Master had given the unfaithful servant an opportunity, a chance to redeem himself. While the servant began with potential, he ended with self-defeat. While he was capable, his negative attitude and laziness revealed a deeper matter of distrust and hatred of the Master. The consequence would be dismissal, removal from the Master's household and realm of authority. Here is where the severity of his banishment tells us something of the warning contained in the parable that is pertinent to Jesus Christ and the Kingdom of God. Outside of the Kingdom of God there is *"darkness"*, a void and separation from the source and giver of life. Outside of the Kingdom of God, death is at work in the inevitable destruction of unbelievers, the disobedient and wicked. The *"weeping"* here is not that of a repentant or redemptive type, it is that of a revengeful and bitter type as evidenced in the *"gnashing"*. The unfaithful servant began "gnashing" his teeth in rebellion before the Master's righteous decision. The judgment of God is both reasonable and necessary. The future of God's Kingdom will be developed upon a "clean slate"; corruption and evil must be purged for a new beginning.

Conclusion: Why is this parable so important?

People without faith and trust in God will often justify their disbelief because they look at all the things that are not perfect, much as the foolish servant looked at the flaws of his master's realm of operation. Instead of trusting in what the master had given him, the foolish servant believed a set of false assumptions. There are many people who believe a set of false assumptions about God, and this keeps them from faith and service in God's Kingdom. For those who have been faithful, they have believed in the word and good will of the Master. They chose to apply themselves with the time, resources and freedom they are granted.

Again, I go back to the dream I was given. There I was, standing upon a ladder at the top of a high skyscraper, holding a box in one arm to be delivered and holding on to the last rung. What is in the box? Why is this delivery important, especially to this perilous location? Why am I the one to deliver the package? Instead of continuing with why questions, I am inspired to think and say, "why not?" The leading of God's Holy Spirit, and the invitation of God's Son Jesus, is to say "yes", thank you Lord for the opportunity. Thank you Lord that you trust me with a great responsibility. I trust that you hold me up in situations of risk and danger. There is nothing that can separate me from your love if I am faithful to your work, in tune with your will and intent on fulfilling your purposes.

There is also another interpretation, one I pray about. What if I am like the unfaithful servant? What if I'm hiding my gift in a lofty unreachable place? I am reminded that the highest and sincerest intentions will not replace humble action and service. Ultimately, the story is about doing the will of God.

Questions for Discussion:

1. In this Parable of the Talents, what are the two essentially different ways that people approach work and opportunity?

2. Why are some people trouble makers? What are the complaints and excuses they use to justify their negative attitudes or complaints?

3. What were the Master's responses to the three servants? What would you have done if you were the Master?

4. Where do false assumptions about God originate from? How are negative beliefs about God, Christians and the Church perpetuated?

5. As you consider your own responsibilities, what is in your "box" of gifts/talents to use or deliver faithfully? What duties and responsibilities has God given you to act upon for His Glory?

Part 9: "God's Judgment in Christ's Coming"

(Praise or punishment: attentiveness or neglect)
Matthew 25:31-46

31 "When the Son of Man comes in his glory, and all the angels with him, he will sit on his glorious throne. 32 All the nations will be gathered before him, and he will separate the people one from another as a shepherd separates the sheep from the goats. 33 He will put the sheep on his right and the goats on his left. 34 "Then the King will say to those on his right, 'Come, you who are blessed by my Father; take your inheritance, the kingdom prepared for you since the creation of the world. 35 For I was hungry and you gave me something to eat, I was thirsty and you gave me something to drink, I was a stranger and you invited me in, 36 I needed clothes and you clothed me, I was sick and you looked after me, I was in prison and you came to visit me.' 37 "Then the righteous will answer him, 'Lord, when did we see you hungry and feed you, or thirsty and give you something to drink? 38 When did we see you a stranger and invite you in, or needing clothes and clothe you? 39 When did we see you sick or in prison and go to visit you?' 40 "The King will reply, 'Truly I tell you, whatever you did for one of the least of these brothers and sisters of mine, you did for me.' 41 "Then he will say to those on his left, 'Depart from me, you who are cursed, into the eternal fire prepared for the devil and his angels. 42 For I was hungry and you gave me nothing to eat, I was thirsty and you gave me nothing to drink, 43 I was a stranger and you did not invite me in, I needed clothes and you did not clothe me, I was sick and in prison and you did not look after me.' 44 "They also will answer, 'Lord, when did we see you hungry or thirsty or a stranger or needing clothes or sick or in prison, and did not help you?' 45 "He will reply, 'Truly I tell you, whatever you did not do for one of the least of these, you did not do for me.' 46 "Then they will go away to eternal punishment, but the righteous to eternal life." Matthew 25:31-46

Introduction: Jesus will come in resplendent glory.

Unlike the analogies and parables of the Kingdom of God that precede this passage, this is a vision, a prophetic telling of an actual, coming, event. The parables were indirect and symbolic, this is direct. Jesus employed analogies to give illustration, and parables to create memorable and understandable narratives, that pointed to a greater reality. This concluding story/vision is a hybrid, built from both the direct warnings and teachings of Jesus and His analogies and parables. From that basis, Jesus could then, logically and powerfully, present a direct vision of what shall come to pass. Jesus is giving away a glimpse of God's plan, a narrative of what God will do. God and His Son Jesus the Christ have a plan that involves the Son coming in power and glory; this will consummate the era of grace that is the hallmark of the "Church Era", eventually being completed at the Day of Judgment, the *separation of the sheep and the goats*". Jesus continues in story language to more directly reveal what the experience of His coming shall involve and what the nature and criteria of judgment shall entail.

The vision Jesus gave here is not only powerful and dramatic, it is engaging, personal and practical. By this time, in this Olivet Discourse, Jesus' disciples were beginning to think about what the practical application of this dramatic prophetic visionary journey presented by their Master. Jesus developed His teaching on the Mount of Olives within a biblically parallel prophetic pattern: 1. Predictions of Woe, 2. Signs of Warning, 3. Narratives for watchfulness, and 4. A revelation of wonder and witness that leads to accountable action for humanity and an ultimate judgment by God (this passage). Everything Jesus has said looking down from upon the Mount of Olives to His disciples will support this final vision of service, and the ultimate monumental unveiling of Christ's authority in His return and the subsequent judgment of all people.

A reverential approach to this passage is essential. If anyone dissects this Scripture without also seeing how it applies to themselves, they are missing Jesus' intent. Jesus taught this lesson for it to change His disciples, to solidify a vision of what the coming Judgment will be like and what their responsibility must be. In the reflection of Scottish Bible scholar, Alexander MacLaren we read:

> *The teachings of that wonderful last day of Christ's ministry, which have occupied so many of our pages, are closed with this tremendous picture of universal judgment. It is one to be gazed upon with silent awe, rather than to be commented on. There is fear lest, in occupying the mind in the study of the details, and trying to pierce the mystery it partly unfolds, we should forget our own individual share in it. Better to burn in on our hearts the thought, 'I shall be there,' than to lose the solemn impression in efforts to unravel the difficulties of the passage. Difficulties there are,*

as is to be expected in even Christ's revelation of so unparalleled a scene. Many questions are raised by it which will never be solved till we stand there. Who can tell how much of the parabolic element enters into the description? We, at all events, do not venture to say of one part, 'This is merely drapery, the sensuous representation of spiritual reality,' and of another, 'That is essential truth.' The curtain is the picture, and before we can separate the elements of it in that fashion, we must have lived through it. Let us try to grasp the main lessons, and not lose the spirit in studying the letter. (MacLaren's Expositions of Holy Scripture).

Outline of Matthew 25:31-46

I. Vision: Jesus will come and judge the peoples of the earth (v.31-33)
   A. Christ Jesus comes in glory with divine authority (31)
   B. All nations will gather for judgment (32a)
   C. Like a Shepherd, He separates the sheep from the goats (32b)
   D. Sheep are on his right, goats on his left (33)

II. Declaration of favorable Judgment for the sheep (v.34-40)
   A. Welcome and blessing from God the Father (34a)
   B. Reward of inheritance of God's Kingdom (34b)
   C. God's plan of redemption since the creation of the world (34c)
   D. Determination of inheritance – faith in action (35-36)
      1. Helping the hungry (35a)
      2. Supplying the thirsty (35b)
      3. Housing the stranger (35c)
      4. Clothing people in need (36a)

5. Caring for the sick (36b)
6. Visiting those in prison (36c)
E. Surprise of the sheep – presence of Jesus in life (37-39)
F. Service for others is service for King Jesus (v.40)

III. Declaration of unfavorable Judgment for the goats (v.41-45)
    A. Banishment of the cursed into the eternal fire (v.41)
        1. The goats are banished (41a)
        2. The devil and his angels are banished in the eternal fire (41b)
    B. Determination of their destruction – no evidence of faith (42-43)
        1. Didn't feed the hungry
        2. Didn't offer a drink to the thirsty
        3. Didn't invite the stranger in
        4. Didn't clothe the naked
        5. Didn't care for the sick or imprisoned
    C. Surprise of the goats – When did we see you? (44)
    D. Missed opportunity of seeing, serving and knowing Jesus (45)
IV. Final Judgment (The Kingdom of Heaven or destruction in Hell) (46)

Study on Matthew 25:31-46

I. <u>Vision: Jesus will come and judge the peoples of the earth</u> (v.31-33)

31 "When the Son of Man comes in his glory, and all the angels with him, he will sit on his glorious throne. 32 All the nations will be gathered before him, and he will separate the people one from another as a shepherd separates the sheep from the goats. 33 He will put the sheep on his right and the goats on his left.

A. Christ Jesus comes in glory with divine authority (31)

31 "When the Son of Man comes in his glory, and all the angels with him, he will sit on his glorious throne.

A time is coming when Jesus the Christ, the *"Son of Man"*, will return to earth. This time, unlike His first incarnation, Jesus' will come vested with power and shining brilliantly with God's glory. There will be no mistaking His identity or Divinity. Christ's authority will be manifest in startling pure light, beautiful and wondrous. A description of Christ's appearance after the resurrection was given by the disciple John from His encounter on the Island of Patmos:

I turned around to see the voice that was speaking to me. And when I turned I saw seven golden lampstands, and among the lampstands was someone like a son of man, dressed in a robe reaching down to his feet and with a golden sash around his chest. The hair on his head was white like wool, as white as snow, and his eyes were like blazing fire. His feet were like bronze glowing in a furnace, and his voice was like the sound of rushing waters. In his right hand he held seven stars, and coming out of his mouth was a sharp, double-edged sword. His face was like the sun shining in all its brilliance. When I saw him, I fell at his feet as though dead. Then he placed his right hand on me and said: "Do not be afraid. I am the First and the Last. I am the Living One; I was dead, and now look, I am alive for ever and ever! And I hold the keys of death and Hades. – (Revelation 1:12-19)

Like the night He was born, the angels will announce and celebrate His arrival; yet this time Jesus is leading the way in their midst, and in the skies. Without delay, the mission of His Second Coming is declared, as Jesus speaks in third person about His own purpose and authority: *"He will sit on His glorious throne"* (Matthew 25:31). Jesus shall come to finish God's work of salvation and judgment.

Where, when and how shall this glorious, and fearsome, throne appearance of Jesus Christ occur? The answer is partially a mystery. Still, it is essential to note that there are two revelations of enthronement pertaining to Christ. These enthronements are revealed after the many details of trial and tribulation, as so written down in the book of Revelation. The first enthronement, the one that Jesus is referring to here on the Mount of Olives, shall be the "Great White Throne" judgment:

> Then I saw a great white throne and him who was seated on it. The earth and the heavens fled from his presence, and there was no place for them. And I saw the dead, great and small, standing before the throne, and books were opened. (Revelation 20:11-12)

In the Second enthronement, Christ shall be seated at the right hand of the Thone of God His Heavenly Father in the New Jerusalem, within the City of God that shall appear at the center of a redeemed New Heaven and New Earth.

> The throne of God and of the Lamb will be in the city, and his servants will serve him. They will see his face, and his name will be on their foreheads. There will be no more night. They will not need the light of a lamp or the light of the sun, for the Lord God will give them light. And they will reign for ever and ever. – (Revelation 22:3-5)

B. All nations will gather for judgment (32a)

32 All the nations will be gathered before him,

In the great judgment of the white throne, all nations will be gathered before Christ Jesus. The complete and universal judgment of God, through Jesus Christ, will include all people of every race, nation and culture who live upon the earth. There are different theories about whether this is a judgment that involves the Church (born again believers), or if the Church would already be among those pardoned and accepted by God's gift of grace received by faith, and thereby they would not be among the great host of the nations who will be gathered before Him at this judgment. This is a mystery, and the best thing to do is be ready, in any event, by being faithful to God's call.

Therefore, while we don't know all the details about where the "taken up" moment of the "Rapture" fits in to this judgment, there are several postulated scenarios to note. One, is that the "taken up" are already in Heaven and are exempt from this judgment. Two, is that the "taken up" will be brought back after the great tribulation to be included in this judgment. Three, is that there is no Rapture or time when the elect will be "taken up", but that all will share in the trials and tribulations of the end times and will need to appear before the Christ. (In this author's opinion, the first scenario makes the most sense and fits best with all of Scripture; the second scenario is not out of the question, and the third scenario denies any sort of Parousia or Rapture).

Ultimately, the important truth here is that Jesus will come again, and He will administer salvation and judgment on behalf of the Kingdom of Heaven as it shall be established upon the earth. His coming and appearance will be truly powerful and His judgment is inevitable.

C. Like a Shepherd, He separates the sheep from the goats (32b)

and he will separate the people one from another as a shepherd separates the sheep from the goats.

Jesus is the Good Shepherd of Ezekiel 34. The shepherds of the world have had their day, and now the presence of God's Son coming in the fulness of God's plan will precipitate judgment. In this event, there shall be a separation of the redeemed from those who are not born of God's Spirit (the unfaithful). Ezekiel spoke about God's judgment involving accountability to the unfaithful shepherds and mercy leading to salvation for the "sheep" or "flock":

9 therefore, you shepherds, hear the word of the Lord: 10 This is what the Sovereign Lord says: I am against the shepherds and will hold them accountable for my flock. I

will remove them from tending the flock so that the shepherds can no longer feed themselves. I will rescue my flock from their mouths, and it will no longer be food for them. 11 "'For this is what the Sovereign Lord says: I myself will search for my sheep and look after them. 12 As a shepherd looks after his scattered flock when he is with them, so will I look after my sheep. I will rescue them from all the places where they were scattered on a day of clouds and darkness. 13 I will bring them out from the nations and gather them from the countries, and I will bring them into their own land. I will pasture them on the mountains of Israel, in the ravines and in all the settlements in the land. 14 I will tend them in a good pasture, and the mountain heights of Israel will be their grazing land. There they will lie down in good grazing land, and there they will feed in a rich pasture on the mountains of Israel. 15 I myself will tend my sheep and have them lie down, declares the Sovereign Lord. 16 I will search for the lost and bring back the strays. I will bind up the injured and strengthen the weak, but the sleek and the strong I will destroy. I will shepherd the flock with justice.*
– (Ezekiel 34:9-17)

Now if anyone assumes that God is uninterested or uninvolved in humanity's "Game of Thrones", where people have tried to manipulate and manage their "flocks" without regard to justice and righteousness, this passage is a reminder that in the final analysis God will hold all people into account, no matter their status or title.

D. Sheep are on his right, goats on his left (33)

33 He will put the sheep on his right and the goats on his left.

According to Jewish legal proceedings, when a decision was reached in the courts of the Sanhedrin, the acquitted (innocent) would be placed on the right, while those found guilty would be placed on the left of the Sanhedrin:

The right hand is always represented as the place of honor and preferment. The Jews in their traditions say that when criminals were tried by the Sanhedrin those who were acquitted were placed on the right hand, and those who were condemned on the left. (J. W. McGarvey and Philip Y. Pendleton. "Commentary on Matthew 25:33". "The Fourfold Gospel" 1914).

God's placement is based upon reasons that God and His Son Jesus may best determine by means of full knowledge and wisdom to apply righteousness, grace, mercy and justice. The separation is God's final decision and division, and must occur for the New Jerusalem to come from Heaven, along with His Heavenly Kingdom.

II. Declaration of favorable Judgment for the sheep (v.34-40)

34 "Then the King will say to those on his right, 'Come, you who are blessed by my Father; take your inheritance, the kingdom prepared for you since the creation of the world. 35 For I was hungry and you gave me something to eat, I was thirsty and you gave me something to drink, I was a stranger and you invited me in, 36 I needed clothes and you clothed me, I was sick and you looked after me, I was in prison and you came to visit me.' 37 "Then the righteous will answer him, 'Lord, when did we see you hungry and feed you, or thirsty and give you something to drink? 38 When did we see you a stranger and invite you in, or needing clothes and clothe you? 39 When did we see you sick or in prison and go to visit you?' 40 "The King will reply, 'Truly I tell you, whatever you did for one of the least of these brothers and sisters of mine, you did for me.'

This first group received by Jesus shall receive a favorable judgment. The Lord rejoices in their salvation and their inheritance to receive the Kingdom of Heaven. Their acceptance into Heaven wasn't only a matter of their good works, their salvation was because they had been born again, and the Spirit of God had begun to work in and through their lives. Their actions of faith were the evidence presented in the court of God to substantiate the change of heart and mind that accompanied being born again of God's Holy Spirit.

Jesus had changed their lives and had entered their hearts and minds. Consequently, their inspired way of looking at the world, and how they internally responded to people and situations of need had motivated their actions. Paul put it this way to the church:

> 1 Therefore if you have any encouragement from being united with Christ, if any comfort from his love, if any common sharing in the Spirit, if any tenderness and compassion, 2 then make my joy complete by being like-minded, having the same love, being one in spirit and of one mind. 3 Do nothing out of selfish ambition or vain conceit. Rather, in humility value others above yourselves, 4 not looking to your own interests but each of you to the interests of the others. 5 In your relationships with one another, have the same mindset as Christ Jesus: 6 Who, being in very nature God, did not consider equality with God something to be used to his own advantage; 7 rather, he made himself nothing by taking the very nature of a servant, being made in human likeness. – (Philippians 2:1-7)

Being united with Christ, having truly received Him, had made the early church believers tender-hearted, compassionate, unselfish, gracious and humble; they were like-minded to the way and leading of their Lord Jesus Christ.

Why the Lord begins with this group is worth consideration. First, God graciously does not leave His people in limbo at the Judgment, they are immediately rewarded. The Lord is eager to shower them with His Kingdom, to clothe them completely in His righteousness. Second, God has an order of entry, those who have been faithful are the first to receive their inheritance. Third, God will bring them in to spare them the painful observance of those who will not enter the Kingdom of Heaven. The difficult matter of administering punishment is something God will complete with Christ working alongside His angels, and it won't be pretty. With the final judgment of the nations, at the great white throne, the redeemed will go into the Kingdom of Heaven, and await the swift cleansing of the earth, the judgment to the goats (the faithless and rebellious), and the destruction of hell and its legion of fallen angels. We read of the face-off between Christ and the devil. As the camp of God's people are under attack within the city that God loves, Christ takes charge by sending fire from Heaven to defeat Satan and then the Lord throws the devil and his minions into the "lake of burning sulfur".

> *9 They marched across the breadth of the earth and surrounded the camp of God's people, the city he loves. But fire came down from heaven and devoured them. 10 And the devil, who deceived them, was thrown into the lake of burning sulfur, where the beast and the false prophet had been thrown. They will be tormented day and night for ever and ever.* – (Revelation 20:9-10)

Further on, we read of the destruction of death and hell (Hades). Again, this cleansing judgment is necessary in God's preparation of a New Heaven and Earth. For those who had not come to faith, who were not born again of God's Holy Spirit, their names would not be found in the *"Book of Life"*, they too would be *"thrown into the lake of fire"*.

> *14 Then death and Hades were thrown into the lake of fire. The lake of fire is the second death. 15 Anyone whose name was not found written in the book of life was thrown into the lake of fire.* - (Revelation 20:14-15)

Now that we have had an overview of this passage, let's take a closer look to go through Matthew 24:34-40, verse by verse.

A. Welcome and blessing from God the Father (34a)

34 "Then the King will say to those on his right, 'Come, you who are blessed by my Father;

The voice of Jesus, the King for our hearts, will say that blessed word, *"Come"*. He shall speak on behalf of God His Heavenly Father's love, and will speak from His own knowledge in loving each of us. All who believe will respond in faith. They shall be brought to the right hand of God's throne, to the side of God's Son, the very place of grace. As noted, the right side of a Hebrew judge was the side of acquittal and forgiveness. The grace and favor of God, to all who believe, is based upon genuine repentance and the reception of internal baptism that is transformative for a person to be born again of God's Holy Spirit. If we are on the Lord's side, trusting in Jesus, we are oriented to the One who has paid our penalty, the One who can defend our case before the Heavenly Father. Jesus is the One who gives new life that is born of God's deposit of grace in the Holy Spirit. This gift is still available to all who believe by faith, and is maintained through devotion and acts of service.

B. Reward of inheritance of God's Kingdom (34b)

take your inheritance, the kingdom

The Kingdom of God is therefore a gift, and we are called to respond in faith. The faith which people come to in response to God's invitation is the same kind of faith that one needs to take in their final step into God's Kingdom by responding to Jesus' final call. Come and *"take"* the *"inheritance, the Kingdom"*. Believe, don't delay. Seize the moment of grace, seize the hope realized in the resurrection. This same hope involves the daily steps we all take toward the New Heaven and New Earth. When God blesses His people, God wants us not to hesitate, but to take what God shall prepare for us. When Jesus broke the bread, and blessed it at Passover, He said: *"Take, eat, this is my body which is broken for you."* The substance of our hope shall one day be realized, Jesus will be revealed in all the wonder and beauty of God's glory. He gave His life, the perfect Lamb of God, for us, that we may inherit the Kingdom of Heaven.

C. God's plan of redemption since the creation of the world (34c)
prepared for you since the creation of the world.

The preparation of Heaven has been God's design right from the beginning. While Adam and Eve began the human experience, God was always planning and preparing for the final stage, His Heavenly Kingdom, to be our destiny. In Genesis, when Adam and Eve were created, Jesus was co-creating with our Heavenly Father. We read:

> *26 Then God said, "Let us make mankind in our image, in our likeness, so that they may rule over the fish in the sea and the birds in the sky, over the livestock and all the wild animals, and over all the creatures that move along the ground." 27 So God created mankind in his own image, in the image of God he created them; male and female he created them.* – (Genesis 1:26-27)

The plan of God was a coordinated effort involving the "Theophany" of God: Father, Son and Holy Spirit. God created human community from divine community. The journey from being created, falling from God's favor, being under a curse by our own rebellion and sin, and then being redeemed through the gift of salvation in God's Son, shall be completed. The Day of the Lord is coming, it will be the day we respond to the final call. It will be the Day when believers in Heaven will be united with believers still on earth. Together, we will hear Jesus say: *"Take your inheritance, the kingdom"*, and we will come together in the unity Jesus prayed for as we take and eat in remembrance of Him who gave His life as a ransom for our sin. God's plan of creating humanity in His image shall be fulfilled, much as a seed reaches maturity after it has grown, endured trial and borne fruit. So too in Christ, the seed of the gospel fulfills God's covenants to Israel and the nations, the Jew and the Gentile. The fruit of God's Spirit in people is evidence of the experience of Christ's redemptive work of saving grace and truth.

D. Determination of inheritance – faith in action (35-36)

> 35 For I was hungry and you gave me something to eat, I was thirsty and you gave me something to drink, I was a stranger and you invited me in, 36 I needed clothes and you clothed me, I was sick and you looked after me, I was in prison and you came to visit me.'

Jesus is not only focused upon the future time of judgment, He desired to prepare people to live in eager and faithful service. The Kingdom is not only something worth waiting for, it involves genuine faith that gives glory to God through compassionate service. As the early Jerusalem Church leader, James, once put it:

> 14 What good is it, my brothers and sisters, if someone claims to have faith but has no deeds? Can such faith save them? 15 Suppose a brother or a sister is without clothes and daily food. 16 If one of you says to them, "Go in peace; keep warm and well fed," but does nothing about their physical needs, what good is it? 17 In the same way, faith by itself, if it is not accompanied by action, is dead. 18 But someone will say, "You have faith; I have deeds." Show me your faith without deeds, and I will show you my faith by my deeds. – (James 2:14-19)

The wisdom of James had developed through a personal walk of faith with the Risen Lord. Matthew 25:35-36 is a practical and powerful moment of Jesus teaching about who will enter the Kingdom of Heaven. He does not present a theological statement of faith that all must memorize and repeat. Jesus presents God's criteria in practical terms: Be faithful to respond to the needs of the world with God's heart; the objective is to see Jesus present in everything and everybody and to then serve in kind.

1. <u>Helping the hungry</u> (35a) *35 For I was hungry and you gave me something to eat,*

Helping others in need reflects God's compassion and mercy. Giving from abundance is easy. However, the kind of giving Jesus modeled was that of giving from sacrifice, even scarcity. Remember how Jesus fed thousands with a few fish and loaves? Sharing food is one of the most basic activities of human nurture and hospitality. We come together through food, we eat at tables and face one another. We take time to share in fellowship and friendship with food. Helping those who are hungry, in the direct sense of sharing a meal socially, has spiritual dimensions as well. Jesus calls people to respond to hunger in ways that are personal and intimate.

Collection of food, and distribution from food pantries, are both important parts of the equation. What Jesus had in mind was the qualitative way that we care, involving that which is invitational and sacrificial. The stomach and body are to be fed and treated with respect; however, the soul is hungry for love, acceptance, companionship and community. Jesus notices whether people help others out of social compliance or out of compassionate concern. Jesus notices when people prepare and cook an excellent meal for others, out of the goodness of their heart and the generosity of their spirit.

Perhaps if you think about it, you will recall someone being kind and hospitable to you with a meal, a basket of food, a dinner in their home, or treating you out for dinner when you were broke. If you can recall these deeds, it is wonderful to realize that Jesus knows about these deeds. When one serves another person, they are serving Christ Himself. Jesus is hungry down at the mission, over at the broken-down hotel, along the street side, or up at the soup kitchen. Are we ready to volunteer, give or cook-up something? Jesus is waiting.

    2. <u>Supplying the thirsty</u> (35b)   *I was thirsty and you gave me something to drink,*

Giving water to the thirsty illustrates an immediate response. People can wait if they are hungry, but when someone is thirsty and weak, good clean water is needed right away. Recently, in the city of Flint, Michigan, the water supply was changed over to a new system that was intended to save money. Upon being implemented, the residents could quickly see that their water was not clean. It smelled weird, left stains and made children, adults and elderly sick. Some of my friends from Flint were warning each other on Social Media, "don't drink the water." Investigators from the city and state tried to cover up the problem, and local officials continued not to listen to the residents or the health community. Lead poisoning was found in people's bloodwork. An independent community effort, with scientific help and testing from Virginia Tech University, revealed the contamination of toxic metals was indeed the core issue and problem. The denial of this problem, compounded by political corruption, and continued drinking of the water, saw an increase of lead in people's brains and bodies. This toxic presence of lead and other metals will have long-term health consequences. The reason for the contamination was traced back to a decision to save money by not adding an essential anti-corrosive chemical into the water that helps to prevent particle disintegration in older metal pipes.

When we care for others by providing clean water, it is vitally important. God's design for the body involves internal and external cleansing and new life. Those who bring clean water to others may not be aware how much Jesus rejoices in their service. God pours out His grace to those who are faithful in their compassion to fill the cup and soul that is thirsty. The Apostle Paul challenged the Church to give water, even to those who would seem to be enemies:

If your enemy is hungry, feed him; if he is thirsty, give him something to drink. In doing this, you will heap burning coals on his head." 21 Do not be overcome by evil, but overcome evil with good. – (Romans 12:20-21)

On the cross, Jesus identified with our thirst. (John 19:28). Jesus is thirsty upon the parched crosses of our communities. He searches for someone to quench people's thirst for truth and grace, righteousness and compassion. Jesus is thirsty in those who thirst. Jesus waits for us to come to people in our communities and then offer the living water that He shall provide from the wellspring of life from God the Father. (John 4).

> *"Everyone who drinks this water will be thirsty again, 14 but whoever drinks the water I give them will never thirst. Indeed, the water I give them will become in them a spring of water welling up to eternal life." 15 The woman said to him, "Sir, give me this water so that I won't get thirsty and have to keep coming here to draw water."* John 4:13-15

3. <u>Housing the stranger</u> (35c)   *I was a stranger and you invited me in,*

People who help to shelter or house the stranger, the traveler, the homeless, the refuge, or the poor college student are offering hospitality to Jesus. The Lord Jesus said: *"Come unto me all you are weary and heavy-laden and I will give you rest for your souls"*. Jesus desired to bless people. As Jesus grew up, His mother Mary may have indeed told Him about the innkeeper who found space when the inn was full, at the humble stable of Bethlehem. His family had to escape Herod's schemes and were transient refugees. The story of Jesus is summarized by the Lord Himself who said: *"Foxes have dens and birds have nests, but the Son of Man has no place to lay his head"* (Matthew 8:20). Those who house the stranger are preparing a place for Jesus to lay His head. The Lord is with the weary and heavy laden. Will we give them rest for their bodies and souls? Jesus is waiting.

4. Clothing people in need (36a)   *36 I needed clothes and you clothed me,*

After the hurricanes of 2017, in Texas, Florida and Puerto Rico (Harvey, Irma and Maria), people became more aware of how important clean and dry clothing is to maintain health. Many people reported problems of mold and mildew, and the lack of laundry cleaning options. Bacteria and disease were contained within the flood waters surrounding the people of Houston, even after a few weeks. For all locations, the donation and provision of clothing had made all the difference between health and sickness. This need has increased to include the people of California, who have just recently lost many lives, thousands of homes and personal property in deadly fires.

When a person has need of clothing and warmth, there is something personal and assuring about a comfortable shirt or fitting pair of pants and socks. Jesus takes the matter of how we view our clothing to a new level when He stated:

If someone takes your coat, do not withhold your shirt from them. 30 Give to everyone who asks you, and if anyone takes what belongs to you, do not demand it back. 31 Do to others as you would have them do to you. – (Luke 6:29-32)

Jesus gives a scenario where people are desperate. Their behavior of "taking" a coat or asking for a "shirt" is unusual. One wonders if the time of tribulation ahead will involve immediate needs requiring attentive and quick discernment. To be even more intentional, will we look through our closets and give sacrificially and generously of our wardrobe to help those in need? Jesus needs clothing. Will we go on waiting for the Salvation Army to come knocking at our door? Jesus is waiting for warmth and garments of compassion.

5. <u>Caring for the sick</u> (36b)   *I was sick and you looked after me,*

The sacred space of caring for the sick is where Jesus identifies with our pain, our suffering. Jesus often went to those who were sick and allowed those who were considered "unclean" to touch Him. Lepers were loved, the sick were healed. In our world, there will be times that people will doubt God's power and healing when the cure is not found or given. There are times when the healing is not in the cure, but in the community of care. The emphasis of Jesus is upon how we *"look after"* others. Jesus did not say "I was sick and you healed me". Instead, the Lord's emphasis is on presence, care, a relationship of being with another even when we do not have the cure. Being with another person will not always be pleasant, it often means bearing with someone in their pain or frustration. Jesus calls us to have mercy and not internalize the projection of people's struggle with sickness. Later, if we persist, pray and endure in love, there is a blessing of grace and a work of transformation.

While we desire the cure, the ultimate healing will be in the resurrection, the new body promised in the Kingdom of Heaven for all who believe. When people stay with those who are sick, and visit those who are in a hospital or nursing home, there is something powerful and profound about the hope that is given. The pain of isolation is eased, the loneliness is lessened.

Being a chaplain, I have discovered that the presence of people encourages a sense of the presence of God. When people are absent, those who are sick or lonely feel a void, a loss of spiritual and emotional support. This is a mystery, but it relates to our being created for community, and why well-being is directly related to being present with others. While there are times where we need solitude and quiet, peace and rest; more often people suffer from loneliness and neglect. Will we be there for others in the tough times of sickness? Jesus waits for us.

6. Visiting those in prison (36c) *I was in prison and you came to visit me.'*

Prison visitation is scary, unpleasant, controversial and inconvenient, just the kind of place that Jesus would want us to go. In fact, Jesus is there behind the gates, walls and iron bars. "Jesus was not a criminal", you say. That was, in fact, how the people treated Him when they yelled: *"Crucify him! Crucify him!"* Pilate found no fault in Jesus, but still the Sanhedrin struck Him and Roman soldiers mocked and tortured our Lord. Jesus was rejected and killed as a criminal, between two criminals. Jesus was about to be buried as a criminal, except for Joseph of Arimathea, who willingly associated himself with Jesus and offered his tomb. It is interesting that God used Joseph's act of hospitality to prepare the way for Christ's resurrection to occur within a secured individual tomb.

The Apostle Paul and other Apostles and disciples were willing to be called criminals and be imprisoned for the sake of sharing the Gospel. For whatever just or unjust reason, people are imprisoned, the call of Jesus Christ is not to condemn prisoners, but to see them as Jesus does. They are loved, they too may be forgiven. There is hope for their souls in the Kingdom of God. Will we go out of our way to visit the prisoner or their family? Jesus is waiting.

E. Surprise of the sheep – presence of Jesus in life (37-39)

37 "Then the righteous will answer him, 'Lord, when did we see you hungry and feed you, or thirsty and give you something to drink? 38 When did we see you a stranger and invite you in, or needing clothes and clothe you? 39 When did we see you sick or in prison and go to visit you?'

A wonderful surprise awaited the faithful who followed Jesus into the tough places of life, as they discovered redemptive relationships of care with others. Little did they know that it was

Jesus in need, and that their care for others was actually care for the Lord. They were simply doing their job, letting their hearts be moved by the things that move the heart of God. Jesus had changed their lives and had enlarged their faith so they could share God's love in practical ways.

F. Service for others is service for King Jesus (v.40)

40 "The King will reply, 'Truly I tell you, whatever you did for one of the least of these brothers and sisters of mine, you did for me.'

Throughout life's journey, the servants were now made aware that Jesus was there in their midst. Jesus was present in the people at need and in their actions of care. The work of the Holy Spirit flows through deeds of love. Into the encounters of life is where people may experience the Lordship and incarnation of Jesus. Within the daily interactions and decisions, Jesus is there. When did we see you?... Jesus: "When did you not see me?" The reality of Jesus is often missed, even by those who do His will. What they have not identified in their satisfaction of caring is that the Lord is blessing their service by His very presence. This may explain why helping and serving others can be energizing and inspiring.

The litmus test of motivation and care (according to Jesus' standard) involves how people either do, or do not, discriminate in their serving. Anyone can care for people who are pleasant and familiar. However, when we care for the least of these, the vulnerable, weak, poor, meek and ignored; then we are caring as Jesus did. We are called to see all people as brothers and sisters in Christ's spirit of ministry. When racial profiling, prejudice, or favoritism toward material wealth and social status affects our judgment of care, we risk making decisions or setting priorities that may lead to our missing God's opening of care. We may not realize it, but we risk shutting out Jesus. In fact, Jesus is calling for our hearts to be moved to care for those who are rejected and despised, misunderstood, lost, depressed and feeling like nobody cares. That is where Jesus is ready to move in, and change hearts and lives. God's desire is for mercy and grace to prevail. Jesus is found where faith, hope and love are given unselfishly and unconditionally.

One year while I was a pastor in Battle Creek, Michigan, at First Baptist Church, we had a visitor who came as a refugee from the Sudan. His name was Yahwehtur Mok. He was tall and thin, and was missing a leg from a time when he and other believers were ambushed by a radical Muslim militia group. "Mok" needed a new coat, an apartment, furniture and some personal items. In addition, he needed friendship and support. I remember taking him around in my car to specifically find a coat at the thrift shop to fill in the gap for items not donated from the church. In looking around there were several options, a suitable polyester coat and a nice brown leather coat. I could tell that he really liked the brown leather coat, and even though I had to pay more than I was expecting, I realized that such a coat would help boost his morale. When Thanksgiving came, and I picked him up for dinner at our home, he was wearing a sweater I gave him and the beautiful brown leather coat. More importantly, Yahwetur Mok was wearing a big smile.

III. Declaration of unfavorable Judgment for the goats (v.41-45)

41 "Then he will say to those on his left, 'Depart from me, you who are cursed, into the eternal fire prepared for the devil and his angels. 42 For I was hungry and you gave me nothing to eat, I was thirsty and you gave me nothing to drink, 43 I was a stranger and you did not invite me in, I needed clothes and you did not clothe me, I was sick and in prison and you did not look after me.' 44 "They also will answer, 'Lord, when did we see you hungry or thirsty or a stranger or needing clothes or sick or in prison, and did not help you?' 45 "He will reply, 'Truly I tell you, whatever you did not do for one of the least of these, you did not do for me.'

The curtain has now been ripped asunder, the facades can no longer be maintained. False religiosity cannot pass for truth and grace. Jesus was right before them in people whose need and situations called for a response of care, compassion and service. One might even say that these "goats", the condemned in God's judgment, were so consumed with their own ultimacy that they neglected the immediate concerns and daily presence of the Lord. Jesus was not far away, Jesus was right in front of them in the people they rejected, bullied, ignored and spoke ill about. Jesus was the hungry beggar, the homeless man pushing the shopping cart, the ragged children of India, Haiti, Appalachia and Ethiopia. Jesus was ignored, missed. Jesus was the sick neighbor, the man sitting quietly in the doctor's office, the woman being wheeled around in the Nursing Home, the rehabilitated sex offender and the young adult imprisoned for drug possession in the county jail.

"Lord, when did we see you?" "Was that you?" "What were we supposed to do?" Their responses and questions are telling of their drift away from God. Because the *"goats"*, the ones to be banished from God's Kingdom, did not have the mind of Christ or the Holy Spirit of God within them, they were already alienated. Their disobedience and rebellion had placed them under a curse of their own free will. They didn't respond to the needs because they were unwilling to respond to the leading of Christ and the Spirit of God's compassion. Faith is not only a matter of what we believe, it's how we believe. God is not only looking for those who worship in "spirit and in truth" (John 4:23-24), God is also looking for those who serve and respond to people in need with "spirit and truth". True worship is lived out from the change and transformation that comes from faith in Christ. The "goats" were spiritually unresponsive and consumed with living for themselves. There are many who claim to be "Christians", or who trust in their own religious observances, who fall into this category.

A. Banishment of the cursed into the eternal fire (v.41)

> 41 *"Then he will say to those on his left, 'Depart from me, you who are cursed, into the eternal fire prepared for the devil and his angels.*

The determination of banishment was soon to be issued by Christ Jesus, the King, in holy and righteous judgment. The "goats" had already seen the group on the right hand of God's throne be rewarded, and enter the Kingdom. What would their lot be? The answer was not protracted or delayed, *"Depart from me"*. They did not know it, but they were already living under the curse of sin and rebellion, as they were alienated from God. Departure was already their mode of avoiding God, now the Lord completed their willful rebellious faithlessness with the final cut of truth. They had not received God's grace, nor responded to Christ's presence. Now, they would no longer be offered God's mercy.

Since they did not honor Jesus in service, and had chosen to deny the needs of others, there would be no honor given to them. Their time and opportunity in life had come, and now it would cease. Those who choose to live by the curse, and do not repent, are destined to die by the curse. The choice is theirs and it is directly tied to the influence of evil thinking that the "goats" subscribe to as they are deceived by the obsessive pursuit of riches, fame, power and temporal pleasures. Judgment shall come to the *"cursed"* in the same way it shall come for the *"devil and his angels"* who have rebelled against God.

1. The goats are banished (41a)

> 41 *"Then he will say to those on his left, 'Depart from me, you who are cursed,*

Those placed to the left of the judge, in Jewish courts, were guilty. They would then await their sentence. King Jesus shall say to them: "Depart from me." The condition of their souls had already become alienated from the Lord of life, and now the consequence of their faithlessness and hardness of heart would be administered. God does not impose Himself on people to believe, it is a free decision to make and requires belief above self. The "goats" were symbolic of stubbornness and rebelliousness. They did not receive the offer of God's grace and had continued to avoid the Lord and rationalize the curse of their own sin. The judgment of removal for the cursed would be final.

2. <u>The devil and his angels are banished in the eternal fire</u> (41b)

into the eternal fire prepared for the devil and his angels.

Hell is the place of punishment in God's judgment for the destruction of the devil, his angels and those who have been deceived by evil and have chosen to live in the curse of sin and its ways. God prepared the eternal fire to have eternal consequences. This fire of hell burns completely to destroy what is wicked and evil entirely. In the plan of God, a new beginning requires the purging of that which was corrupt and evil. This is a work that only God has the power and authority to implement, and this through Jesus Christ His Son and His Holy Angels.

B. Determination of their destruction – no evidence of faith (42-43)

42 For I was hungry and you gave me nothing to eat, I was thirsty and you gave me nothing to drink, 43 I was a stranger and you did not invite me in, I needed clothes and you did not clothe me, I was sick and in prison and you did not look after me.'

Will God relent from harsh judgment on the Day of the Lord if people were kind and compassionate? The answer to that question belongs to God and to Jesus Christ. Ultimately, how people live is closely related to what they believe deep down. Will only Christians and Jews be in the Kingdom of Heaven? Some people will be mad that I have even asked this question. That will be up to the Lord Jesus Christ on the Day of Judgment. The important matter is not that of labels, but that of belief, actions and heart. God has given His Son Jesus Christ the authority to make the decision. Jesus will know if someone is a genuine believer and disciple by the criteria of faith leading to evidence of obedience, and to the presence of God's Holy Spirit that is deposited in a soul who is forgiven and regenerated by the gift of God's cleansing grace.

Jesus clarified God's criteria to Nicodemus: *"No one can see the kingdom of God unless they are born again"* (John 3:3). Consequently, where God's Holy Spirit is given, in congruence with following Jesus Christ, the activity of a person becomes like-minded with Jesus. The mystery of how King Jesus will judge is not simply a matter of theological correctness of words in the final analysis, it is a matter of genuine faith that receives new life in the Holy Spirit from Christ Jesus. Such a faith seeks knowledge and theological development alongside practical application. The evidence of God's Holy Spirit is service, and when service is absent, the ministry of Jesus suffers neglect along with the Lord Himself.

1. <u>Didn't feed the hungry</u> (42a)   *42 For I was hungry and you gave me nothing to eat,*

An infant's first needs, after a breath of air, is to be bathed, clothed, held and fed. The hunger of an infant is expressed through audible and visual cues: Crying, rooting of the mouth and waving of the arms. The child has an innate ability to communicate to the parents, it is up to the parents to respond lovingly with nurture and provision. This care must extend beyond the obvious needs of our own young, our own families and groupings. Jesus called people to see that the stranger, the neighbor, the beggar and the sick are also part of God's family. The failing of the goats was that they could not be bothered with the needs of people beyond themselves and their immediate families and friends. Jesus said,

> 32 "If you love those who love you, what credit is that to you? Even sinners love those who love them. 33 And if you do good to those who are good to you, what credit is that to you? Even sinners do that. 34 And if you lend to those from whom you expect repayment, what credit is that to you? Even sinners lend to sinners, expecting to be repaid in full. 35 But love your enemies, do good to them, and lend to them without expecting to get anything back. Then your reward will be great, and you will be children of the Most High, because he is kind to the ungrateful and wicked. 36 Be merciful, just as your Father is merciful. – (Luke 6:32-36)

Jesus called for the kind of love that was born of God's grace, full of mercy, pressed down through adversity, and flowing with unconditional generosity. Jesus was hungry, and they did not stop to help.

Jesus had talked about the great Wedding Feast in Heaven, and that many were invited (Matthew 22:1-14). Still, the hall was empty, and the servants were sent out into the highways and byways to invite more to come. What happens to the servants if they don't obey the master and do their part to invite people in? That's something the servants will not want to find out. Indeed, the Master will lead his servants to go to anyone they can find to extend His Kingdom invitation. Will believers, disciples, "the servants" be faithful to deliver the invitation?

2. Didn't offer a drink to the thirsty (42b) *I was thirsty and you gave me nothing to drink,*

One night our plane circled Chicago O'Hare Airport for several hours while we waited for clearance to land. After thirty more minutes of circling, the pilot informed the passengers that we were still waiting for airport clearance, and to be patient. Another forty minutes later, the pilot continued to assure passengers that we were still hoping to land soon. By this time, people were getting thirsty while others were getting agitated in needing to use the restrooms. The holding pattern was causing issues. Fifteen minutes later, the pilot came on and said we were being routed to Milwaukee, where we could refuel and take a moment to rest. While reasons for the holding pattern and delay were beyond our control, it became apparent that all of this could have been anticipated and people's needs better respected.

Recognizing other's needs is a priority in Jesus' teaching and example. Jesus will often be found in others, outside of our own personal sphere of need and satisfaction. Indeed, we are called to be concerned and responsive to those around us who are thirsty. The thirst for both water and righteousness are to be respected. When we carry a pitcher of water to others, hand someone a water bottle, or offer a cool glass to the stranger, it is Jesus that we are ultimately giving it to. When one misses their moment to offer relief, to help satisfy someone's thirst, they may miss a moment to serve the Master. When you miss Jesus, you miss what is most important for the quenching of your soul and another's soul.

3. <u>Didn't invite the stranger in</u> (43a)   *43 I was a stranger and you did not invite me in,*

Being a pastor and living next to churches in parsonages has been a mix of blessing and burden. People will knock on the door, often looking for help in a meal, a place to stay, counsel or assistance with utilities. For the most part, I have opened the door and have taken time to listen, to hear and understand, to respond to the needs of others. I may not always be able to offer the kind of assistance someone is wanting or requesting, but I do seek to discern the wisdom of Jesus in what I can do to help. Jesus did not stress offering people a quick solution or just giving a swift referral. He did emphasize hospitality, care and respect of people. If we don't invite people in to our worlds, if we keep people at a distance, we may indeed be keeping Jesus at a distance. Will we invite Him in? Jesus knocks at our doors.

4. <u>Didn't clothe the naked</u> (43b)   *I needed clothes and you did not clothe me,*

To be clothed, and to care for others to be clothed, is both a practical expression of care and a theological expression of belief in God's grace. Through faith in Jesus Christ a person is re-clothed in the garments of God's righteousness.

> *10 I delight greatly in the Lord; my soul rejoices in my God. For he has clothed me with garments of salvation and arrayed me in a robe of his righteousness, as a bridegroom adorns his head like a priest, and as a bride adorns herself with her jewels. – (Isaiah 61:10)*

Jesus will evaluate your garments. Jesus is not interested in the designers and trendsetters. Jesus is interested in whether you shared your garments of grace with others who needed mercy and love. Jesus wants people to share the threads of kindness, the scarf of sacrifice, the warm gloves of gentleness and the costly coat of compassion. Imagine Jesus wearing what we have given to others. Don't let Jesus be naked, or left poorly clad and cold. After all, you can't bring your wardrobe to Heaven, so give it away on earth.

5. <u>Didn't care for the sick or imprisoned</u> (43c)   *I was sick and in prison and you did not look after me.'*

People who are imprisoned are often neglected and ostracized by society. Prisons have become so focused on holding people securely, that they seldom rehabilitate. There are conditions of overcrowding, violence and abuse. Reform is greatly needed, especially in how minorities are unable to afford legal representation. The current system of incarceration perpetuates entrapment among certain groups. Jesus will hold individuals, and our societies, in judgment as to whether we cared or whether we tried to make things better when we were given the opportunity. Instead of casting stones, we are called to help break the chains of bondage that have contributed to crime and addiction. Jesus was sick and in prison, did we go to see Him? Did we bother to look after Him? Did we seek justice, pursue peace and show mercy?

C. Surprise of the Goats – When did we see you? (44)

> 44 *"They also will answer, 'Lord, when did we see you hungry or thirsty or a stranger or needing clothes or sick or in prison, and did not help you?'*

Spiritual blindness is more a matter of allowing our sin to keep us from beholding what God has placed before us. Just because we can't see something does not mean it is not there. How many times have you misplaced something only to discover it was right near you or underneath something beside you? People must not be quick to dismiss the needs of others, even if on the surface people seem to be alright. The issue of discernment is at hand, and requires intentionality, concern, critical thinking and compassion to look deeper, to listen and to respond. God's Spirit will direct the path of the faithful, and counsel them to discover ways to help. The faithful can look back and realize that it was indeed a "God moment" when someone helped them, or they were able to help others.

The "goats" didn't see it that way. They saw the problems, the people in need, but they did not perceive the leading and presence of God's Spirit. Jesus was right before them, even at times helping to meet their needs through someone who was being faithful, yet they chose not to believe or give thanks to God. The goats might have even responded from guilt or compulsion, but still their hearts stayed cold. The faithless chose not to let their hearts be moved, their hands to care, or their arms to carry. The unwillingness of the "goats" was a symptom of the deeper disease of the hardness of their hearts to humanity and the resistance of their souls to God.

D. Missed opportunity of seeing, serving and knowing Jesus (45)

45 "He will reply, 'Truly I tell you, whatever you did not do for one of the least of these, you did not do for me.'

For six years, I pastored in a small town in southern central Michigan, at Union Church of Quincy. The population was about 1,910 strong (not including cattle and pigs), and there were a few interesting characters who loved to stop by and talk with "the pastor". One of these persons, a young man who seemed a bit off and quirky, was "D". In coming to know "D", my initial impressions of curiosity were replaced with admiration and respect. "D" had been hit by a car while riding his bicycle when he was in High School. "D" works as a volunteer at the hospital and is always participating in community events and fund raisers. Though "D" has had challenges speaking straight and laughing uncontrollably, his heart is pure gold. "D" has a special gift of calling a variety of people by phone on special holidays and on their birthdays to tell them "God bless you buddy". I can still count on "D" to regularly call me, even after 4 years of moving away as a pastor from his town. "D" has not forgotten me, and I have not forgotten him. "D" is not understood by many people, and is on the list of the least in some people's minds. For me, "D" is right up there near the top of faithful believers.

How well do we remember people, reach out and show the love of God? The reply of the Lord to the unfaithful servants related to their lack of concern, care and remembrance. The conscience of God's Spirit, when yielded to, will lead us to be sensitive, remember people, and express care for others. To live otherwise is to lose our identity as children of God; to not show care is to deny the presence of Jesus. When was the last time you called someone, wrote a note or visited as the Spirit led? Don't miss the opportunity to open your heart to someone today, before it is too late. Also, don't be surprised if Jesus shows up in your life through humble and unusual people. The Kingdom of Heaven comes near us in ways and through people, quite often, unexpected and unsuspecting.

IV. Final Judgment (The Kingdom of Heaven or destruction in Hell) (46)

46 "Then they will go away to eternal punishment, but the righteous to eternal life."

So here it is! The final judgment of God shall be issued by His Son Jesus, the Christ, the coming King of Glory. What is at stake? God has given His Son Jesus Christ the authority to decide our fate. Will it be Heaven or hell, inclusion or exclusion from God's Kingdom at the final judgment? There are people who will find this objectionable, the whole matter of God's love involving judgment and eternal consequence. There are those who believe in the universal acceptance of all people into the Kingdom of Heaven. This is not the picture Jesus gives, nor is it consistent with all of Scripture. Furthermore, the persistent problem of people being judgmental and "playing God" is not the issue here. In this prophecy from Matthew 24 and 25, Jesus is referring to the Day of the Lord, the inevitable work of God's accounting, the determination of mercy and/or justice. At stake is God's culmination of redemptive, covenantal, history; all this in the transformative work of Christ Jesus for the salvation of those who have been forgiven, faithful, believing. Eternal punishment can never be a matter of human account or knowledge, this belongs to the One who created and redeems. The words *"go away"* indicate that the punishment is that of removal, the *"second death"*. The "redeemed" or "elect" shall not taste the *"second death"*. We read more about this from the Risen Jesus as He spoke to the 7 Churches of Asia Minor:

> *11 Whoever has ears, let them hear what the Spirit says to the churches. The one who is victorious will not be hurt at all by the second death.* – Revelation 2:11

The Lord spoke once more about the *"second death"* later in the Revelation to John, Christ has a message for the Church and for everyone to be forewarned and to repent:

> *7 Those who are victorious will inherit all this, and I will be their God and they will be my children. 8 But the cowardly, the unbelieving, the vile, the murderers, the sexually immoral, those who practice magic arts, the idolaters and all liars—they will be consigned to the fiery lake of burning sulfur. This is the second death."* Revelation 21:7-8

The point of all this warning from Jesus in the Olivet Discourse from Matthew 24-25 is to prepare the disciples. He gave them a vision, purpose and message of potency regarding the coming of God's Kingdom to earth. The coming of God's Kingdom would not arrive in the way that many of the Jews, disciples, or early Christians may have imagined. Indeed, it would be far greater and more extensive. Jesus taught His disciples in a way that inspired a movement of humility and service. Christ's prophetic vision helped them to enlarge their faith so they could be pliable to follow and discover Christ in daily service. The disciples were given important signs and parables that helped their faith become more intentional and committed. Jesus provided answers and direction that would allow them to discover God's big plan of salvation and judgment.

Conclusion: Why is this vision of Jesus so important today?

The vision of Jesus is poignant and powerful. His prophetic Word is as relevant as ever. For within Jesus' words we are forewarned, given signs to watch for, taught wisdom for discernment, and are guided to prepare for God's coming Kingdom through practical actions of love. Jesus inspires us through His amazing foreknowledge of future events, and through vivid illustrations and parables.

To conclude His "Olivet Discourse" (Matthew 24 and 25), Jesus relayed His Heavenly Father's call for readiness through being service-minded, and by caring directly for others. This is not abstract and "out of reach", the call of following Christ is practical and achievable. By following Jesus and applying His example, we do the work of God's kingdom; and if we have our eyes and hearts open, we shall discover the presence of our Lord daily.

Questions for Discussion:

1. Why is this vision of Jesus so important today?

2. List signs of our times that indicate why it is important to be ready by serving in Jesus name?

3. What is comforting in the reward given to the "sheep"? What criteria did God use?

4. What is challenging about the punishment given to the "goats"? What was missing in their lives?

5. Where do we see Jesus today in the needs of people in the world? What are we called to do to serve our Lord and Savior?

Conclusion:
"Staying with", a witness through the storm.

The Church is the Body of Christ in this era of grace, this time in which the Gospel seed is still being spread, nurtured and grown. The witness and presence of God's Kingdom hope is evidenced in faith and service that is true to the character of Christ Jesus. For believers to represent God's Kingdom faithfully, it is essential that the faithful hold on, run the race, and stand firm through the storms. The way for the Church, for believers, to do this is not through trying to create heaven on earth through political or legal maneuvering. That is how false messiahs operated in Israel's history (and in world history), and that will be how false messiah's will arise in our times. When false messiahs are followed, the people of God lose sight of who their true King and Master is. The truth of God's Sovereignty, and coming Kingdom, in the powerful return and judgment of Jesus Christ, has sadly been replaced by hope in human leaders or movements. The call of Jesus to His disciples then, and the disciples since then, is to be watchful, enduring, faithful and ready through serving Jesus in practical ministry and care. This is not a duty for clergy alone, but for all disciples through faithfulness and obedience to the inspiration and leading of God's Holy Spirit.

While writing the last several chapters of this book, I have been at the home of my wife's sister in the suburbs of Chicago. The reason we were there was because one of the family members was going through her last days of life with an inoperable and untreatable cancer that had aggressively advanced. Many people had visited our beloved Felina, and family took turns to provide support, comfort measures, companionship and prayers. Often, we found that practical service, caring presence and faith filled prayer were the most meaningful things we could offer to her. After one of the prayers, my sister-in-law opened her heavy eyes and said: "Thank you for praying for me". I said: "That's the least I can do." Quick-witted, she replied: "No, prayer is the best you can do."

End of life care is a model for the ministry of the Body of Christ in our times. While the scientific community postulates ways for humanity to survive by space travel and repopulation on another planet far off in another part of the Milky Way Galaxy; the hope of the people of God is that our Creator Heavenly Father is not done with humanity or the earth. In preparation for a New Heaven and New Earth, God's plan is for salvation, and this shall involve a shake up and a Judgment as a prelude to this new beginning.

The ministry of the Church, the people of God, is that of presence and care. This is different from the illusive idea of the Church creating a theocratic "holy nation", which assumes that the Church is meant to usher in the Kingdom of God of its own good work (God have mercy). Instead, the model of the Church being the presence of Jesus Christ, giving evocative, accompanying, comforting and hopeful presence is what needs to be recovered and promoted. This is what Jesus modeled, and it was the mode of operation for the Early Church and has been the hallmark of faithful, servant-minded, missiology. The Church must trust in the Spirit of God that is at work in and amidst the world's peoples. God is calling the nations and our neighbors to note that the Lord is not far off, and that the Prince of Peace, the King of Kings, is walking, breathing and caring for the world, even in and through His people who are His Bride, the Body of Christ. Eventually, Jesus will come again. Until then, the Gospel is to be preached in deed and word to all the nations. The question of how ready people will be, is in fact, a matter of urgent and compassionate mission as the Day of the Lord draws nearer.

While walking in the neighborhood during our time in Chicago, I noticed that there was a Horse Chestnut Tree with spikey shells of mature nuts fallen on the ground. This reminded me of such trees that were in Alma, Michigan in front of Alma College. As a child, when I was 8-10 years old, I fondly remember knocking these spikey shells down, and then opening them to discover the beautiful cherry/mahogany colored nuts inside. My brother and I would save them in our red Radio Flyer wagon. I would bring a few of them to school in my pocket, and show them to my classmates. They collected them too, and for a least a couple weeks, we could hold them and feel the smooth polished surface. Sometimes I would ponder how beautiful they were, and as a child I believed that there must be a God to create something so special. Now, there I was walking about many years later, many miles and years away, in Chicago. I picked up the horse chestnuts and held the polished gems in my hands. God's Spirit spoke to my mind and heart to consider the parable of the fig tree as it evidenced maturity, and to prepare, for the harvest is near, it is right at the door:

> 28 "Now learn this lesson from the fig tree: As soon as its twigs get tender and its leaves come out, you know that summer is near. 29 Even so, when you see these things happening, you know that it is near, right at the door. - Mark 13:28-29

Jesus gave us a promise of His return, and He gave us plenty of things to make note of in the journey that His Church, His Body, His very flock and family, would go through in their time of service and witness. Only God the Father knows the day and hour of Christ's return, there are many people becoming increasingly anxious, even fearful, about the times we are living in. Is the coming of Jesus Christ very near? Once again, I think about how people die. That is part of my calling as a pastor and chaplain. Who is to know about their own personal time of being *"taken up"*? Who is to know about God's time of saying *"come, receive the Kingdom"* or *"depart from me"*? I thought about Jesus' promise in John 14:

> *"Do not let your hearts be troubled. You believe in God; believe also in me. My Father's house has many rooms; if that were not so, would I have told you that I am going there to prepare a place for you? And if I go and prepare a place for you, I will come back and take you to be with me that you also may be where I am."* – (John 14:1-3)

Once again, at the bedside of my beloved sister in law, I felt the Lord's presence and could hear His words of promise, *"I will come back and take you to be with me"*. These are essential words to live by, not only in the face of death, but also to face the storms of this world at the "End Times". Christ's Second Coming draws near. How will people navigate through the hazards of these times? Will people heed Christ's teaching? Will people be forewarned and prepared? I pray that people will carefully consider, believe and apply Jesus' invitation and instruction. Jesus calls people, even now, to become His disciples in the Good News of God's Kingdom. In addition, I pray that people will also take caution of Jesus' words of woe, warning and watchfulness, as He gave these to us as a survival guide and inspiration for service.

Joseph P. Bishop wrote about the painful experience he and his wife endured at the death of their 19-year-old son to a tragic and unexplainable car accident:

"A week after Peter's death I was walking along the lip of the sea when suddenly before me was a pure white stone, smooth and round. I have never seen one like it before or since. I picked it up with such excitement there was a buzzing in my head. Just that summer I had been meditating again on that mysterious sentence in the second chapter of Revelation, "To him who conquers I will give a white stone with a new name written on the stone which no one knows except him who receives it." I held the stone in the palm of my hand, like a sacred wafer...

A few years later his wife died with cancer, and so Joseph Bishop wrote of his faith:

Whatever the human trauma – whether disease or accident, the loss of a job, the breakup of a marriage, the disappointment of a hope – the way out is always the way through a narrow tunnel of truth. My hope in sharing my own very personal "way through" is not to suggest that your truth will be the same as mine, but that the very center of every storm is peace, and at the end is light." (Joseph P. Bishop, "The Eye of the Storm", p., 26, 31, Chosen Books, 1976).

Going through life's storms is tough, but God is there to help us through. There are dangers all around us. I think of a few close friends who have also gone through some tough storms of loss and grief. The pain is difficult to navigate, only going through the storm do we find the power of God's presence and the reality of peace.

One summer as a family, we took a road trip that brought us out-west to Yellowstone National Park. There are many areas where you walk amid super-hot water springs and geysers. I liken the experience to walking between heaven and hell, for indeed once one realizes that this whole area is the top of a large volcanic

Caldera, you see this beautiful and dangerous wilderness in a different light.

One of my close friends, Mark, told me about a time he went trout fishing on the Lamar and Madison rivers in Yellowstone. While catching cutthroat trout, buffalos grazed about and then swam next to them; all this beauty amidst geysers and hot springs. With one false step someone could go through the thin crust into an instant boil of scalding hot water. The dangerous reality is that the earth at Yellowstone is in a state of temporary balance. Pressure is released from the ancient caldera, life is held in a fragile state. Someday the dynamic forces underneath shall erupt, but for now these forces work together and allow for a marvelous place of beauty and danger. So too, our earth and its people, live on the edge of beauty and danger. There are dynamic and powerful forces being held at bay so that life may continue as the Lord has ordained it to by grace. A time of great change will come, the forces that are in balance will tip. What we now know will be replaced by a new order.

This past summer, I had to patch up some rust on my old car so that it would pass the state inspection. While I was waiting for the fiberglass resin to harden, I had to hold the body repair patch in place over the sanded and prepared rust hole. The hardening process took longer than I had anticipated. I realized that I had not put enough of the chemical hardener into the mixture. I waited 10 minutes, then 20 minutes, then finally at 30 minutes (my arms getting tired) the patch solidified. The chemical transformation took time and it involved holding on and waiting, trusting that the resin and hardener would set. Did Jesus know I would be working on this car? Yes. Did he know that I would be sitting there on the dirt driveway holding the fiberglass patch on the car for 30 minutes until it dried? Yes. Did Jesus know that in that time of "holding on" I would see the connection of "holding on to the patch" as being comparable to the Church's waiting for the transformation of God's Kingdom to come? Yes. The Good News is that God is planning for something more than a patch. God has something substantially better planned.

God has a plan for a New Heaven and a New Earth. Have faith to believe, be born again, hold on and serve well. Know that Christ Jesus and God our Heavenly Father are rooting for us, undergirding our faith with all-sufficient grace. Indeed, by faith and God's mercy we discover that God is present through the storms, and present through the waiting times, to hold on to us. In the fulness of time the chemistry of God's Kingdom, the very catalytic forces of truth and grace shall solidify. All that is wrong in the world, evil, will be removed. All who have faith and are currently in flux amid suffering and waiting, shall be transformed. We are promised entrance into the Kingdom of Heaven through a faith relationship with Jesus Christ. This shall involve letting go of our old bodies and receiving the resurrection body. Jesus will come again. The time of Judgment, of Christ's return may be near or far away in our understanding of time. Ultimately, God is planning for our reunion, to bring His Kingdom to earth as it is in Heaven. Beyond the big events, the cosmic shake up ahead, God has a timetable for bringing the New Jerusalem to earth. How sweet it will be when the City of our God, the New Jerusalem, comes within a New Heaven and Earth.

> 1 Then I saw "a new heaven and a new earth," for the first heaven and the first earth had passed away, and there was no longer any sea. 2 I saw the Holy City, the new Jerusalem, coming down out of heaven from God, prepared as a bride beautifully dressed for her husband. 3 And I heard a loud voice from the throne saying, "Look! God's dwelling place is now among the people, and he will dwell with them. They will be his people, and God himself will be with them and be their God. 4 'He will wipe every tear from their eyes. There will be no more death' or mourning or crying or pain, for the old order of things has passed away." Revelation 21:1-4

Bibliography

Arnold, Scott T. "Soul Fruit, Bearing Blessings through Cancer", Shine Press, Quincy, MI. 2009

Arnold, Scott T. "Prelude: The Kingdom of God: Salvation, Signs and Service", Shine Press, Quincy, MI 2012

Barclay, William. "The King and the Kingdom", Westminster Press, Philadelphia PA 1968.

Bishop, Joseph P. "The Eye of the Storm", Chosen Books, Fleming Revell, Old Tappan, NJ. 1976

Bendiksen, Jonas. "Messiahs" National Geographic. 8/2017. P. 86

Benson, Joseph. "Benson's Commentary"

Boice, James M. "The Gospel of Matthew: The Triumph of the King – Matthew 18-28.", Baker Books, Grand Rapids, MI. 2001. p. 499 – 539.

Boeree, George C. "The Emotional Nervous System". 2009. http://webspace.ship.edu/cgboer/onlinetexts.html

Bosley, Harold A. "He Spoke to Them in Parables", Harper and Row, New York. 1963

Connolly, Peter. "A History of the Jewish People in the Time of Jesus" Reference to Josephus. 1983 p. 66

Doran, Robert, "Birth of a Worldview", Westview Press, Oxford England, 1995. P. 51-63.

Ellicott, Charles. "Ellicott's Commentary", 1897

Exell, Joseph S. and Henry Donald Maurice Spence-Jones (Editors). The Pulpit Commentary. 23 volumes. First publication: 1890.

Fintel, William and McDermott, Gerald. "Cancer", Baker Books, Grand Rapids, MI 2004. P.14-21

Goodman, Martin. "Jerusalem and Rome: The Clash of Ancient Civilizations" A. Knoff Press, New York, NY 2007

Hagner, Donald A. "Word Biblical Commentary: Volume 33B, Matthew 14-18", Word Books, Dallas, TX. p. 682-747.

History.com, "This Day in History", March 26, 1997

Josephus, "The Jewish Wars", Penguin Books, Middlesex England.

Ladd, George E. "The Gospel of the Kingdom", Eerdmans, Grand Rapids, MI. 1959.

Laughlin, Greg, Don Korycansky and Fred Adams. Nasa Ames Research Center in California.

Lewis, Jack P. "The Gospel According to Matthew, Part II", Sweet Publishing, Austin, TX. 1976

MacArthur, John. "The MacArthur New Testament Commentary: Matthew 24-28". Moody Publishers, Chicago, IL. 1989.

MacLaren, Alexander. "MacLaren's Expositions of Holy Scripture"

McGarvey, J. W., and Philip Y. Pendleton. "Commentary on
    Matthew 25:33". The Fourfold Gospel, 1914

Maier, Paul, "Eusebius" p. 26-27. Kregel publishing, 2007

Nolan, Steve. "Spiritual Care at the End of Life (The Chaplain as a
    Hopeful Presence)", Jessica Kingsley Publishers, London and
    Philadelphia, 2012.

Peters, F.E., "Jerusalem", Princeton University Press, Princeton, N.J.
    1986. p. 120-121

Skinner B.F. "Walden two". New York: Macmillan; 1976.

Tenney, Merrill C., "Interpreting Revelation", Eerdmans, Grand
    Rapids, MI. 1957.

Thoreau, Henry David. "Walden". 1854

All Scriptural references are from: The New International Version of
the Holy Bible. (2011)

www.ingramcontent.com/pod-product-compliance
Lightning Source LLC
Chambersburg PA
CBHW071206090426
42736CB00014B/2728